No Mercy

Jean Stefancic
Richard Delgado

No Mercy

How Conservative Think Tanks

and Foundations Changed

America's Social Agenda

Foreword by Mark Tushnet

TEMPLE UNIVERSITY PRESS

PHILADELPHIA

Temple University Press, Philadelphia 19122
Copyright © 1996 by Temple University
All rights reserved
Published 1996
Printed in the United States of America

♾ The paper used in this publication meets the
requirements of the American National Standard for
Information Sciences—Permanence of Paper for
Printed Library Materials, ANSI Z39.48-1984

Text design by Erin Kirk New

Library of Congress Cataloging-in-Publication Data

Stefancic, Jean.
No mercy : how conservative think tanks and
foundations changed America's social agenda /
Jean Stefancic, Richard Delgado.
p.   cm.
Includes bibliographical references and index.
ISBN 1-56639-469-4 (cloth : alk. paper). —
ISBN 1-56639-470-8 (pbk : alk. paper)
1. Social movements—United States. 2. Social
problems—United States. 3. United States—Social
policy—1980–1993. 4. United States—Social
policy—1993–   5. Conservatism—United States.
6. Research institutes—United States.   I. Delgado, Richard.
II. Title.
HN65.S718   1996
361.1′0973—dc20   96-14145

The quality of mercy is not strain'd;

It droppeth as the gentle rain from heaven

Upon the place beneath: it is twice bless'd;

It blesseth him that gives and him that takes:

'Tis mightiest in the mightiest; it becomes

The throned monarch better than his crown;

His sceptre shows the force of temporal power,

The attribute to awe and majesty,

Wherein doth sit the dread and fear of kings;

But mercy is above this sceptred sway, —

It is enthroned in the hearts of kings,

It is an attribute to God himself;

And earthly power doth then show likest God's

When mercy seasons justice.

———————————————————

WILLIAM SHAKESPEARE

The Merchant of Venice. 4.1.184–97

Contents

Foreword

The Italian political theorist Antonio Gramsci distinguished between political "wars of maneuver" and "wars of position." The war of maneuver occurs as parties face off against each other in elections and other confrontations. The war of position, in contrast, occurs as political actors develop their ideological stances, which Gramsci believed was an essential precondition to success in the war of maneuver.

No Mercy describes in detail how conservatives have conducted a successful war of position over the past decades. It demonstrates how a network of think tanks supported by generous foundation grants produced position papers, op-ed articles, and books that shifted the ground of discussion away from liberal solutions to what many Americans believed were real social problems, and toward conservative solutions, sometimes to "problems" of conservatives' own creation.

Why were liberals unable to counter with their own moves in a war of position? *No Mercy* concludes with some speculations. Conservatives have correctly understood that liberals have indeed conducted their own "culture wars" in the academy and are winning those wars. Liberals have been unable, however, to translate those victories into even a modest holding action in the policy arena.

In part the reasons are straightforward. Liberal intellectuals have on the whole found their homes in the academy. As Russell Jacoby has argued, liberal academics can attain and preserve their positions and prestige within the academy only by writing for their professional colleagues. Academic writing has its own conventions, which are rarely helpful in policy discourse.

Then, too, liberal academics have full-time jobs as academics. They have to teach classes, grade papers and examinations, and help run their universities. The network of conservative think tanks supports people who have no obligations other than advancing the conservative cause.

Finally, many left-leaning academics believe that left politics for the foreseeable future must build on "identity politics," the assertion of claims by groups distinguished from each other by race, ethnicity, gender, and sexual orientation. That strategic judgment may prove to be correct as the war of position continues, but it has made it difficult for liberal academics to develop public policy positions that are tightly connected to the identity politics they defend in the academy.

Why have liberal foundations done far less than conservative ones to give liberal intellectuals a financial alternative to working in the academy? Here again *No Mercy* sketches the story. Liberal foundations are typically far more interested in "action" projects than in "merely" intellectual ones. In Gramsci's terms, they are attentive to wars of maneuver but not wars of position.

When a war of maneuver is actually occurring, of course, such a judgment is entirely sensible. It is equally sensible if one already has a defensible position during a war of position. In the 1960s, for example, the Democratic Party's Great Society programs garnered substantial foundation support, in part because they represented a war of maneuver against reactionary forces and in part because they were living off the intellectual capital accumulated during the long post–New Deal Democratic ascendancy.

That capital dissipated as the United States' position in the world economy changed. The pieties of New Deal and Great Society liberalism are inadequate in today's war of position. To some extent, liberal foundations have failed to adapt to changed circumstances. *No Mercy* may induce some reflection on their part.

Two additional features of liberal foundations deserve mention, however, for they suggest that liberal intellectuals may continue to struggle at a disadvantage in the current war of position. First, foundations are created by those who have accumulated substantial wealth as capitalists. One should not be surprised to discover that foundations with such origins hesitate to support the development of intellectual positions that might cast some doubt on the virtues of capitalism—or at least that the distribution of foundation resources would be skewed in the direction of supporting those who support capitalism.

Second, liberal foundations are liberal not simply in terms of their vague commitments to social justice, but more deeply in their commitment to principles of neutrality that make them uncomfortable with making grants that seem too "political." A liberal foundation can readily give money to support a hospital or medical research on illnesses that afflict the poor. It will find it more difficult to give money to support research on why poor people get sick so often, and even more difficult to give money to support research on why poor people are poor. Again, the point should not be overstated. Liberal foundations do support some research with a thrust critical of capitalism, but they cannot do so systematically without betraying their liberal commitments to politically neutral scholarship.

No Mercy is hardly politically neutral, but it surely is scholarship—and fascinating scholarship at that. Its analysis may help liberal intellectuals to understand how it came about that current policy debates are conducted on premises that seem to us quite inappropriate and indeed peculiar. Its recommendations may also help us gain some ground in the current war of position. In these troubled times, even such modest gains must be counted as a major achievement.

Mark Tushnet

Acknowledgments

WE WISH TO THANK our editor, Doris Braendel, for her inspiration and encouragement; our copyeditor, Debby Stuart, for exemplary attention to structure and detail; Jennifer Bradfield, Pamela Compo, Peter Johnson, Blaine Lozano Milne, Kim Quinn, Linda Ramirez, and Melissa Richards for unflagging and high quality research assistance. Marge Brunner, Cynthia Carter, Anne Guthrie, Linda Spiegler, and Kay Wilkie prepared the manuscript with intelligence and care.

Our gratitude goes to the Rockefeller Foundation Scholar-in-Residence Program at Bellagio, Italy, where many of the ideas in Chapter 8 were developed, and to the countless investigative journalists on whose work we relied. Many of the organizations studied were kind enough to send us annual reports and literature; for this, we are grateful.

Evelyn Hu-deHart, Michael Olivas, and Katheryn Russell supplied notes, articles, and encouragement. They give new meaning to the term colleague. Gene Nichol, dean of the University of Colorado Law School, provided both a supportive atmosphere and material assistance without which this book would not have been written. We also acknowledge the generous support of the IMPART program at University of Colorado, which enabled us to complete this project in a timely fashion.

No Mercy

Introduction

THE CONSERVATIVE SURGE began quietly, in the late 1960s. While the rest of the country was marching for civil rights, protesting the war in Indochina, and experimenting with drugs and freedom from convention, small groups of conservatives were meeting to plan their long-range agenda and deciding what to do when they returned, as they knew they would, to power. Some of the think tanks we meet in this book formed and began raising money among the faithful.

The conservative elite bided their time. With Richard Nixon's election in 1968, moderate conservatism became fashionable. Little innovation occurred, however, until about 1978, when William Simon, secretary of the treasury under Presidents Nixon and Ford, called for a radical rethinking of conservative principles. His book *A Time for Truth* urged the right to rise above the homilies of both classical liberalism and Goldwater-era conservatism and forge a new set of institutions capable of leading America into a new age. He also urged corporations to support counter-intellectuals in their struggle to come. The Reagan era was a time of consolidation and experiment. Supply-side economics came and went. Religion, family values, and patriotism came to stay.

Beginning about 1985, all the careful preparation began to pay off. The new conservative movement exploded on the national scene. One successful campaign followed another: official English, immigration reform, welfare revisionism, limits on affirmative action, rollbacks in women's procreative rights. As we write, conservatives in Congress are well on the way toward enacting House Speaker Newt Gingrich's Contract with America. In the last election, nearly two-thirds of white males voted Republican.

How did this happen? This book is about the role of conservative think tanks and foundations—brains and money—in bringing about the conservative revolution. Our guiding premise is that America works best when it receives a roughly equal infusion of ideas from the right and the left. For nearly two decades, this balance has been tilting sharply. Today, society is out of kilter, the right in full cry, the left defeated and listless. Most new programs and initiatives come from the right. The left has had little to do with setting the country's agenda and seems unable to mount any sort of effective resistance to the conservative juggernaut.

Out of the belief that this is harmful for the country, we wrote this book. Realizing that we could not address every aspect of the right-wing surge, we examine seven selected campaigns that the right wing mounted, all with remarkable success, over the last dozen years: official English; Proposition 187 and immigration reform; IQ, race, and eugenics; affirmative action; welfare; tort reform; and campus multiculturalism. We look for what enabled conservatives to wage these battles so effectively, focusing particularly on the roles right-wing think tanks and foundations have played in backing and guiding these movements. In the final chapter, we summarize what we have learned and address why it proved so easy for conservatives to transform America's landscape practically overnight. We tell what will happen if liberals do not marshal more effective opposition than they have managed so far. And we conclude with a few suggestions for reformers determined to get America back on course.

Although we consider ourselves well to the left end of the political spectrum, and expect the audience for this book to be so as well, we must concede our grudging respect for certain aspects of the way the right does business. We wrote this book out of concern over what the conservative movement is doing to causes—social equity, civil rights, personal freedom— that we hold dear. Yet, as we wrote, we could not help being impressed with the professionalism and cold precision with which the right has been waging and winning struggle after struggle. Leftist, progressive readers may find (as we do) the ideas and principles that animate the conservative program unappealing. We have little admiration for the substance of the right's social agenda—its rollback of affirmative action, welfare for the needy, aid to college students and its attack on the multicultural canon and on all the other programs discussed in this book. But the dedication, economy of effort, and sheer ingenuity of much of the conservative machine are extraordinary. We wrote this book to inform the American public how that machine operates—not to celebrate, but to deplore it. We wrote to encourage the left to get busy and counter it before it is too late. If liberals are to bring this country back nearer the center they must understand—and even at times emulate—the strategies and approaches deployed by their opposite numbers on the other side of the political spectrum.

Seven Campaigns That Changed

the Face of America

"It's precisely because of the large numbers of
Hispanics who have come here, that we ought to
remind them, and better still educate them to the fact
that the United States is not a mongrel nation. We
have a common language, it's English and we're damn
proud of it."
— Terry Robbins, former head of U.S. English
operations in Florida

Official English

BY THE YEAR 2000, the number of non-English-speaking residents in
the United States is expected to reach 40 million. Many find this alarming,
worrying that we will become a fractured society, unable to understand one
another, transact business, or perpetuate our common culture. Public interest groups such as U.S. English and lobbying groups such as English
First have capitalized on these fears, organizing and agitating on behalf of
an English-only agenda. A proposal in 1982 by the late Senator S. I.
Hayakawa (R-Calif.) to make English the official language of the United
States fired the opening salvo.[1] Hayakawa, a semanticist whose Japanese
immigrant family had settled in bilingual Canada, co-founded an organi-
zation called U.S. English. Although subcommittees of the Senate and
House Judiciary Committees held hearings on his proposed official-
English constitutional amendment, the measure did not pass.

Undeterred, the movement shifted its focus to the state level, where it
achieved rapid success. In the November 1986 election, California passed
Proposition 63 by a 3–1 margin, making English its official language. Over
$1 million was spent in support of the measure,[2] including $500,000 from
Hayakawa's U.S. English,[3] by then the nation's largest and most powerful

English-only activist group. With half of its membership residing in California, the organization was well situated to make the state its trial run. The initiative was critical to the movement as well because of its far-reaching wording; of the six states that had passed official-English legislation, California's was the first to require the legislature to undertake *affirmative measures* to "preserve and enhance the use of English." Passage of the initiative also indicated a change in public sentiment since previously California had enacted broad legislation protecting nonspeakers of English.[4]

Building on the momentum of the California campaign, supporters of English-only returned to the federal level, lobbying and petitioning conservative Republicans Senator Steven Symms of Idaho and Representative Norm Shumway of California to sponsor several of the six bills introduced into the U.S. Senate and House in 1987 to amend the Constitution and make English the official language. Shumway, who later became chairman of U.S. English, believes that bilingualism is a threat to national unity and could lead to social unrest. Other supporters argue that the bills will help minorities assimilate and advance more quickly in American society.[5] None of the early bills passed; but at the time of writing, a new generation of bills was on the floor of the 104th Congress. One, jointly proposed by Representative Bill Emerson (R-Mo.) and Senator Richard Shelby (R-Ala.), is the most popular, with 160 Republican co-sponsors. It would make English the official language, with an exception for emergency services. Another bill requires citizenship ceremonies to be performed in English. A third calls for printing ballots in English only, while a fourth does away with bilingual education.

Not Going Quietly into the Night: The Groups and Their Connections

A main player in the English-only movement, U.S. English is a national nonprofit organization founded in 1983 by Hayakawa and John Tanton, a retired Michigan ophthalmologist. Tanton, formerly a liberal conservationist, in his previous guise belonged to a web of groups with overlapping interests and agendas, including population control and immigration reform. After holding various offices in the Sierra Club and Planned Parenthood, he went on to become president of Zero Population Growth. When his position that immigration was the main cause of overpopulation became unacceptable to that group, he founded the Federation for American Immigration Reform (FAIR). Tanton founded U.S. English when FAIR refused to embrace the English-only movement, although staff members still move between the two groups, which share the same office space, direct-mail consultant, general counsel, and funding benefactor.[6] Boasting over 620,000[7] members nationwide, the group's ultimate goal is to make English the official language of the U.S. government through a constitutional amendment. Other goals include: "action to end policies which require government agencies to conduct their official business in multiple languages; enforcement of English language and civics requirements for naturalization; English proficiency as a national priority; expanded opportunities to learn English quickly in our schools and in the workplace."[8] Unlike other groups, however, the organization does not support English-only workplaces.[9] Foreign-speakers may still, for example, discuss their homeland during breaks, or ask each other how to use safety equipment or find the bathroom in their native language.

In 1986 Tanton wrote a controversial paper for a private study group known as WITAN, a word derived from the Old English *witenagemot*, meaning wise men who advise the king—a kind of prototypical Anglo-Saxon think tank.[10] In the paper Tanton asks a series of questions on a variety of topics dealing with the consequences of immigration in California, some of which are:

> "To govern is to populate." Will the present majority peaceably hand over its political power to a group that is simply more fertile?
>
> As Whites see their power and control over their lives declining, will they simply go quietly into the night? Or will there be an explosion?
>
> Can *homo contraceptivus* compete with *homo progenitiva* if borders aren't controlled? Or is advice to limit one's family simply advice to move over and let someone else with greater reproductive powers occupy the space?
>
> Perhaps this is the first instance in which those with their pants up are going to get caught by those with their pants down?
>
> Since the majority of the retirees will be Non-Hispanic Whites, but the workers will be minorities, will the latter be willing to pay for the care of the former? They will also have to provide the direct care: How will they get along, especially through a language barrier?[11]

The document was never intended to become public, but in 1988 it was discovered and disclosed by the *Arizona Republic* during the state's official-

English initiative campaign. It created a sensation. Arthur J. Kropp, president of People for the American Way, called for the immediate resignation of U.S. English board members, declaring, "The scandal has laid bare the ugly core of the English-only movement. The real motivation for too many of the movement's leaders is racism, plain and simple. The leaders of U.S. English have grossly misrepresented their real purpose."[12] Amid the controversy Tanton resigned as chairman, as did advisory board members Linda Chavez, former executive director of the U.S. Commission on Civil Rights, and Walter Cronkite.[13] One who did not resign was Alistair Cooke, award-winning television host for PBS's *Masterpiece Theatre*. Cooke, an immigrant from England in 1941, holds that a common language is necessary to maintain national unity and dismisses charges of racism toward the movement as simply "inevitable."[14]

To temper the charges against it, U.S. English points out that a majority of its leaders, as well as a large number of its members, are minority immigrants.[15] The organization also paints itself as the real champion of ethnic and linguistic nondiscrimination. Because over 150 languages are spoken in the United States, the impracticability of printing government and official documents in all of them would entail discriminating against groups who do not speak Spanish or another major world language.[16] Leaders also point to the current troubles in Yugoslavia, arguing that without a common language the United States is headed in the same direction.[17] Many of these justifications and comparisons, of course, are the same ones the public heard in connection with proposed legislation at the national level—not surprising since they were made by many of the same people.

Beset by power struggles within and criticized nationwide in the press, U.S. English spent two years recovering from the disclosure of John Tanton's WITAN memo. Fiscal problems in 1990 led to an Internal Revenue Service examination. In spite of it all, U.S. English regrouped and retained the loyalty of most of its members, who continued to contribute a major portion of its budget through direct-mail solicitations.[18] In January 1991, the organization commissioned a Gallup Poll, which purportedly showed 78 percent of registered voters favoring making English the official language of the United States and requiring that all government forms, proceedings of the legislature, and other business take place in English.[19] Soon afterward, the organization launched a national "Campaign for Our Common

Language," kicked off by a rally in Washington, D.C., in September 1991 that attracted hundreds of supporters from more than a dozen states.[20]

Funding for the English-only movement comes from a miscellany of sources. In 1993, U.S. English reported total contributions in excess of $6 million.[21] Apart from member dues (approximately $20 a year), funding for the organization comes from the Laurel Foundation[22] and reportedly also from the Pioneer Fund[23]—two groups that have backed a number of dubious ventures and that appear several times later in this book. The Laurel Foundation, established by Cordelia Scaife May, a Mellon family heiress with a keen interest in Third World birthrates and population control, has supported the Tanton network for many years. According to an examination of IRS records by investigative reporter James Crawford, between 1983 and 1989 May donated at least $5.8 million to the U.S. English Foundation (formerly U.S. English), FAIR, Population-Environment Balance (formerly Environmental Fund), and U.S. Inc. (Tanton's umbrella corporation).[24]

Laurel also gave $5,000 toward the distribution of the first United States translation of Jean Raspail's 1973 novel *The Camp of the Saints*, which describes the overrunning of Europe and the United States by "swarthy hordes" from the Third World. Although former U.S. English board member Linda Chavez calls it "the most vehemently racist book I have ever read,"[25] it is said to have been a big hit with staff members at the organization. Laurel also helped fund Garrett Hardin's 1993 book, *Living Within Limits: Ecology, Economics, and Population Taboos.*[26] Hardin, professor emeritus at the University of California at Santa Barbara, is a co-founder of Zero Population Growth, a WITAN participant, and a member of FAIR. He supports incentives for sterilization and argues that multiculturalism leads to chaos and loss of freedom. Like U.S. English, he points to the former Yugoslavia as a prime example of cultural disintegration. An equal opportunity alarmist, Hardin also warns that the United States is turning into the France Raspail depicts in his novel.[27] The Pioneer Fund also supported Hardin's book[28] as well as controversial research by J. Philippe Rushton, Richard Lynn, Arthur Jensen, and Michael Levin, figures that also appear later in this book.[29]

U.S. English directs and funds a strange assortment of groups working for its cause, including Mothers of Multicultural English (MOME), Learning English Advocates Drive (LEAD), and the Institute for Research in English Acquisition and Development (READ). MOME, a New York City group composed of immigrant mothers who want their children to be taught in

English only is directed by Anita Cloutier De la Garza. Not herself Hispanic but married to a Mexican American surgeon, De la Garza argues that to survive in today's United States and get a decent job, immigrant children must have a thorough command of English—something she believes bilingual education impairs. Although MOME is under the direction of U.S. English, the group denies that it is anti-immigrant or anti-Hispanic.[30]

LEAD, founded in 1987 by Sally Peterson, a Los Angeles Unified School District elementary school teacher, receives financial support from U.S. English and English First as well as from ten-dollar membership dues. Like De la Garza, Peterson believes that bilingual education is ineffective and that immigrant children should be taught subjects such as math and history only in English. In 1989, LEAD opposed a proposal that would have awarded certified bilingual teachers in Los Angeles special stipends for their language abilities.[31] In 1993, LEAD appeared at hearings for the reauthorization of the federal Bilingual Education Act, which allows students whose native language is not English to be taught in that language, arguing on the side of flexibility—school districts should be able to do whatever they think works. By 1993 the group boasted about twenty thousand members nationwide, many in Dade County, Florida, San Francisco, and New York City, where the Hispanic immigrant population is large.[32]

A sister organization, the READ Institute, was founded in 1989 to carry out research into the failings of bilingual education. READ received a start-up grant of $62,000 from U.S. English. In addition, it receives support from the Laurel Foundation and English Language Advocates, another Tanton organization. Rosalie Porter, author of *Forked Tongue: The Politics of Bilingual Education* and advocate of English-only instruction, took over as director in 1991. Board and advisory panel members have included Abigail Thernstrom, senior fellow at the Manhattan Institute; Christine Rossell, professor of political science at Boston University; and Richard Estrada, former research director of FAIR.[33] READ studies profess to show that native-language teaching harms the foreign-born by delaying their acquisition of English with little compensating gain. They insist that English as a Second Language (ESL) classes are more effective and less costly in the long run. Ignoring evidence by such organizations as the Mexican American Legal Defense and Education Fund that total immersion programs will cause the dropout rate for Hispanic students to rise precipitously,[34] READ urges that federal and state governments cease requiring bilingual or native-language instruction entirely.

U.S. English bills itself as a national public interest group, thereby making it eligible for 501(c)(3) status as a tax-exempt charitable organization under Internal Revenue Service regulations. Taking advantage of this status, in some years it has used up to the maximum amount allowed (20 percent of its annual budget) for lobbying expenditures. It does this, James Crawford points out, by transferring part of its tax-exempt revenue (up to 20 percent) to the U.S. English Legislative Task Force, which in turn passes it on to state lobbying groups. Thus, taxpayers, regardless of their views, are subsidizing part of the cost of U.S. English campaigns.[35]

A spin-off of U.S. English, English First is a Springfield, Virginia-based lobbying organization founded by Lawrence Pratt in 1986. Claiming approximately 250,000 members, by 1991 it had raised $7.1 million, according to official reports filed with the U.S. Senate.[36] It has three basic goals: "make English America's official language; give every child the chance to learn English; eliminate costly and ineffective multilingual programs." The organization, whose logo is the Statue of Liberty (donated by France!), attempts to achieve those goals through grassroots movements across the country. English First adopts a harsher tone than its parent organization, although its basic belief—that English unites the country—is the same. English First sponsors two associated groups to help its cause: the English First Foundation, which distributes pro-English books to school libraries, educates the public on English-only, and writes briefs on research dealing with official English and the English First Political Victory Fund, a fundraising arm that supports English-only candidates.[37]

Members of English First are convinced that the downfall of the English language in America started in the 1960s when the federal government for the first time mandated multilingual teaching.[38] A 1987 English First fund-raising letter describes non-English-speaking groups as "remain[ing] stuck in a linguistic and economic ghetto, many living off welfare and costing working Americans millions of dollars every year."[39] The organization quotes immigrants who support its cause, including Josephine Wang, a former member of the National Advisory and Coordinating Council on Bilingual Education, and Sandor Balogh, executive secretary of the National Federation of Hungarian Americans and head of University Professors for Academic Order. English First funds itself, in part, through annual membership dues of approximately twenty-eight dollars per year.[40]

English First supported the 1987 congressional movement for official

English and presented Senator Symms with over two hundred thousand signatures on petitions supporting a constitutional amendment. It also advocates English-only workplaces, arguing that if an employee is allowed to use her native language, she could secretly conspire against co-workers or supervisors. Furthermore, a Spanish-speaking worker could be harassing another Spanish speaker in that language, with impunity, if the supervisor speaks only English. English speakers would, thus, be subject to penalties for harassment that Spanish speakers would not—a situation that Jim Boulet, legislative director of English First, insists is radically unfair.[41]

English First is also active at the state level. In April 1995, Boulet wrote a letter to the editor of the *Atlanta Journal and Constitution* decrying Georgia's English-only bill because it authorized the printing of official documents in other languages and allowed the right to speak a language other than English in court.[42] The bill ultimately passed, only to be vetoed by the governor.[43] In Allentown, Pennsylvania, English First sent four thousand letters to voters asking them to support city council candidates who had sponsored the city's new English-only law. English First jumped into this seemingly innocuous election because the Department of Housing and Urban Development was making an inquiry into the new law.[44]

A third group that has recently entered the fray is English Language Advocates (ELA). Still standing by his WITAN memo, John Tanton founded this new organization as an even more hard-line version of U.S. English.[45] ELA's chairman is Bob Park, who is also the chairman of Arizonans for Official English. ELA unsuccessfully appealed, on behalf of Arizonans for Official English, a 1994 ruling from the United States Court of Appeals for the Ninth Circuit striking down Arizona's official English initiative as unconstitutional. Like all the other organizations mentioned so far, ELA argues that the official English initiative preserves a sense of community and that without it the government would become a Tower of Babel.[46]

An Intricate Web

Although English-only groups are sometimes in competition with one another, they are closely connected in terms of personnel, rhetoric, and method of operation. The key players, also ever-present in right-wing circles, crop up throughout this book. Consider, for example, the career of

Lawrence (Larry) Pratt. English First president, Pratt is also secretary of the Council for Inter-American Security (CIAS), which sees increasing Hispanic immigration as a threat to the United States. The council issued a document in 1986 declaring, "Hispanics in America today represent a very dangerous, subversive force that is bent on taking over our nation's political institutions for the purpose of imposing Spanish as the official language of the United States."[47] Earlier it published *On Creating a Hispanic America: A Nation Within a Nation*, which warned that bilingual education "could feed and guide terrorism in the United States."[48] During the 1980s CIAS also championed Lt. Col. Oliver North, former National Security Council member under Reagan, in his covert attempts to fund and supply the contras in Nicaragua with guns.[49]

Pratt established English First in 1986 as a subsidiary of his Family Foundation, a nonprofit organization he had founded in 1980. Among other initiatives the foundation has called for a quarantine for those with AIDS; in 1990 it raised almost $150,000 to pay expenses and fines incurred by Randall Terry's Operation Rescue, a radical antiabortion group.[50]

In 1992, Pratt, in yet another guise—executive director of Gun Owners of America (which lobbies for private ownership of machine guns)—participated in a three-day strategy session in Estes Park, Colorado, where he addressed a gathering of members of Pete Peters' Christian Identity, an organization that has ties to Aryan supremacist groups, the militia movement, and survivalists. Exhorting the crowd, he advocated the right for citizens to own the military assault weapon of their choice and to belong to people's militias, which in his 1990 book *Armed People Victorious* he declared should replace professional law enforcement.[51]

The indefatigable Pratt is also a member of the Coors-funded Council for National Policy (CNP), which writer Russ Bellant has called "a secretive group of the foremost right-wing activists and funders in the United States." Founded in 1981 by Nelson Bunker Hunt, a Texas billionaire and John Birch Society council member, T. Cullen Davis, another wealthy Texan, and Tim LeHaye of Moral Majority as the right's answer to the mainline New York–based Council on Foreign Relations, CNP focuses on setting national policy for the conservative movement. Its first executive director, Woody Jenkins, told members, "I predict that one day before the end of this century, the Council will be so influential that no President, regardless of party or philosophy, will be able to ignore us or our concerns or shut us out of the highest levels of government." Members of the council have included Paul M. Weyrich, architect of conservative causes for the past two decades; direct-mail king Richard Viguerie; Heritage Foundation president Edwin Feulner; Tom Ellis, one-time director of the Pioneer Fund; Senator Jesse Helms (R-N.C.); Morton Blackwell of the Leadership Institute; J. A. Parker of the Lincoln Institute; one-time presidential candidate Pat Robertson; television evangelist Jerry Falwell; singer Pat Boone; Richard DeVos of the Amway Corporation; Joseph and Holly Coors; Edwin Meese III; Arnaud de Borchgrave; Henry Salvatori; Phyllis Schlafly; as well as military figures Lt. Col. Oliver North and retired generals John Singlaub and Gordon Sumner.[52] (Many of these people, too, reappear throughout this book.) Most recently Pratt agreed to step down as Patrick Buchanan's campaign co-chairman when his connection to para-military groups came to light during the 1996 presidential primaries.[53]

Conservative causes are generally funded in one of two ways: by business-oriented foundations, or by grassroots contributions from middle- and working-class people. Rarely is there much crossover. The foundations support curricular reform, such as teaching economics in junior high schools and educating judges and law students in law and economics approaches to deregulation. By contrast, movements promoting immigration reform, school prayer, family values, and English-only target worried lower- and middle-class people and garner support from a large number of contributors of modest means.

Official English is a nearly pristine case of the latter type of financing. Although the movement receives occasional support from conservative foundations and think tanks, this support tends to take the form of encouragement and research, not dollars. Most of the money appears to come from membership dues and direct mail campaigns emphasizing such themes as the need to preserve a common culture and for immigrants to assimilate into it as soon as possible—even in the face of social science evidence showing that most immigrants want to learn English quickly and that linguistic diversity has never in this country's history been associated with social unrest. Fundraising material capitalizes on workers' fears of multilingual confusion, linguistic ghettos, and the draining of resources from Social Security and other programs that aid the elderly and poor who are already citizens. As such, it is a true *nativist* movement—it exploits the country's fear of social upheaval and limited resources and argues for a return to core values and practices in order to cope with change.

The movement has proven highly effective in mobilizing those fears. Direct-mail appeals and newspaper ads use provocative questions ("Would you want . . . ?") and scare scenarios (for example, comparisons to the former Yugoslavia) to frame the issue as that of protecting a priceless national heritage. Advocates orchestrate the movement carefully, picking and choosing their states, cycling and recycling leaders and members, and using money shrewdly. Progressives, who have scored no comparable victory in at least three decades on any issue, should take note.

The people are tired of watching their state run wild and become a third world country.

If you catch 'em [illegal aliens] you ought to clean 'em and fry 'em.
— Harold Ezell, former western regional commissioner of the Immigration and Naturalization Service

2

Proposition 187 and

Immigration Reform

CALIFORNIA, whose ethnic and racial diversity has long been considered a source of strength, has in recent years turned into a field of battle. The cry was sounded on October 5, 1993, when a ten-person group, most of them unknown to one another, were summoned to a meeting by Ron Prince, an unemployed accountant, to discuss illegal immigration, something they all agreed had grown to dangerous proportions. By the end of the day, they agreed to launch a statewide drive for an initiative to deny public benefits to illegal immigrants.[1] The measure became known across the state and nation as Proposition 187.

Former Immigration and Naturalization Service (INS) officials Alan Nelson and Harold Ezell, widely credited with creating the initiative, were only two of the ten at the meeting. Others included Prince and Republican Assemblyman Richard L. Mountjoy, political consultants Robert Kiley and Barbara Kiley (mayor of Yorba Linda) and police employee Barbara

Coe.[2] Nelson and Ezell had become full-time activists in the immigration reform movement, forming a national organization, Americans Against Illegal Immigration (AAII), which was later to aid the coalition of grassroots groups that sprang up to support Proposition 187. Seed money for AAII came from Howard Jarvis Taxpayers Association and Butcher, Forde and Mollrich, the political consulting firm that successfully directed the Proposition 13 campaign that limited California property taxes in 1978.[3] Coe, along with former INS border agent Bill King, had led a network of grassroots political groups (Citizens for Action Now) that dabbled in various conservative causes. After the October meeting, Coe and Prince joined forces and formed an organization, the California Coalition for Immigration Reform, that proved to be instrumental in the drive to punish aliens and foreign workers. In unconscious irony, the group chose the name "SOS" (Save Our State) for the campaign, while eating at a Mexican restaurant.[4]

Proposition 187 passed on November 8, 1994, by a vote of 59.2 percent to 40.2 percent. Its key provisions prohibit illegal immigrants from attending public schools and universities or obtaining nonemergency medical care at facilities receiving public funds. Proposition 187 also requires schools, hospitals, and social service agencies to report suspected illegal immigrants, including parents of native-born children, to state and federal authorities. Finally, the measure bars illegal immigrants from social service programs such as disability insurance, family planning, and foster care.[5]

The Juggernaut

Proposition 187 was endorsed by numerous influential people and groups, including California Governor Pete Wilson, the California Republican Party, United Organizations of Taxpayers, Inc., Ross Perot's United We Stand America of California, Federation for American Immigration Reform (FAIR), Americans Against Illegal Immigration (AAII), California Coalition for Immigration Reform, Stop the Out-of-Control Problems of Immigration Today (S.T.O.P.-I.T.), and two-time GOP presidential candidate Patrick J. Buchanan.[6]

Proposition 187 encountered opposition from some of the state's most powerful institutions including Taxpayers Against 187, formed by four groups that stood to suffer losses if the initiative passed: California Teachers Association, California Medical Association, California State Council of the Service Employees International Union, and California Labor Federation, AFL-CIO.[7] Other opponents included President Bill Clinton, U.S. Senator Dianne Feinstein (D-Calif.), Los Angeles County Sheriff Sherman Block, California Parent-Teacher Association, California School Boards Association, California State Employees Association, the Peace Officers Research Association of California, the California Organization of Police and Sheriffs, League of Women Voters, Mexican American Legal Defense and Education Fund, Los Angeles City Council, Los Angeles County Board of Supervisors, Sierra Club, American Jewish Congress, and the editors of the *Wall Street Journal, USA Today, Los Angeles Times, San Francisco Chronicle,* and *Orange County Register.*[8]

Although Proposition 187 garnered much conservative support, a few influential Republicans opposed the initiative, including Ron Unz, an adjunct scholar at the Center for Equal Opportunity who challenged Governor Pete Wilson in the 1994 California Primary. Unz, whose agenda otherwise opposed affirmative action, bilingual education, abortion, and welfare, persuaded influential national conservative William Kristol, who in turn convinced William Bennett and Jack Kemp to oppose the initiative.[9] Kemp, a former U.S. representative, and Bennett, former U.S. secretary of education, are co-directors of Empower America, a conservative think tank that has supported school choice in Milwaukee and California, antitakings measures in Arizona, "Three Strikes and You're Out" in California and Washington, and repeal of rent controls in Massachusetts.[10] Kemp and Bennett staunchly oppose illegal immigration but nevertheless warn against "a series of fundamentally flawed, constitutionally questionable 'solutions' which are not consonant with our history; which would prove ineffectual; and which would help contribute to a nativist, anti-immigrant climate."[11]

In addition to Empower America, several other conservative think tanks opposed the initiative. Steve Moore, an analyst for the Cato Institute, led prominent conservatives, including Milton Friedman, as well as representatives of the Heritage Foundation, the American Enterprise Institute, and the Christian Coalition, in a letter-writing campaign against it.[12] Leaders from the Alexis de Tocqueville Institution and the Reason Foundation signed a statement warning that Proposition 187 would turn health care workers and educators "into de facto INS agents and Border Patrol guards, forcing them to investigate the citizen status of every child and parent." According to de Tocqueville executive director Cesar V. Conda, "It's a Big Brother, big government scheme that will do little to deter illegal immigration."[13]

Funding the Juggernaut

Opponents of Proposition 187 raised a huge amount of money, $836,973, as of September 30, 1994. The largest contributions were $321,896 from the California Teachers Association, $139,837 from the California State Council of Service Employees, and $100,000 from Univision Television Group, Inc., a New Jersey–based Spanish television network with stations in Los Angeles and San Francisco. Monica Lozano, associate publisher of the Los Angeles–based newspaper *La Opinion*, contributed $5,000.[14]

Supporters of Proposition 187, by contrast, ran a relatively low-budget campaign, relying mostly on an army of volunteers. As with official English, the initiative received funding from many sources, including the founders themselves: Prince—though unemployed and with no assets at the time, according to his former attorney, William Baker, to whom he owed $9,643—donated $2,000 to get the campaign started and loaned it another $20,000 in May 1994, while Coe contributed $15,000.[15] John Tanton, founder of FAIR, made a small contribution.[16] But much of the funding came from a large number of individuals, many of them retired: Of contributions in which occupations were listed, 58 percent were from retirees. Although the largest seniors' advocacy group, AARP (American Association of Retired Persons) opposed Proposition 187, talk show appearances by Proposition 187 advocates produced a heavy flow of contributions from retired people. Consultants attributed retirees' support to resentment over bilingualism and the belief that their benefits are endangered by the cost of services to illegal immigrants.[17]

Although small contributions from retirees accounted for much of the funding, donations from wealthy individuals, large institutions, and political groups played a substantial part as well. Of the $486,044 the campaign raised from January 1, 1993, to September 30, 1994, $136,482 consisted of in-kind contributions, including $43,500 from Assemblyman Richard Mountjoy. The Republican Party contributed $86,678 cash, Mountjoy $27,850, and California state senator Don Rogers $25,000. Americans Against Illegal Immigration donated $15,740.[18]

Like Fair Skin? Try FAIR and Learn Why America Should Be as White as Possible

One source of funding for the Proposition 187 campaign that sparked considerable controversy was Federation for American Immigration Reform (FAIR), the national organization founded in 1979 by English-only activist John Tanton that seeks to end illegal immigration and sharply curb the legal variety. FAIR had quickly gained fifty thousand members with direct mail appeals emphasizing protection of American jobs, culture and language.

When the Proposition 187 campaign started up, Alan Nelson, one of its co-authors, was serving as a part-time consultant and lobbyist for FAIR.[19] This connection proved controversial when opponents of Proposition 187 learned of FAIR's receipt of money from the Pioneer Fund, which has promoted the eugenics movement and sponsored research seeking to prove the genetic inferiority of minorities. (See Chapter 3.) Pioneer was established in 1937 by Wickliffe Draper, an independently wealthy New England textile industrialist. Its first president, eugenicist Harry Laughlin, was influential in lobbying for anti-immigration legislation in 1924. Basing his proposals on alleged genetic inferiority, he sought to prevent Russian Jews escaping persecution from entering the United States. During the 1930s Pioneer supported the translation of Nazi eugenics texts into English for sale in the United States. After World War II, Draper supported Senator Joseph McCarthy, fought against the decision in *Brown v. Board of Education*, and advocated repatriating blacks to Africa. In response to critics, Pioneer Fund's current president, Harry Weyher, asserts that the fund does not engage itself in any way in the research projects it supports—it merely gives them money—nor does it take any positions on the political issues brought up by such research.[20] Nonetheless, Proposition 187 opponents circulated a background paper to reporters entitled "The Ideas and People Behind Proposition 187," urging them to investigate the link between FAIR and the Pioneer Fund.[21]

One source of FAIR's funding has indeed been the Pioneer Fund: The fund gave FAIR $1.1 million between 1982 and 1992,[22] making it the second largest of Pioneer's twenty-two grant recipients.[23] FAIR insists that this amounts to only a small portion of its $3.5 million annual budget and that it receives contributions from forty other foundations, including the Leland Fikes ($50,000, 1992), Weeden ($25,000, 1993), Carthage ($70,000, 1992), S. H. Cowell ($36,000, 1992), and Henry Luce ($25,000, 1993) foundations, as well as the Pasadena Area Residential Aid-A Corporation ($19,000, 1993).[24]

The fund does seem constitutionally incapable of finding any anti-immigrant group it dislikes. It supports, for example, the American Immigration Control Foundation (AICF), according to the fund's president Harry Weyher, because the foundation's aims coincide with those of the fund—ending Third World immigration in the United States. AICF has received $200,000 over the years from the fund, and Pioneer grant recipients serve on its board.[25] AICF recently published John Tanton and Wayne Lutton's *The Immigration Invasion*, a book seemingly inspired by Jean Raspail's *The Camp of the Saints*, which depicts starving refugees from the Third World swarming over Europe, causing chaos and disruption. Tanton, who read the novel while establishing FAIR, has compared Raspail's "prescient" fictional catastrophe to recent pictures of Albanian and Chinese refugees clinging to boats or falling overboard.

FAIR's executive director, Dan Stein, professes not to be troubled about FAIR's financial backing from the Pioneer Fund, saying, "I don't [care] what they do with their money. . . . My job is to get every dime of Pioneer's money. . . . And if [FAIR's critics] don't like what Pioneer is doing . . . why don't they take it up with Pioneer?"[26] Furthermore, he points out, environmental groups like Negative Population Growth and Carrying Capacity Network also support immigration reform, and the Sierra Club is considering the issue.

If FAIR was not engaged with the California initiative from the beginning, it certainly became so not long after the campaign started to gain momentum. One congressional staff member noted, "These guys at FAIR have come out of nowhere to damn near shape the whole immigration debate." FAIR takes credit for passage of four bills in California in 1993: New driver's licenses will not be issued without proof of legal status; local sanctuary decrees will not be honored; undocumented prisoners will be deported; and government jobs for illegal immigrants will be banned.[27]

FAIR's initial support of Proposition 187 was premised on the belief that providing services for illegal immigrants drains taxes. But when several studies by conservative think tanks, as well as one by the Urban Institute released in late September 1994, concluded that economic losses associated with illegal immigration are more than offset by gains for private industry,[28] FAIR responded by changing its strategy to focus on the scourge of over-population. As FAIR-California media director Ira Mehlman put it: "The U.S. is more than an economy. Do we really want a society with a half-billion people in it?" He added, "American birth rates are more or less stabilized. Burgeoning growth comes primarily from immigration—two new San Franciscos every year."[29] FAIR also emphasized reports that have reached conclusions contrary to those reached by the Urban Institute, including one written by Donald Huddle of Rice University that concludes that high levels of legal as well as illegal immigration endanger the host country. Huddle's report was underwritten by Carrying Capacity Network, a nonprofit Washington-based group that promotes the connection between environmentalism and population control.[30]

Today California, Tomorrow the World?

Immediately after the passage of Proposition 187, the ACLU filed two lawsuits seeking temporary restraining orders: The first, in state court in San Francisco, challenges the denial of educational benefits; the second, in federal court, asserts the unconstitutionality of the proposition itself. Implementation of health care cut-offs was delayed under an executive order issued by Governor Pete Wilson until the state Department of Health Services developed emergency regulations.[31] On December 14, 1994, district court judge Mariana R. Pfaelzer enjoined the major provisions of Proposition 187 until trial; the case is still pending.[32]

California's adoption of Proposition 187 emboldened FAIR to seek immigration reform in Congress. "Proposition 187's success sends the unequivocal message to the new House and Senate that the people of California and the people of our nation won't accept a few extra border guards—they want comprehensive reform," said spokesman Dan Stein, adding: "Proposition 187 has pushed immigration reform to the front burner for the 104th Congress."[33] On November 18, 1994, Wilson, in an address to the Heritage Foundation, proposed that Congress adopt a federal version of Proposition 187. Congress, he declared, should either fully reimburse states for the cost of providing public services to illegal immigrants or end requirements that states provide them.[34]

Wilson's view has received support from the Washington Legal Foundation (WLF), a conservative public interest law group. Speaking on behalf of the organization, attorney David Andrew Price charged that the obligation for states to provide free public education to illegal immigrants is one of the largest unfunded federal requirements. Even prior to the battle in California, the foundation, on behalf of forty U.S. senators and representatives, had filed an amicus curiae brief against the federal government on the ground that various mandates arising from illegal immigration constitute intrusions into state sovereignty. [35]

Frustrated by the slow pace of court action, WLF published a legal opinion letter entitled "Judicial Activists Subvert Will of Majority on Proposition 187," setting forth statistics that illustrate why the majority of Californians voted for Proposition 187: 43 percent of all illegal immigrants in the United States, 1.7 million, reside in California; the state has more illegal immigrants than some states have residents; and the annual cost to taxpayers of providing public education to illegal immigrants is $1.5 billion, of health care $395 million, and of incarceration $474 million. But now, the letter concludes, "the will of 4.6 million voters has been overridden by the decision of two judges, . . . and lawyers are busy churning up huge fees (which the public may have to pay), and illegal immigrants are free to consume costly public services and public education (at taxpayer expense) without fear of apprehension or deportation." [36]

After the California election, FAIR warned that if the federal government does not take steps to deal with the problem of illegal immigration, other states where immigration is a major political concern are likely to follow California's lead. Ira Mehlman named six others where immigration is a major political concern—Arizona, Florida, Illinois, New Jersey, New York, and Texas. His prediction is proving correct. Floridians for Immigration Control closely followed the measure in California, then asked Proposition 187 proponents for help in drafting a similar initiative there. A spokesperson for the Austin Citizens Committee for Fair Immigration announced that the organization was awaiting the outcome of the lawsuits against Proposition 187 before lobbying for a similar measure in Texas, and a spokesperson for the Illinois Citizens for Immigration Reform declared that the organization would submit a proposal similar to Proposition 187 to the state legislature. [37]

Although many states are considering similar measures, Florida, with an initiative process like California's, has taken the lead. Several groups, including Floridians for Immigration Control, Citizens of Dade United, and the regional chapter of FAIR, are gearing up to put a similar measure on the state ballot in 1996. According to Dave Ray, the regional director of FAIR who has organized several meetings across Florida to raise awareness, "Polls show that immigration is the No. 2 issue on people's minds after crime, . . . even bigger than education and taxes."[38]

On May 4, 1995, a political committee—FLA-187—unveiled state constitutional amendments that would deny public education, welfare, and other social services, except for emergency health care, to illegal immigrants and also make English the official language at all levels of government. "We are concerned that our nation needs not only an immigration policy, but an assimilation policy," declared executive director Robert Ross. FLA-187 received support from Floridians for Immigration Control, Citizens of Dade United, FAIR, and the ubiquitous Barbara Coe, co-founder of the California Coalition for Immigration Reform.

Although Florida citizens have reacted to messages like these with alarm, statistics from many Florida state and federal agencies suggest that illegal immigration in Florida is not as widespread as it is perceived to be. According to 1992 statistics, more new residents moved to Florida from Alabama than from Cuba; fifteen times more moved to Florida from other parts of the United States than from all Spanish-speaking countries combined; and people who moved from other states outnumbered immigrants from all foreign countries eight to one. Florida residents who claim Hispanic heritage constitute less than 12 percent of the state's population, and the majority of them are American citizens. But according to David May, eastern regional field director for FAIR, statistics do not matter—perception does: "Look, it's South Florida that has the immigration problem now. But there is a perception that the problem is creeping northward. And in Broward and Palm Beach counties, they believe that once the problem starts, it can't be stopped."[39]

Scholarship for Hire

FAIR leaders appear ready to advance even stricter controls on illegal immigration and a moratorium on the legal variety. According to Frank Sharry, executive director of the National Immigration Forum, which lobbies in support of immigrants, "FAIR wants to take advantage of the energy of 187 proponents, and try to get them to buy into their agenda, which is to attack legal immigration. It will be interesting to see how far the 187 people will go in embracing FAIR's extreme restrictionist views."[40] Perhaps he was thinking of views like those FAIR published in a March 1995 booklet entitled "Ten Steps to Ending Illegal Immigration." The booklet recommends enforcing a moratorium against all legal immigration, inspecting and shutting down job sites for illegal workers and their employers, withholding citizenship from children born in the United States of illegal immigrants, jailing more illegals while they await deportation, and requiring every citizen to carry a work eligibility card.[41]

Passage of Proposition 187 also led conservative think tanks to conduct studies on the effects of illegal immigration. One supporter of Proposition 187, Tom Tancredo, president of the Independence Institute (a conservative think tank in Golden, Colorado), believes the initiative is not a racial or a civil rights issue: "It's economic. . . . What we see in this proposition passing in California is part of a bigger phenomenon. . . . There's a strong anti-federal government feeling. The government has been unable to control the border in California. The people voted to take care of the problem."[42] California spends $2.8 billion on services for 1.7 million illegal immigrants. How about Colorado? The Independence Institute commissioned a study to determine just that.[43] It also organized a conference in Denver to encourage a petition drive to place a measure similar to Proposition 187 on the Colorado ballot in 1996. Representatives of the institute admitted that they knew it would probably be declared unconstitutional but added that they needed Proposition 187 to unite a large conservative constituency that would then mobilize to promote the institute's agenda of eliminating multicultural curriculums and bilingual education in schools.[44]

Independence completed its study, entitled "Compassion or Compulsion: The Immigration Debate and Proposition 187," in late April 1995, finding that of Colorado's 3.5 million population, 142,000 are non-U.S. citizens and about 50,000 illegal immigrants. It also found that Colorado taxpayers pay as much as $22 million a year for welfare and health care for noncitizens, $8 million a year to jail illegal aliens, and between $5 million and $13 million a year to educate the children of illegal immigrants. In discussing the sociopolitical expense of immigration, the study sounds a familiar refrain: "Immigration and the multiculturalism it feeds are threatening to dissolve the bonds of common nationhood and the underlying sense of a common national destiny, bringing forward the danger of a Balkanized America." Tancredo went on to announce that "a common language is an extremely important element of nationhood" and called for elimination of bilingual education, which is "both educationally unsound and politically divisive."[45]

Intriguingly, other conservative think tanks reached contrary conclusions. In mid-November 1994, Jack Kemp and William Bennett of Empower America and Linda Chavez, then director of the Center for the New American Community at the Manhattan Institute, held a press conference to mark the release of the Manhattan Institute and Pacific Research Institute's book, *Strangers at Our Gate: Immigration in the 1990s.* The book contains an index of leading immigration indicators and concludes that immigration is a net benefit, not a drawback to the regions in which immigrants settle. Bennett attacked Governor Wilson of California for legalizing over one million illegal immigrants as part of a Seasonal Agricultural Worker Program and then complaining when illegals kept coming and few returned to their native countries. Kemp pleaded for Republicans to turn to immigrants and blacks to strengthen the party. Chavez warned of the danger of letting legitimate concerns about illegal immigration "spill over to turn us into an anti-immigration, close the borders, restrict legal immigration fervor." She charged that this was the goal of groups like FAIR who focus on illegal immigration because for years they have been unable to get enough support for measures that would control the flow of legal immigrants.[46]

The press conference led FAIR and the Manhattan Institute to release their own, competing "leading immigration indicators." FAIR cited numbers showing that immigration accounts for nearly half the country's population growth, that the number of legal immigrants on welfare is increasing, and that illegal immigrants are more likely to be in prison than legal residents. Manhattan responded by re-emphasizing that legal immigrants are more likely than natives to participate in the labor force, hold a doctorate degree, and stay married;[47] that the percentage of immigrants in the population is less than half of what it was during the great European migrations at the turn of the century; that states with larger percentages of immigrants, such as Texas, have lower unemployment rates; and that immigrants earn roughly $700 more a year per capita than natives, with those who entered the United States before 1980 earning nearly $4,000 more.[48]

Republican Dilemma: The Immigrant as Parasite or Modern-Day Horatio Alger?

The increasing focus on immigration reform at the federal level after the passage of Proposition 187 unveiled a sharp division within the Republican Party. "If Proposition 187 goes national," Kemp predicted, "that would be something on which the soul of our party would be decided."[49] William F. Buckley Jr., founder of the *National Review*, wrote that while "the dispute on immigration policy within the right had up until just now exercised itself in the theoretical playing grounds," after the success of Proposition 187, "the two camps are now out in the open, moving towards one another with sabers drawn."[50]

The split within the party arises from a growing conflict between two fundamental conservative notions. On one hand, Republicans strongly support cuts in government spending, particularly for health care and welfare. On the other, Republicans promote the entrepreneurial values that immigrants, legal and illegal, often exhibit. Indeed, statistics released in the Manhattan Institute's report show that immigrants, especially those who arrived before 1980, are more likely even than the native-born to own their own businesses.

Upon taking control of Congress in January, 1995, Republicans were forced to face the conflict almost immediately. Their "Contract with America," which would come to a floor vote within one hundred days, included a provision that would end many services even to *legal* immigrants.[51] House Republicans quickly drafted legislation excluding most legal immigrants from sixty federal programs such as housing assistance, Medicaid, childhood immunizations, and subsidized school lunches. Steve Moore of the Cato Institute supported the legislation, explaining, "Our belief is that nobody should get these programs, but if welfare is not going to be eliminated outright, then we argue that it should be for citizens only."[52]

On January 5, 1995, Senator Richard Shelby (R-Ala.) introduced major reform legislation, the "Immigration Moratorium Act," which would place a five-year moratorium on legal immigration, reducing it by at least two-thirds, down to 325,000 a year instead of the current 1 million. Dan Stein, executive director of FAIR, applauded: "We will not have real immigration reform unless Congress reduces legal immigration numerically, structurally, and radically." FAIR also predicted that if Congress fails to pass tough legislation in 1995, immigration reform will play a major role in the 1996 presidential election.[53] Reaction from corporate America, especially the high-tech sector, to measures like these, has been intensely negative.[54]

Like the English-only movement, the movement to cut services to immigrants draws on a set of anxieties that typify the struggling blue-collar and middle classes. Many of the more principled or "blue chip" Republican organizations and spokespersons have declined to endorse the mean-spirited nativist sentiments that fuel these movements. But the Republican Party has partially endorsed immigration reform, and both movements have had little difficulty in obtaining funding from the smaller and more ideological think tanks and foundations on the right, as well as from many small, individual donors, including the retired. The coalition of activists who successfully pressed for English-only reforms includes many who simply moved over to immigration reform when the first campaign proved successful. By the same token, many of the same constituencies that donated money for the first cause went on to contribute to the second. None of this should be surprising—the movements share a common set of concerns: fear of engulfment by waves of immigrants; a dislike of foreignness; and a sense that the nation's unity is threatened when too many cultures, languages, and experiences enter the American mix too rapidly. The movements also tap economic anxieties that the middle and working classes feel more acutely than do those at the top—fear that immigrants will take jobs, that they will require too many services thus increasing the tax burden for U.S. workers, and that English, the great binding tie, will diminish in importance.

Conservatives have pressed these and related campaigns with notable success. They have shrewdly manipulated fears and then adroitly solicited funds from the newly insecure. They have capitalized on economic dislocations to scapegoat a class of people—immigrants—that is by and large hard working and self-supporting. As with official English, they have selected their targets carefully and spent money where it would count. They shuttle talent and resources from one successful issue to other embryonic ones. They make good use of personnel, deploying the hard-hitting shock troops, more moderate academics, and senior figureheads as the situation calls for them. Little money or effort is wasted. The liberal opposition has managed none of these. It has been disorganized, sporadic, and largely ineffectual, countering mainly with despairing rhetoric and an occasional lawsuit.

We have in mind a high-tech and more lavish version
of the Indian reservation for some substantial minority
of the nation's population, while the rest of America
goes on about its business.
—Richard J. Herrnstein and Charles Murray,
The Bell Curve

3

IQ, Race, and Eugenics

UNLIKE ENGLISH-ONLY and immigration reform, the race-IQ/eugenics movement is not a grassroots but an elite effort. English-only and immigration reform did not need an intellectual justification beyond a few simple assertions, forcefully and dogmatically repeated ("If we don't close our borders . . ."). Funding and support for these movements, then, had their roots in populist, nativist sentiments and fears. Support for the eugenics movement today, however, like that for its early twentieth-century predecessors, originates with an autocratic elite. It relies on science and pseudoscience; its purpose is to persuade policy leaders that withdrawing support for affirmative action, Head Start, and welfare is not only permissible but sensible and just. It seems unlikely that 2 million retirees or 4 million blue-collar workers would donate twenty dollars apiece for a university-based program of research designed to demonstrate the intellectual inferiority of American blacks, or for a large-scale twins study to show the extent to which personality traits and aptitudes track genetic categories. Nevertheless, studies of this sort are important for the conservative agenda. They rationalize withdrawal of support from social programs for those in need.

In our society at least, programs of this sort could only be carried out through private grants, relying on a few well-financed organizations and donors, sponsoring research carried out in relative secrecy and on a decentralized basis. This the Pioneer Fund and a few other wealthy donors . have been able to accomplish with exceptional dispatch and skill. Often, a landmark book or study will appear almost out of the blue, taking the world by surprise, yet seeming to be exactly what is needed at the time. *The Bell Curve*,[1] for example, was launched at a major celebration and press conference hosted by the American Enterprise Institute, following which it was covered by virtually every major newspaper, news magazine, and talk show in the land.[2] The dubious science and even more dubious political premises on which it rests were not brought out until later, when of course they received less publicity than the book's supposed breakthroughs.

Liberals have their intellectual stars, too—Jennifer Hochschild, Derrick Bell, Andrew Hacker, and John Rawls, just to name a few—but their work tends to be not as well financed as that of their counterparts on the right; not so narrowly focused at supporting an action agenda, and not so shrewdly coordinated and centralized as is the research program underwritten by the Pioneer Fund. Liberals surprised and shocked by the direction this country has taken, and by the speed at which the changes of the 1960s have been rolled back, would do well to heed the effective tactics employed by their counterparts on the other side of the political spectrum.

An Idea with a Long History

Publication of *The Bell Curve: Intelligence and Class Structure in American Life* and its authors' reliance on research underwritten by the Pioneer Fund precipitated a spirited debate about the relationship between race and IQ. The main premises of *The Bell Curve* are: Intelligence is inherited and unchangeable; biological determinism foils market-based reforms, as well as government-sponsored social reform; social problems of minority groups (mainly blacks), such as poverty, crime, and teenage pregnancy, are attributable to low IQ and cannot be remedied by programs such as Head Start, welfare, or affirmative action. These conclusions renewed a controversy over eugenics that started almost a century ago. Beginning as a branch of the new field of anthropology in nineteenth-century England, eugenics took on the trappings of science when Charles Darwin's cousin, Francis

Galton, published *Hereditary Genius* in 1869. Influenced by his experiments with selective breeding of plants and animals, Galton concluded that a superior race of humans could be produced by judicious matings of members of eminent families over several generations. Galton coined the term "eugenics" from the Greek—meaning of good stock—in 1883.[3]

In 1905, less than a decade after the Supreme Court decided *Plessy v. Ferguson*,[4] social Darwinists in the United States founded the American Eugenics Society. While the Court declared that the black and white races should remain separate but equal, the eugenicists held that the races are not equal, that the white race is superior to all others, with Nordic whites at the top. In 1916, Madison Grant, a New York aristocrat and promoter of the American Eugenics Society, published *The Passing of the Great Race*, setting out such a hierarchy. The preface was written by Henry F. Osborn, director of the American Museum of Natural History, who warned of the gradual demise of the white race. A few years later, in 1920, Theodore Lothrop Stoddard, reacting to the great waves of migration from southern and eastern Europe, China, and Japan, published *The Rising Tide of Color Against White World Supremacy*. In 1923 Carl Campbell Brigham, in *A Study of American Intelligence*, declared that Nordic white intelligence in the United States was being diluted because of the introduction of inferior Negro stock. A few years later, Brigham designed an intelligence test that professed to measure native ability but incorporated a bias that would award high scores for knowledge of facts associated with Anglo culture. Shortly thereafter, Brigham became director of testing for the College Board; his test became known as the Scholastic Aptitude Test and is still given to millions of high school students today. The organization has not repudiated his teaching; as Stanley Fish points out, the library at the College Board's Educational Testing Service still bears Brigham's name.[5]

In 1924 Congress enacted the National Origins Quota Act restricting immigration by those deemed to be of "inferior stock." Harry Laughlin, the eugenicist who later became Pioneer Fund's first president, testified in favor, reporting that IQ studies showed that 83 percent of Jews are feebleminded and urging that Jewish immigration be sharply curtailed. In 1922 Laughlin had written the Model Eugenical Sterilization Law, adopted by nearly thirty states, under which tens of thousands of persons accused of feeble-mindedness were forcibly sterilized.[6]

Laughlin, who could trace his lineage to pre-Revolutionary forebears, was serving as superintendent of the Eugenics Record Office when the case of Carrie Buck came to the attention of a Virginia appellate court. A seventeen-year-old single woman who had just given birth to a daughter, Buck had been committed to the Virginia Colony for Epileptics and the Feebleminded, where she was pronounced a moral imbecile. Buck's mother previously had been committed to the same institution. Without examining Buck, her mother, or her daughter, Laughlin declared that she belonged to "the shiftless, ignorant, and worthless class of anti-social whites of the South," and that her feeblemindedness was inherited. Buck's case was appealed in 1924 to the U.S. Supreme Court, which affirmed her sterilization order by a vote of eight to one. In contorted logic, Justice Oliver Wendell Holmes, a believer in the eugenics movement, reasoned that if the best citizens could lay down their lives for the state, then the worst should be willing to make sacrifices as well—in Buck's case, submitting to sterilization "in order to prevent our being swamped with incompetence."[7]

Laughlin's law caught the attention of Nazi leaders, who passed similar laws resulting in sterilization of more than two million people. In 1936, the University of Heidelberg conferred an honorary degree on Laughlin, who called the Nazi sterilization program "a most exciting experiment." Shortly thereafter, Laughlin suggested that Adolf Hitler be made an honorary member of the Eugenics Research Association.[8] By 1937, Harry Laughlin was serving as the first president of the Pioneer Fund, whose charter states that it is "committed to the proposition that people of different ethnic and cultural backgrounds are, on the basis of their heredity, inherently unequal and can never be expected to behave or perform equally."[9]

Although eugenics is controversial today because of its use by the Third Reich, it at one time attracted the support of social and intellectual elites on both sides of the Atlantic. Influenced by theories of intellectual merit, Alfred Binet created IQ tests to identify fast learners. Educators in the United States, England, and Europe used the tests to reform public education from the 1930s until the early 1960s. Labour Party intellectuals in England promoted the meritocratic ideal by espousing more and better—but differentiated—education for all classes of citizens.[10] The discussion of intelligence broke into two opposing camps, simply described as nature versus nurture. Some believed that intelligence is largely inherited, while others held that cultural and environmental factors (which are subject to change) have as much to do with determining IQ as does biological makeup. In England, intelligence researchers who held sway promoted a more fluid definition of intelligence and demanded rigorous proof from researchers such as William McDougall and Raymond Cattell that their theories of race-based intelligence were scientifically correct. Consequently, a number of British scientists who believed in the link between race and intelligence emigrated to the United States and Canada.[11]

Bored with Electrical Engineering? Want to Branch Out? Try the Pioneer Fund

The main source of grant money for race-based intelligence research in the English-speaking world today is the Pioneer Fund. Between 1971 and 1992, the fund dispensed at least $4,631,332 to support work relating race to IQ. When Wickliffe Draper established the Pioneer Fund's endowment in 1937 and appointed Harry Laughlin president, he also appointed four other directors, including Frederick Osborn, nephew of Henry Osborn and secretary of the American Eugenics Society. The fund's charter proposed aiding parents "descended predominantly from white persons who settled in the original thirteen states prior to the adoption of the Constitution of the United States" and conducting research into "racial betterment." Draper applauded Laughlin's success in obtaining the Nazi propaganda film *Erbkrank* (Hereditary Defective) advocating "eugenic cleansing" of the Jewish population, which he had offered to three thousand high schools in the United States. Draper also wanted to repatriate black Americans to Africa.[12]

The current unpaid president of the fund serving since 1958, Harry Weyher runs the operation out of his New York City law office. John Marshall Harlan, a New York lawyer and Pioneer Fund director, recommended Weyher's name to Draper. Harlan soon afterward became a Supreme Court justice who sat on the Warren Court and joined with Weyher on a crime-commission project. Weyher, a North Carolina native, University of Glasgow and Harvard Law School graduate, appealed to Draper because he vehemently opposed the *Brown* decision. Still implacably opposed to *Brown*, Weyher recently lamented, "It was supposed to integrate the schools and everybody said we'd mix 'em up and the blacks' scores would come up. But of course they never did. All *Brown* did was wreck the school system."[13]

Others associated with Pioneer include Henry E. Garrett, a Columbia University psychology professor and one-time fund director, who testified in favor of segregation in *Brown*. Garrett has also been a member of the White Citizens Councils. R. Travis Osborne, a retired University of Georgia psychology professor, received $386,900 from the fund for research, some of which has been distributed by neo-Nazi mail-order outlets. He testified in an unsuccessful appeal to overturn *Brown* that blacks inherit an intellectual deficit that makes it difficult for them to compete with whites. John B. Trevor Jr., son of anti-immigration advocate John B. Trevor Sr. (booster of the national origins quota system) and a longtime official of the Coalition of Patriotic Societies, was serving as the group's treasurer when, in 1962, it demanded the release of all Nazi war criminals and announced that it supported apartheid in South Africa.[14]

Pioneer's links to other far-right organizations are eye-opening. Thomas Ellis, fund director from 1973 to 1977, serves as adviser to Senator Jesse Helms (R-N.C.) and founded the organization Fairness in Media (FIM) in 1985 to counteract a supposed liberal bias in the media. FIM, which unsuccessfully attempted to take over CBS, was represented by Harry Weyher's law firm. Ellis is also chair of Coalition for Freedom, another cog in the Helms machine. In 1983, the coalition received $10,000 from Pioneer. Like others with Pioneer ties, Ellis is anti-*Brown*. "The eventual goal of [school integration]," he once stated, "is racial intermarriage and the disappearance of the Negro race by fusing into the white."[15]

Even though Weyher insists that Pioneer does not participate in the research projects it supports or take positions on political issues implicated by such research, the individuals and organizations it supports, such as the Federation for American Immigration Reform (FAIR), have a predictable cast—they support population control, white superiority, limits on immigration, and overt opposition to affirmative action, school desegregation, and welfare reform.[16] Arthur Jensen, educational psychology professor at the University of California at Berkeley, has received well over $1 million from Pioneer since 1971. Jensen published a controversial article in the *Harvard Education Review* in 1969 in which he declared that programs such as Head Start are useless because they can do little to raise the IQ levels of poverty-level black children. This article was based on his previous work in which he argued that blacks may be genetically inferior to whites, possessing an average IQ fifteen points lower.[17]

The late William Shockley, Stanford electrical engineering professor, Nobel laureate, and contemporary of Jensen, received almost $200,000 from Pioneer. An amateur geneticist, Shockley advocated on talk shows and in a letter to the National Academy of Sciences in 1970 a sterilization bonus plan to deter low-IQ people from reproducing. Those whose IQ fell below 100 (the median for whites) would be given $1,000 for each point under 100 if they agreed to be sterilized. Shockley had no doubts about his own intelligence, however, and is perhaps as famous for his donation to the Nobel Prize winners sperm bank, which he proudly announced in 1980, as for his receipt of the award itself.[18]

Until recently, the Pioneer project that received the most attention was Thomas Bouchard's twins study at the University of Minnesota. Bouchard, director of the University of Minnesota's Center for Twin and Adoption Research, designed and led a study of more than fifty pairs of identical twins raised apart to determine the heritability of intelligence and personality traits. His work continued the line of research begun by the famous educational psychologist Cyril Burt, whose findings were challenged shortly after his death in 1971. Bouchard's data, published in 1990, conclude that 70 percent of intelligence variation is attributable to genes. Researchers at Minnesota are now investigating the genetic propensity for such characteristics as professional aptitude, religious tolerance, and political radicalism.[19]

Bouchard's work rests squarely on the side of hereditarianism in the nature-nurture debate. It reinforces the convictions of those who call for elimination of social programs and provides legitimation for scientific programs like the Human Genome Project, which, at the cost of $3 billion, seeks to identify one hundred thousand genes in the human body, probably including ones governing criminal behavior. Pioneer has granted Bouchard close to $1.3 million since 1980 to support his research. [20]

Michael Levin, a philosophy professor at City College of New York (CCNY), bases his work on statistics like Jensen's that show that blacks, as a group, score about fifteen points lower than do whites on standardized IQ tests. He believes blacks' lower intelligence scores make them likely to become criminals, and he supports policies that would allow police to detain blacks solely because of their race: "What's so outrageous if a policeman sees three Asian boys go in one store and three blacks go into another, he wants to prevent shoplifting and he's got to choose—why couldn't he use race as a factor?"[21]

Although Levin insists he keeps these views out of the classroom, CCNY attempted to remove him from his position in response to pickets and protests after his views became public. Represented by the ultra-conservative Center for Individual Rights (see Chapters 4 and 7), Levin sued, won, and remained at CCNY.[22] His case has been compared to that of his colleague, Leonard Jeffries, who, at the other end of the political spectrum, has been called a black supremacist and denounced for his Afrocentrist views.

In 1991 Levin began receiving support from Pioneer that now totals nearly $125,000.[23] Some conservative organizations, however, have backed away from him. The National Association of Scholars asked him to step down from his board position. Neoconservative leaders David Horowitz and Peter Collier, co-directors of the Center for the Study of Popular Culture, rescinded an invitation to give a paper on race at a Second Thoughts conference.[24]

Levin is implacably opposed to affirmative action—"I'm interested in innocence for whites. . . . Race differences show whites aren't at fault for blacks being down, and making whites pay for something they're not responsible for is a terrible injustice." He recriminates against school integration—"The reason [integration is not working] is two basic and unalterable black characteristics: less intelligence and greater proneness to violence." Regarding black communities, he declares, "Left to themselves, blacks will form societies whites would find intolerable and that it takes whites to prop them up." Ending welfare, he believes, "would automatically have a very excellent demographic effect." And eugenics, Levin says, is "a perfectly respectable idea. I think it may be making a comeback."[25]

Another Pioneer Fund grantee, Linda Gottfredson, professor of educational studies at the University of Delaware, focused her research on race-norming, the practice of evaluating government employment test results in comparison only to those of the same race, rather than the entire test pool. Ultimately the practice was eliminated in the Civil Rights Act of 1991. The university, however, was concerned about the conflict between its commitment to racial and cultural diversity and the goals of the Pioneer Fund. When it attempted to bar Gottfredson from accepting an additional Pioneer grant, she sued and with the help of—who else?—the Center for Individual Rights reached a settlement.[26]

In 1988 Gottfredson's work on race and intelligence was cited by the National Alliance, a white supremacist group, in its bid to get AT&T to drop its affirmative action policies. The Alliance first purchased one hundred shares to enable it to have a vote at the annual stockholders meeting. Then it submitted its proposal, which AT&T rejected because it feared that accepting the proposal would injure its ability "to qualify for government business." Since 1988 Gottfredson has received $335,000 from the Pioneer Fund.[27]

Shopping Malls and Cranial Sizes

J. Philippe Rushton, psychology professor at the University of Western Ontario, used part of $770,000 granted him by Pioneer to finance a survey at a local shopping mall. He targeted 150 male participants—one-third black, one-third white, and one-third Asian—asking them to fill out a questionnaire about their penis size, how many sexual partners they had had, and at what age they had had their first sexual experience. The previous year he had measured the heads of 200 students, correlating cranial size to IQ.[28] In 1989, he presented his findings in a paper delivered at the annual meeting of the American Association for the Advancement of Science (AAAS). Rushton argued that blacks have smaller heads, larger penises, and more sex partners than whites and that this is part of an evolutionary strategy in which whites rely on brains, while blacks rely on rapid breeding, to assure perpetuation.[29]

Reaction was passionate and immediate. Rushton's fellow scientists warned that his conclusions would be used to institute a racial "pecking order." Ontario premier David Peterson called for his dismissal. The province's attorney general considered prosecuting him for hate speech.[30] Rushton, who was born in South Africa and educated at the University of London, objects to the terms "inferior" or "superior" that others use to describe his categorization of racial groups, saying, "If you take something like athletic ability or sexuality—not to reinforce stereotypes or some such thing . . . it's a trade-off: more brain or more penis. You can't have everything."[31] Yet in his recent book, *Race, Evolution, and Behavior*, he divides races into three subsets he calls Mongoloids, Caucasoids, and Negroids and ranks them in that order for intelligence, brain size, family stability, and sexual restraint.[32]

Insisting that he maintains a value-free position on the implications for his research, Rushton nevertheless does not refrain from commenting on the use of eugenics. In a 1986 article in *Politics and the Life Sciences* he attributes the Third Reich's military excellence to the purity of its gene pool and comments that white supremacists who oppose abortion may, ironically, be contributing to their own demise by allowing blacks and Latinos to reproduce prolifically. After the AAAS debacle, he co-authored a new paper arguing that blacks are more disposed to contract AIDS because of an "inherited genetic reproductive strategy" that makes them more promiscuous than whites.[33]

Another Pioneer grantee, Richard Lynn, on the other hand, is an out-and-out believer in eugenics who advocates attention to the possibility that the world is burdened by inferior peoples who should be "phased out." "Who can doubt that the Caucasoids and the Mongoloids are the only two races that have made any significant contribution to civilization?" he asks in a 1991 article, "Race Differences in Intelligence: A Global Perspective."[34] A psychology professor at the University of Ulster in Northern Ireland, Lynn attributes racial differences to ancestral migration patterns. Groups of early hominids who migrated from Africa to the harsher and more demanding environments of Europe and Asia developed, in time, advanced levels of intelligence. To continue this Panglossian line of thought, the Pioneer Fund awarded Lynn $325,000.[35]

Roger Pearson, an English anthropologist and émigré to the United States, has received at least $775,000 from the Pioneer Fund. Pearson advocates the creation of a "supergeneration" from the sperm of "the fittest and most capable whites." Now head of the Institute for the Study of Man, Pearson earlier founded the Northern League, which fosters "the interests, friendship, and solidarity of all Teutonic nations."[36] In 1966, he proposed that "if a nation with a more advanced, more specialized or in any way superior set of genes mingles with, instead of exterminating, an inferior tribe, then it commits racial suicide."[37] In 1978, Pearson organized a World Anti-Communist League conference featuring among others Giorgio Almirante, a leader in Mussolini's fascist government, and Willis Carto, founder of the ultra-right Liberty Lobby.[38]

In 1981, Pearson's institute acquired, with a grant of $59,000 from Pioneer, the papers of Donald Swan, a University of Southern Mississippi anthropology professor, Pioneer Fund recipient, and eugenics advocate who had devised research projects on Anglo-Saxon intelligence. His attraction to Nazism became apparent when he was arrested for mail fraud in 1966 and a police raid of his apartment uncovered a collection of Nazi flags, helmets, and weapons, as well as a stash of anti-Semitic and anti-Catholic literature and pictures of Swan with members of George Lincoln Rockwell's neo-Nazi organization.[39]

Earlier Swan had mentored students sent to him by Ralph Scott, an educational psychology professor at the University of Northern Iowa, whose campaign against busing to achieve integrated schools in turn was financed by his Pioneer Fund grant. Scott served as chair of the Iowa Advisory Commission on Civil Rights as part of a Reagan administration shakeup of civil rights enforcement in the mid-1980s. Scott also served as vice president of the German-American National Congress, which has been charged with Nazi revisionism.[40] Both Scott and Pearson headed University Professors for Academic Order, a group opposed to the purported liberal takeover of university campuses.

Pearson's Institute for the Study of Man publishes the journal *Mankind Quarterly*, which during the 1970s was edited by former Nazi scientist Otmar, Baron von Verschuer, who had tutored Joseph Mengele and recommended him as camp director at Auschwitz. Other editors have included Corrado Gini, a supporter of Mussolini; segregationist Henry Garrett; and Hans Wilhelm Jurgens, who believes hereditary "anti-socials" should be sterilized. One issue of the journal, devoted to the inferiority of blacks, proclaims that "pure Negroid blood never evinced highly intelligent abilities." Pioneer Fund recipients who have published articles in *Mankind Quarterly* include J. Philippe Rushton, Richard Lynn, Linda Gottfredson, Ralph Scott, Hans Eysenck, and Roger Pearson.[41]

Charles Murray insists that he and Richard Herrnstein, co-authors of *The Bell Curve*, received no money from Pioneer for the project. (Pioneer, however, would have funded Murray and Herrnstein "at the drop of a hat," according to Harry Weyher, the fund's current president;[42] all they had to do was ask.) Although it may be true that Murray and Herrnstein received no money from the Pioneer Fund, they liberally cite its grantees in *The Bell Curve*. They cite five articles published in *Mankind Quarterly*, and their bibliography includes seventeen *Mankind Quarterly* authors, ten of whom have served on its editorial board. In particular they give liberal praise to Lynn and Rushton.[43]

Murray first argued against welfare in *Losing Ground*. (See Chapter 5.) A symposium on the book brought Murray and Herrnstein together in 1984. Upon discovering their common interests, the two authors decided to collaborate on an exploration of the links between race and intelligence. Earlier, Herrnstein had written an article for *The Atlantic* simply titled "I.Q.," which caused an uproar in the academic community. In it he maintained that IQ is inherited and an accurate predictor of academic success and social standing. He subsequently wrote *I.Q. in the Meritocracy*, and in 1985 put forth a biological basis for criminal activity in *Crime and Human Nature*, co-authored with James Q. Wilson. Herrnstein declared, "In times to come the tendency to be unemployed may run in the genes of a family about as certainly as bad teeth do now." Herrnstein died of cancer before the book came out, leaving Murray alone to defend its thesis and controversial premises.[44]

Meanwhile, the Pioneer Fund is spending money as though it is going out of business—over $500,000 a year from total reserves of about $5,000,000—which it actually may be. "It seemed to make more sense to spend the money than to save it, so we spent it. Once it's gone we'll just quit," said fund president Harry Weyher.[45] Once the fund is dead, will the idea follow suit?

But the British tribe's greatest legacy extends far
beyond its physical assets and investments . . . . in a
host of critical fields—from accounting and advertising
to culture, science, and, finally, the operations of
government—the Anglo-Saxon created standards not
just for their own race, or for their colonies, but also
for the entire modern world.
—Joel Kotkin, senior fellow, Center for the New West,
in *Tribes: How Race, Religion, and Identity
Determine Success in the New Global Economy.*

4

The Attack on Affirmative Action

THREE DECADES AFTER ENACTMENT of the Civil Rights Act of 1964,
the campaign against affirmative action has reached fever pitch. The movement's roots can be traced to the early Reagan days, when conservatives first
began questioning whether affirmative action could be squared with trea-
sured American principles of equal opportunity and merit. But it is only recently that the anti–affirmative action campaign has captured the nation's
consciousness with the drafting of the California Civil Rights Initiative,
Supreme Court decisions narrowing affirmative action, and bills in Congress aimed at the same result.

The battle against affirmative action features some of the same players,
rhetoric, and funding sources that appear in previous chapters. But in some
respects this is a different kind of campaign. For one thing, the racism is
less overt than, for example, in the efforts against immigrants or in eugenics and race-IQ research. The coalition is broader. Virtually every conservative and even some mainstream think tanks and foundations play important roles; the sharp-edged Pioneer Fund virtually disappears from the
scene. Moreover, the campaign against affirmative action has a national

scope, whereas those others tend to be waged, at least initially, in regions with large immigrant populations.

Yet, in a quite real sense, the campaign against affirmative action builds on those earlier battles, mobilizing many of the same fears, hatreds, and constituencies. In this sense, it sits at the apex of a pyramid, its foundation built by what has come before. Precisely because those earlier efforts legitimized previously unthinkable attacks on minorities and the poor, the more "cerebral" campaign against affirmative action has been able to gain ground. Expectations and code-words that originated in campaigns against nonspeakers of English, immigrants, and "baby-factory" women of color have been recycled into new forms.

In early 1995, two things happened: the House of Representatives voted for the first time to kill an affirmative action program, and House Speaker Newt Gingrich indicated that abolishing racial-preference laws would be a top GOP priority after the House completed his one-hundred-day Contract with America. A short time later, Senate Majority Leader Bob Dole of Kansas, a longtime supporter of affirmative action, opened his presidential campaign attacking it, as did Senator Phil Gramm of Texas. Gingrich and Dole are working with Clint Bolick of the Institute for Justice to cut off funding for the 160 affirmative action provisions in various federal laws. Even Democratic Senator Daniel P. Moynihan of Massachusetts, the former Harvard professor who helped create President Lyndon B. Johnson's affirmative action policy in 1965, has declared that it may now be doing more harm than good.

Affirmative action has become a difficult issue for Democrats. Although blacks, Hispanics, feminists, liberals, and civil service unions—all important groups within the Democratic Party—support it, affirmative action is markedly unpopular among blue-collar whites ("Reagan Democrats") whose votes are necessary for a Democratic victory. But the debate does not fall entirely along racial lines. Some of the sharpest attacks on affirmative action have come from black intellectuals such as Thomas Sowell, Shelby Steele, and Walter E. Williams. Nonetheless, the central political force in the affirmative action debate is the "angry white male." The Republican share of the white male vote went from 51 percent in 1992 to 63 percent in 1994; nearly 4 million white men changed from Democrat to Republican according to a USA Today poll.

The drafting of the California Civil Rights Initiative focused national attention on the debate over affirmative action. The initiative, which will appear on the 1996 ballot, was drafted by two academics, Thomas Wood and

Glynn Custred. It would ban preferential treatment based on race or gender in state government hiring, education, and contracting. Support comes from unexpected sources, including Ward Connerly, an African American member of the University of California Board of Regents who led the board in voting to end affirmative action in admissions, and Hispanic columnist Roger Hernandez. California Governor Pete Wilson, once a strong proponent of affirmative action, announced his support for the initiative.

The initiative campaign is fueled by many newly empowered Proposition 187 activists who complain that affirmative action, originally designed to help African Americans, has been wrongly appropriated by others, including illegal immigrants. (See Chapter 2.) Prominent Proposition 187 backers who simply moved over to the new campaign include Ron Prince, architect of the Save Our State initiative, Glenn Spencer, founder of the Voice of Citizens Together, a principal supporter of Proposition 187, and Ezola Foster, founder of Black Americans for Family Values, who charges that affirmative action stigmatizes and stereotypes black Americans. Also in favor are many supporters of Ross Perot's United We Stand America movement, who earlier were among the leading activists working for Proposition 187.

Like the anti-immigration movement that followed Proposition 187, the campaign to ban affirmative action has moved to other states. John Nelson, a Colorado attorney, has drafted a similar initiative to ban preference programs in his state, and conservatives in several other states have followed suit. Frederick R. Lynch, Sarah Scaife Scholar at the Salvatori Center at Claremont McKenna College and author of *Invisible Victims: White Males and the Crisis of Affirmative Action*, notes that affirmative action did not become a widespread issue until the success of Proposition 187, which showed that "issues of race and class were open to political debate."[1]

The anti-affirmative action campaign proceeds essentially on two fronts—litigation and policy analysis.

Lost a Bid or the Scholarship of Your Choice? Mad Enough to Sue? Try the Washington Legal Foundation

Founded in 1977 by attorney Daniel J. Popeo, the Washington Legal Foundation (WLF) has played a key role in the campaign against affirmative action since at least 1985. In that year, Paul D. Kamenar, the organization's executive director, wrote a report entitled *Revising Executive Order 11246: Fulfilling the Promise of Affirmative Action.* In it, he urged Reagan to change the order so as to eliminate the requirement that federal contractors use goals and timetables when hiring. The effects of goals and timetables (which the foundation terms "quotas") were outlined in another WLF monograph by Professor Herman Belz of the University of Maryland entitled *Affirmative Action from Kennedy to Reagan: Redefining American Equality.* Both men argued that quotas have not helped any minority group, have hurt some, and fly in the face of the American ideal of equal treatment.[2]

With an annual budget of approximately $3 million and a staff of eighteen to twenty-four, including six full-time attorneys, WLF has engaged in litigation in a big way. The foundation filed an opposition brief in *Metro Broadcasting v. FCC,*[3] in which the Supreme Court upheld a Federal Communications Commission policy that gives minorities preference in the awarding of broadcast licenses. A short time later, WLF sued the federal government on the ground that its policy of permitting colleges to set aside scholarships for minorities constitutes unlawful reverse discrimination in violation of Title VI of the Civil Rights Act of 1964.[4] In another WLF case, *Podberesky v. Kirwan,*[5] a federal court of appeals upheld a Hispanic student's constitutional challenge to a University of Maryland scholarship program under which only African Americans were eligible. WLF also lent its support to the Mountain States Legal Foundation in *Adarand Constructors v. Pena.*[6] In that case, Mountain States successfully represented a white highway subcontractor who challenged a Department of Transportation program under which prime contractors were provided incentive payments for hiring disadvantaged business enterprises as subcontractors. WLF is looking for more cases to test the new standard set in *Adarand* and eventually strike down affirmative action altogether.[7] The foundation also offered wholehearted support for Clarence Thomas, a black conservative opposed to affirmative action, in his nomination to the Supreme Court, holding news conferences and preparing reports analyzing his background and concluding that he was "eminently qualified to serve on the Supreme Court."[8]

WLF has grown from a relatively small organization with an annual budget of $800,000 in 1977[9] to a powerful one with an annual budget of $3 million in 1995, with the money coming from over five hundred companies and foundations, as well as countless individuals.[10] The organization receives support from over four hundred of the one thousand largest corporations in America, including Aetna, AMAX, Archer-Daniels-Midland, Ashland Oil, CIGNA, Citicorp, Duke Power, Emerson Electric, Exxon, Ford Motor, General Motors, GTE, Litton, Phillips Petroleum, Rockwell International, Texaco, UNOCAL and Westinghouse.[11]

In recent years, WLF has received funding from the following foundations:

- Allegheny Foundation—$200,000, 1992 (for tort reform)
- Carthage Foundation—$300,000, 1992 (for general operating support)
- JM Foundation—$25,000, 1994 (for Free Enterprise Education Center)
- Thomas and Dorothy Leavey Foundation—$25,000, 1992
- M. J. Murdock Charitable Trust—$225,000, 1993 (for conference center and audio/visual equipment)
- Samuel Roberts Noble Foundation—$15,000, 1993 (for tort reform)
- John M. Olin Foundation—$25,000, 1993 (for litigation on regulatory activities of FDA)
- Henry Salvatori Foundation—$50,000, 1993 (for lectures to students on founding values of America)
- E. L. Wiegand Foundation—$119,000, 1993 (for conference center furnishings)[12]

It has also received contributions from Richard Mellon Scaife and Joseph Coors.[13] Coors has served on WLF's national board of advisors, as have U.S. Senators Jesse Helms (R-N.C.) and Orrin Hatch (R-Utah).[14] In addition to financial contributions, no fewer than forty-eight law firms donated pro bono services to WLF in 1993, including megafirms Arnold & Porter, Covington & Burling, and Vinson & Elkins.[15] Its governing body is a legal policy advisory board made up of fifty-five lawyers, judges, and law professors.[16]

Hate Government Regulation? Try the Center for Individual Rights

Like the Washington Legal Foundation (WLF), with which it frequently cooperates, the libertarian Center for Individual Rights (CIR) stands at the center of the campaign against affirmative action. CIR was founded in 1989 by Michael McDonald and Michael Greve, who met when they worked at WLF. CIR has become best known for defending the "politically incorrect" on college campuses, including alleged victims of reverse discrimination and men charged with sexual harassment.[17] (See Chapter 7.)

CIR has attacked affirmative action in the courts as well as in articles and other publications. In addition to trying to restore a Pioneer Fund grant to the University of Delaware professor Linda Gottfredson for research on race-norming, the center served as an amicus party along with the WLF in *Metro Broadcasting v. FCC*.[18] In April 1991, CIR defended Georgetown University Law Center student Timothy Maguire after he was reprimanded for breaking a nondisclosure agreement while working in the admissions office. Maguire revealed confidential information in an article critical of affirmative action entitled "Admissions Apartheid."[19] Greve later wrote a column entitled "The Newest Move in Law Schools' Quota Game" for the *Wall Street Journal*, concluding that law school admission policies, including that of Boalt Hall Law School at the University of California at Berkeley, amount to racial quotas in disguise.

What some have called the most serious attack on affirmative action in thirty years was led by the CIR in *Hopwood v. Texas*.[20] Described as the "first full-blown constitutional challenge to racial preferences in student admissions since *Regents of the University of California v. Bakke*,"[21] *Hopwood* was filed in September 1992 by four white applicants to the University of Texas School of Law who alleged that they were denied admission because of their race under a policy that reserved 15 percent of all seats in each class for African Americans and Hispanics. In August 1994, the court held that the law school's admission procedure violated the applicants' equal protection rights and awarded them one dollar each in damages and the right to reapply without paying an application fee. Unsatisfied, CIR appealed, winning an even broader decree.[22] Currently, CIR is representing Jerry Henry, a white man and president of the Henry Painting Company, who filed suit against Ohio State University when notified that he could no longer compete for work at the university because it had decided to award all painting contracts to minorities. The center is also representing a fourteen-year-old white girl denied acceptance at a study camp sponsored by the National Science Foundation and operated by Texas A&M University, because, according to McDonald, it was "reserved exclusively for blacks, Hispanics, and Native Americans."[23]

CIR receives 90 percent of its support from conservative foundations,[24] including the following:

- Lynde and Harry Bradley Foundation
    - $50,000, 1992 (for Academic Freedom Defense Fund)
    - $50,000, 1993 (for Academic Freedom Defense Fund)
- Carthage Foundation—$100,000, 1992 (for general operating support and expansion of Academic Freedom Defense Fund)
- F. M. Kirby Foundation—$25,000, 1992 (for Property Rights Litigation Program)
- John M. Olin Foundation
    - $100,000, 1992 (for Academic Freedom Defense Fund)
    - $25,000, 1993 (for litigation programs on property rights, civil rights, and the First Amendment)
- Smith Richardson foundation—$100,000, 1992 (for case reserves)
- Stranahan Foundation—$10,000, 1992[25]

CIR also receives support from the Adolph Coors, de Tocqueville, JM, Scaife, and E. L. Wiegand foundations, as well as the Pioneer Fund.[26]

Mountain States Legal Foundation

The Mountain States Legal Foundation was co-founded in 1977 by Joseph Coors, who served as its main financial backer, and James G. Watt, President Reagan's first secretary of the interior and an ardent anti-environmentalist.[27] Since its early days, the foundation has taken a leading role in challenging affirmative action programs in court. In *Wygant v. Jackson Board of Education*,[28] it represented ten senior white teachers who lost their jobs. Black teachers with less seniority were retained because the district's plan called for the same black-white ratio among teachers as among students. The Supreme Court, in its first decision on the constitutional implications of affirmative action in the workplace, agreed with their position, holding that layoffs imposed too intrusive a burden on nonminority teachers and that the Board of Education did not have a compelling governmental interest in retaining less senior minority teachers.

Mountain States also presented the first gender-based affirmative action challenge to reach the Supreme Court in *Johnson v. Transportation Agency, Santa Clara County.*[29] Paul Johnson, a white male, lost a promotion to a woman who scored lower than he in two interviews. Johnson challenged the agency's affirmative action plan, which sought a work force in which the proportion of women in all job levels and categories mirrored that of women in the county labor pool. The Supreme Court upheld the plan, finding it consistent with Title VII and the type of case-by-case, voluntary action that may be taken by a public employer to eliminate discrimination and improve the representation of minorities and women in the work force.

Mountain States' most significant victory came in *Adarand v. Pena.* Randy Pech, owner of Adarand Constructors Inc., submitted the lowest, but losing, bid on a subcontract to put up guardrails on a new highway. The subcontract was awarded to a small, disadvantaged Hispanic-owned enterprise. For his part, the prime contractor received an additional $10,000 under the Federal Subcontracting Compensation Clause to help cover expenses in working with a smaller, disadvantaged business. Pech sought legal representation from Mountain States and challenged the Department of Transportation program, alleging it resulted in reverse discrimination. The foundation had been looking for a case that would allow it to argue that the strict scrutiny legal standard, held to apply to state and local set-aside programs in *City of Richmond v. J. A. Croson Co.*,[30] should apply to federal programs as well.

Before *Adarand*, the Court had applied a less rigorous, more deferential standard of judicial review to federal affirmative action measures. But in *Adarand*, the Court held that the federal government must show that the programs serve a compelling state interest and therefore meet the "strict scrutiny" test, effectively overturning two earlier decisions, *Metro Broadcasting v. FCC* and *Fullilove v. Klutznick*,[31] which applied a much more lenient one. The decision represented a major victory for affirmative action opponents since many federal programs are not likely to pass this stricter test. Mountain States Legal Foundation has received funding from the following foundations: $15,000 from the Boettcher Foundation in 1993 for operations; $30,000 from the Adolph Coors Foundation in 1993 for general operating support; $15,000 from the Gates Foundation in 1992 and 1993 for general operating support; and $31,250 from the Ruth and Vernon Taylor Foundation in 1993.[32]

Ever Want to Be a Professor? Neglect to Get Your Ph.D.? Join the Heritage Foundation and Make Federal Policy

The Heritage Foundation was founded in 1973 by Paul M. Weyrich, now head of the Free Congress Foundation, with $250,000 from Joseph Coors and Richard Scaife. Within two years, Heritage reported annual revenues of over $1 million. Money flowing into the foundation increased rapidly; it is now Washington's largest and best-funded think tank, with an annual budget of over $25 million. Heritage specializes in producing conservative books, monographs, newsletters, policy papers, and reviews on domestic and foreign issues, including tort reform, deregulation, and affirmative action, which are often delivered to several hundred policy makers in Congress and the administration and mailed to thousands of journalists and academics. Most of the publications are designed to meet the "briefcase test"—succinct enough to be read in the time it takes for an official to be driven from Washington's National Airport to a congressional committee hearing on Capitol Hill (about twenty minutes).[33]

Heritage played a key role in kicking off the campaign against affirmative action under the Reagan administration. Ten days after Reagan won the presidency, the foundation issued a three-thousand-page, twenty-volume report entitled *Mandate for Leadership* to the Reagan transition team to serve as "a blueprint for the construction of a conservative government." The one-hundred-thousand-dollar report argued for color- and gender-blind approaches to civil rights policy. It called the Civil Rights Division a "radicalized" agency and attacked the actions of many civil rights offices in federal departments. The report also urged that President-elect Reagan revoke all executive orders requiring affirmative action for minorities in government hiring and contracting and recommended that the Justice Department require proof of intent to discriminate before taking legal action.[34] In November 1981, the foundation issued a follow-up report entitled *The First Year*, which found that about 60 percent of the initial report's recommendations had been effectuated.[35] A short time later, Heritage published *Agenda '83*, in which it urged that the U.S. Justice Department essentially switch sides and begin challenging affirmative action programs. It recommended that the administration shift its "top legal priority" from crime prevention to civil rights, conduct studies to show how affirmative action programs increase racial resentment, and frame a new definition of discrimination that eliminates the concept of affirmative action and focuses on practices "having a discriminatory intent, as the result of identifiable policies . . . and with clearly identifiable victims." The foundation also urged that the administration amend Executive Order 11246 "to outlaw quotas, goals, and timetables for federal contractors and to require nondiscrimination policies across the board."[36]

For more than a decade Heritage has been publishing an outpouring of articles on the drawbacks and shortcomings of affirmative action in the *Heritage Foundation Policy Review*. Many prominent scholars have contributed essays, including Walter E. Williams, Linda Chavez, William R. Beer and Frederick R. Lynch, Ron Unz, and Ward Connerly.[37] The foundation also has sponsored lectures and reports on affirmative action by journalist and television host Tony Brown, Paul D. Kamenar, Clint Bolick, Clarence Thomas, and others, as well as seminars and conferences featuring conservative leaders such as Judge Robert Bork, former Attorney General Edwin Meese III, and Linda Chavez.[38]

And in the can-you-top-this fashion possible only in a conservative think tank that feels itself truly on a roll, in January 1994 Heritage held a seminar entitled "The Conservative Virtues of Martin Luther King." The seminar's speakers included Robert Woodson, head of the National Center for Neighborhood Enterprise, and William Bennett, Reagan's education secretary whose conservative credentials include John M. Olin Fellow at the Hudson Institute, distinguished fellow for the study of cultural policy at the Heritage Foundation, and co-founder of Empower America. The speakers argued that King's dream of seeing his children valued for their character instead of disparaged for their skin color has been betrayed by affirmative action and reverse discrimination.[39]

Heritage has used the 1994 Republican victory in gaining control of Congress as an opportunity to get its affirmative action agenda across to key committees. For example, all of the congressional reform provisions of Gingrich's Contract with America appeared in a 1992 Heritage study of Congress entitled *The Ruling Class*. In December 1994, the foundation held a week-long orientation session in Baltimore for freshman Congress members that rivaled that of Harvard's Kennedy School of Government.[40] It also held an affirmative action strategy session early in 1995, with two dozen Hill staffers, lawyers, and conservative activists.[41]

Like other think tanks, Heritage has been linked with the infamous book *The Bell Curve*. A highly favorable review of Charles Murray's earlier book, *Losing Ground: American Social Policy, 1950–1980*, was published in the *Heritage Foundation Policy Review*. (See Chapter 5.) While affiliated with Heritage, Murray had written an earlier version of the book, a pamphlet entitled "Safety Nets and the Truly Needy," in which he argues that America has been losing the war on poverty and that massive and misdirected federal spending is a prime reason.[42] Information for a section of *The Bell Curve* on the "degradation of intellectual requirements" on police officer hiring exams cited the work of an editor of the *Heritage Foundation Policy Review*.[43]

Richard Scaife serves on the foundation's board of trustees, which also includes W. Grover Coors, heir to the Coors fortune. The Sarah Scaife Foundation played a major role along with Joseph Coors in establishing Heritage in 1973 and has remained its largest contributor.[44] Richard M. Larry, Scaife's president, forced Heritage to abandon its antagonism to New Right cultural conservatism, which emphasizes patriotism, family, and other traditional values. In response to Larry's concern about lack of attention to cultural issues, the foundation hired William Bennett, who was director at the Sarah Scaife Foundation, to head a new program for the study of culture, examining media, families, churches, and schools.[45]

In 1993, the two major Scaife foundations gave at least $17.6 million to 150 nonprofit public policy groups, with the largest amount, $1.6 million, going to Heritage.[46] The Heritage Foundation has also received funding from the following foundations:

- Alcoa Foundation—$30,000, 1992
- Lynde and Harry Bradley Foundation
    - $555,101, 1992 (for continued support of Bradley Resident Scholars Program)
    - $11,850, 1992 (for book project on Anita Hill)
    - $265,076, 1993 (for Bradley Resident Scholars Program)
    - $175,000, 1993 (for Domestic Policy Studies Program)
    - $175,000, 1993 (for Foreign Policy Studies Program)
    - $170,000, 1993 (for continued support of Bradley Resident Scholars Program)
    - $75,000, 1993 (for Bradley International Fellowship)

—$24,850, 1993 (for series of meetings on domestic policy issues)

—$20,000, 1993 (for study of American conservatism)

- Shelby Cullom Davis Foundation—$100,000, 1992
- William Stamps Farrish Fund—$10,000, 1993
- FMC Foundation—$10,000, 1992
- Rollin M. Gerstacker Foundation—$12,000, 1992
- William Randolph Hearst Foundation—$25,000, 1994 (toward Health Care Reform Project)
- Herrick Foundation—$25,000, 1992 (for general support)
- Conrad L. Hilton Foundation—$15,000, 1993
- Jaquelin Hume Foundation—$100,000, 1993 (for grant made in form of stock)
- F. M. Kirby Foundation—$40,000, 1992
- McCamish Foundation—$10,000, 1992
- Philip M. McKenna Foundation—$80,000, 1992 (for McKenna Fellow in Regulatory and Business Affairs)
- Montgomery Street Foundation—$17,500, 1992 (for program of public policy research)
- Samuel Roberts Noble Foundation
    —$500,000, 1992 (for operating support)
    —$450,000, 1993 (for operating support)
- John M. Olin Foundation
    —$100,000, 1992 (for John M. Olin Fellowship in Political Economy)
    —$100,000, 1993 (for John M. Olin Fellowship in Political Economy)
    —$87,500, 1993 (for Domestic Policy Studies Program)
    —$75,000, 1993 (for Cultural Policy Studies Program)
- Henry Salvatori Foundation—$200,000, 1993 (for fellowship and awards for exhibiting American values)
- Sarah Scaife Foundation
    —$1,000,000, 1992 (for general operating and program support)
    —$800,000, 1993 (for general operating and program support)
- Starr Foundation
    —$150,000, 1993 (for continued support)
    —$150,000, 1994 (for renewed support)

- Stranahan Foundation—$35,000, 1992
- Ruth and Vernon Taylor Foundation—$25,000, 1993
- Jay and Betty VanAndel Foundation—$250,000, 1992 (for general support)
- E. L. Wiegand Foundation—$57,500, 1993 (for privatization/free market economics projects)[47]

In 1993, over two hundred thousand individual donors provided more than $18 million of Heritage's $22.9 million budget; foundations and corporations provided the remainder. Other foundations that contributed to Heritage in 1993 include Carthage, Castle Rock, the Grover M. Hermann Foundation, the M. J. Murdock Charitable Trust, Reader's Digest Association, and the Scaife Family Foundation.[48]

Can't Stop Writing? Join the Manhattan Institute for Policy Research

Founded in 1978 by William J. Casey, who went on to become CIA chief under Reagan, the Manhattan Institute has an annual budget of $5 million and a staff of about thirty. It gained national attention in the early 1980s by sponsoring two books widely regarded as influencing the Reagan administration's social and economic thinking: *Wealth and Poverty* by George Gilder and *Losing Ground* by Charles Murray. Since then, the institute has underwritten books, articles and seminars on affirmative action, tort reform, and other such issues. It also publishes the quarterly *City Journal*, an outlet for conservative thought. Manhattan has been compared to the Heritage Foundation in that, like Heritage, its focus is not just on scholarship but also on idea brokering. For its size, the Manhattan Institute publishes more op-ed articles, including many on affirmative action, than any other think tank.[49]

Manhattan has sponsored conferences on affirmative action and underwritten books by some of its most vocal critics, including *Out of the Barrio: Toward a New Politics of Hispanic Assimilation* by Linda Chavez, in which she argues that Hispanics should not depend on government assistance and that affirmative action and bilingual education programs hurt Hispanics and hinder assimilation. The institute also supports the work of senior fellow

Abigail Thernstrom, whose book *Whose Votes Count? Affirmative Action and Minority Voting Rights* opposes special measures to increase minorities' political influence. In June 1995, Thernstrom attacked both race- and class-based affirmative action in "A Class Backwards Idea: Why Affirmative Action for the Needy Won't Work."[50] Thernstrom has criticized affirmative action on *Morning Edition* of National Public Radio[51] and the *MacNeil/Lehrer Newshour*,[52] which also interviewed Boston University president John Silber, black neoconservative writer Shelby Steele, and Ward Connerly on the subject.

Charles Murray got his start at Manhattan as a Bradley Fellow. In 1982, William Hammett, president of the institute, offered the then-unknown Murray a position as a senior research fellow and the institute's full financial backing to complete *Losing Ground*. The institute raised $125,000 to promote Murray's book and pay him a $35,000 stipend, most coming from Scaife, which gave $75,000, and Olin, $25,000. Upon publication, it sent seven hundred free copies to academics, journalists, and public officials worldwide, sponsored seminars on the book, and funded a nationwide speaking tour for Murray that was made possible by a $15,000 grant from the Liberty Fund.[53]

Murray remained with Manhattan for eight years, leaving when the institute refused to support his research on differences in intelligence between blacks and whites and taking with him his annual $100,000 foundation grant from the Bradley Foundation for salary, overhead, and other expenses. Murray approached the Brookings Institution about the project but ended up at the American Enterprise Institute.[54] Manhattan appears to have forgiven him: Shortly after *The Bell Curve* was published, the institute sponsored a luncheon to honor Murray and the book, in which he proposes a genetic explanation for the fifteen-point difference in IQ between blacks and whites that is the basis for his dismissing affirmative action policies as futile.[55] (See chapter 3.)

One of Manhattan's major sources of funding is the Bradley Foundation, which has given it over $1 million since 1986, mostly for specific book projects.[56] Although the institute receives funding from such conservative foundations as Sarah Scaife, Olin, and Smith Richardson, it also receives contributions from a few mainstream foundations, including the J. M. Kaplan Fund and the Commonwealth Fund.[57] Manhattan has received funding from the following foundations:

- Lynde and Harry Bradley Foundation
    - $45,000, 1992 (for book project on term limitations)
    - $70,000, 1993 (for biography of Saul Bellow)
    - $40,000, 1993 (for seminar series at Center for Educational Innovation)
- Carthage Foundation — $15,000, 1992 (for publication)
- William H. Donner Foundation — $25,000, 1992
- Gilder Foundation — $225,000, 1992
- JM Foundation — $20,000, 1994 (to increase circulation of *City Journal*, quarterly magazine aimed at revitalizing American urban policy)
- J. M. Kaplan Fund — $10,000, 1992 (to establish ContractWatch in *City Journal*)
- John and Mary R. Markle Foundation — $125,000, 1993 (to continue work on books outlining future directions for telecommunications policy)
- John M. Olin Foundation
    - $100,000, 1992 (for research fellowship)
    - $40,000, 1992 (for *City Journal*)
    - $60,000, 1993 (for completion of book, *The New Protectionism*)
    - $45,000, 1993 (for research fellowship)
    - $40,000, 1993 (for *City Journal*)
    - $30,000, 1993 (for completion of book *Beyond Pluralism*)
    - $25,000, 1993 (for John M. Olin Research Fellowship)
- Frederick P. and Sandra P. Rose Foundation — $20,000, 1992
- Sarah Scaife Foundation — $150,000, 1992 (for general operating support)
- Scaife Family Foundation — $25,000, 1992 (for publication of *The Divided Mother*)
- Smith Richardson Foundation
    - $65,000, 1992 (for *City Journal*)
    - $90,000, 1992 (for Judicial Studies Program)
    - $29,080, 1992 (for research and writing on integration and race relations in three American cities)
- Starr Foundation — $400,000, 1993 (for renewed support of legal, education, and New York City programs)
- Robert W. Wilson Foundation — $25,000, 1992[58]

Deny Language Rights and Affirmative Action for Everyone—Join the Center for Equal Opportunity

The Center for Equal Opportunity (CEO) was founded in 1995 by Linda Chavez, former John M. Olin Fellow at Manhattan. The first think tank in Washington concerned exclusively with race, ethnicity, immigration, and public policy, CEO currently is focusing its attention on three areas: immigration, racial preferences, and multicultural education. Chavez, who used Olin money to fund CEO, said she established the center to move "toward a society in which race/ethnicity is not the most important factor in deciding who gets a job or gets into a school." Though she tried unsuccessfully for years to stir debate on affirmative action, even Reagan backed away, she said, out of fear of a backlash.[59]

The center has held several conferences on affirmative action, beginning with a March 1995 panel discussion on the California Civil Rights Initiative that included Glynn Custred, the initiative's co-author. CEO also sponsored Custred's four-day trip to Washington in April 1995 to testify before a House Judiciary subcommittee hearing. It then held a press briefing in which Custred reaffirmed his effort to place the California initiative on the November ballot. It also arranged a meeting with Dole.[60] On April 9, 1995, CEO held another panel discussion entitled "The Case for and Against Socioeconomic Affirmative Action," which included Clint Bolick of the Institute for Justice,[61] and, a few months later, a conference entitled "What Comes Next: An Alternative to Affirmative Action," which examined a privately managed, race-neutral program by the National Council of Contractors Association that is said to have an 85 percent minority participation rate.[62]

Chavez has strenuously opposed affirmative action in the press, at congressional hearings, and in speeches at colleges across the country. In a panel discussion on the future of affirmative action programs sponsored by the National Press Foundation entitled "Affirmative Action: Where Do We Go from Here?" she expressed support for Florida Republican Charles Canady's proposed "Civil Rights Act of 1995," which would prevent the federal government from using race, ethnicity, or gender criteria when awarding jobs or contracts.[63] She testified, along with Ward Connerly, before the subcommittee on employer-employee relations of the House Economic and Educational Opportunities Committee in a hearing on affirmative action in

March 1995, maintaining that affirmative action neither serves the purpose for which it was intended nor benefits those for whom it was designed.[64]

Like Going to the Opera on Opening Night— Everyone Is There at One Time or Another: American Enterprise Institute for Public Policy Research

The American Enterprise Institute (AEI), founded in 1943 by industrialist Lewis Brown, who hoped to match the influence of Robert S. Brookings of the Brookings Institution, was the first major conservative think tank and has served as home base of many well-known public figures, including former President Gerald Ford, Irving Kristol, Supreme Court Justice Antonin Scalia, and Milton Friedman, the 1976 Nobel Prize winner in economics. More recently, it has been the home of Ben J. Wattenberg, a former speech writer for President Johnson and host of *Think Tank*, Judge Robert H. Bork, affirmative action critic Dinesh D'Souza, and race-IQ researcher Charles Murray.[65]

AEI's legal expert, Bruce E. Fein, has published a torrent of articles and books analyzing affirmative action decisions. Another legal eagle, Robert Bork, the former Supreme Court nominee who was viewed as the judicial savior of Reagan's wavering social agenda of ending abortion and affirmative action, also has written about the subject. When the Supreme Court upheld affirmative action admissions in *Bakke* in 1978, Bork wrote in the *Wall Street Journal* that the program "offends both ideas of common justice and the Fourteenth Amendment's guarantee of equal protection to persons, not classes." Before *Bakke*, Bork warned that the Court's approval of affirmative action would induce other groups, such as white ethnics, to insist on preferential treatment.[66] In 1989, Bork took part in a Heritage panel discussion, along with Linda Chavez and Edwin Meese III, blasting recent Supreme Court civil rights decisions.[67] Recently, Bork declared that affirmative action fosters hostility between racial groups and should be terminated for every group except blacks, for whom it should be gradually phased out.[68]

One of the most outspoken critics of affirmative action, Dinesh D'Souza gained national attention with his books *Illiberal Education: The Politics of*

Race and Sex on Campus and *The End of Racism: Principles for a Multiracial Society*. D'Souza charges affirmative action with increasing racial tensions on campuses and with setting up minority students for failure. For D'Souza, affirmative action sets up a vicious cycle in which students are falsely assured of their qualifications at the same time they are told that their problems can be attributed to racism. The search for the source of that racism can then trigger a backlash. At the same time, the resulting "academic mismatch" causes frustration among minority students who cannot live up to expectations, leading them to retreat to the safety of their groups, further increasing balkanization and distrust. Any rise in racial violence, hate speech, anonymous leaflets, and similar acts, he concludes, is attributable to embittered white students understandably lashing out at perceived injustices. D'Souza proposes replacing race-based affirmative action with one based on socioeconomic disadvantage.[69]

Like D'Souza, Charles Murray has stirred up controversy in the affirmative action debate. Shortly after joining AEI as a Bradley Fellow after the Manhattan Institute declined to back his project on the relationship between race and IQ, Murray warned that the Rodney King verdict opened "a dangerous period in race relations," which have been "spiraling downwards for many years now without yet provoking American white leaders to confront the sources of the antagonism." Murray cited affirmative action as one of two main sources of antagonism that have changed the nature of whites' attitudes toward blacks.[70]

Although Murray has written extensively, he is most famous for *The Bell Curve*, in which he and co-author Richard J. Herrnstein charge affirmative action with "leaking poison into the American soul" and dividing American society more so even than crime, abortion, or taxes. They conclude that affirmative action has backfired severely, especially on the minorities it is supposed to benefit. It dooms blacks and Hispanics to low educational performance because they are always overmatched and focuses white resentment on them as recipients of special privileges. According to Murray and Herrnstein, affirmative action in employment is even more dangerous. A student denied admission to a college does not know who was accepted in his or her place; at work, however, people can see who is promoted and on what basis. The two authors favor abandoning affirmative action and returning to college admissions based on merit; only when candidates have comparable test scores should other factors such as ethnic diversity be considered. Employers also should be permitted to administer intelligence tests in order to make hiring practices more efficient.[71]

Not content with supporting the individual contributions of its fellows to the campaign against affirmative action, AEI has attempted to mobilize public opinion by sponsoring forums and polls on the subject. In 1984, it held a forum on civil rights in which Linda Chavez, speaking for the Civil Rights Commission, expressed the commission's opposition to affirmative action, declaring that because the Constitution envisions a color-blind society, preferential treatment is unconstitutional.[72] A widely cited poll on the differences in views between black society and its leaders also pushed AEI into the national spotlight. In 1985, AEI published results of a survey in its *Public Opinion* journal that professed to show that a majority of blacks do not support the liberal views of their black leaders, 77 percent of whom favored affirmative action, while 77 percent of the black public opposed it. The poll was attacked by Jesse Jackson, who questioned its connection to AEI, "a right-wing institution." The Joint Center for Political and Economic Studies pointed out that its own Gallup poll found that only 37 percent of blacks believed they were making progress and only 27 percent were against affirmative action.[73]

The John M. Olin Foundation, which earmarks grants for specific individuals, has been an important source of financial support for the American Enterprise Institute. Through AEI, Bork, Kristol, and D'Souza received Olin grants totaling $375,000 in 1991: Bork, holder of the Olin chair in legal studies, received $150,880; Kristol, an Olin fellow, $125,400; and D'Souza, recipient of an Olin Research Fellowship, $98,400 as well as an additional $20,000 in Olin money to pay for the promotional costs for *Illiberal Education*.[74] In addition, Olin provides funding for *Think Tank with Ben Wattenberg*, as does the William H. Donner Foundation, the Randolph Foundation, and the JM Foundation.[75] Olin also helped fund another show hosted by Wattenberg called *Wattenberg in the 90s: Trends*, providing $45,000 in 1990.[76]

AEI has received funding from the following foundations:

- Alcoa Foundation—$50,000, 1992
- Armstrong Foundation—$15,000, 1992
- Lynde and Harry Bradley Foundation
    —$350,000, 1992 (for general program activities)

—$56,500, 1992 (for social policy research)
  —$50,000, 1992 (for establishment of Bradley Distinguished
    Fellowship program)
  —$63,500, 1992 (for continued support for Bradley Lecture Se-
    ries)
  —$750,000, 1993 (for foreign and defense policy program)
  —$113,000, 1993 (for social policy research)
  —$50,000, 1993 (for establishment of Bradley Distinguished
    Fellowship Program)
  —$33,500, 1993 (for Bradley Lecture Series)

- FMC Foundation—$45,000, 1992
- Rollin M. Gerstacker Foundation—$15,000, 1992
- John and Mary R. Markle Foundation—$50,000, 1993
- Philip M. McKenna Foundation—$15,000, 1992 (for work of
  Michael Novak)
- Ambrose Monell Foundation—$250,000, 1992 (for general sup-
  port)
- J. P. Morgan Charitable Trust—$15,000, 1993
- Foundation for the National Capital Region—$15,000, 1993
- John M. Olin Foundation
  —$106,950, 1992 (for John M. Olin Research Fellowship)
  —$79,950, 1992 (for Program on Religion, Philosophy, and
    Public Policy)
  —$60,200, 1992 (for John M. Olin Fellowship)
  —$50,000, 1992 (for work on U.S. living standards and income
    distribution)
  —$148,480, 1993 (for John M. Olin Chair in Legal Studies)
  —$122,800, 1993 (for John M. Olin Distinguished Fellowship)
  —$54,750, 1993 (for John M. Olin Research Fellowship)
  —$50,000, 1993 (for Health Care Policy Program)
  —$42,780, 1993 (for Program on Religion, Philosophy, and
    Public Policy)
  —$25,000, 1993 (for research on U.S. living standards and in-
    come distribution)
- Philip D. Reed Foundation—$25,000, 1993 (for general support)
- Roberts Foundation—$18,415, 1992 (for unrestricted support)
- Billy Rose Foundation—$50,000, 1992

- Henry Salvatori Foundation—$50,000, 1993 (to disseminate founding principles of organization)
- Sarah Scaife Foundation
  - $225,000, 1992 (for general operating and policy studies support)
  - $240,000, 1993 (for cultural and security projects)
  - $75,000, 1993 (for environmental research project)
- Starr Foundation—$450,000, 1993 (three-year grant; for renewed support)
- Matilda R. Wilson Fund—$25,000, 1992 (for operating support)[77]

How to Keep Busy When There's No War and Too Much Peace: Hoover Institution on War, Revolution, and Peace

The Hoover Institution was founded in 1919 with a $50,000 gift from Herbert Hoover. Moderately conservative in orientation, it served as an important source of policy advice and personnel during the Reagan administration: affiliates Martin Anderson and Darrell M. Trent served on the White House staff; others served elsewhere in the federal government.[78] Several key opponents of affirmative action are associated with the institution, including Thomas Sowell, Shelby Steele, and John H. Bunzel. Sowell has written innumerable books and articles criticizing affirmative action, arguing that it stigmatizes blacks, destroys their incentive and self-esteem, causes resentment among the rest of the population, and has done little to help the undereducated, underemployed blacks who are most in need of assistance. His book *Ethnic America* examines the success of various ethnic groups and shows that factors other than race are at work. *Civil Rights: Rhetoric or Reality?* analyzes the shortcomings of actions taken in the name of "civil rights." In *Preferential Policies: An International Perspective*, Sowell identifies common patterns found in affirmative action programs around the world: benefits favor the elite of the receiving group disproportionately; programs focus on goals rather than results; social groups become polarized and start to hate each other.[79] A prolific anti–affirmative action writer, Sowell's other books include *Race and Culture: A World View*; *Markets and Minorities*; and *The Vision of the Anointed*.

An equal opportunity conservative, Sowell gets around. When not at Hoover, he graces other right-wing think tanks such as the Heritage Foundation, where he holds the rank of adjunct scholar. Sowell attacked affirmative action in "By the Numbers,"[80] an article published in the *Heritage Foundation Policy Review*. In a lecture to the same foundation in 1990, Sowell described affirmative action programs as a complete failure.[81] A few years earlier, he participated in a debate on affirmative action sponsored by the Manhattan Institute in which he challenged the views of Alfred Blumrosen of the Rutgers University Law School, author of *Black Employment and the Law* and supporter of goals and timetables in hiring and promotion.[82] In 1981, Sowell formed a national black organization called Black Alternatives Association, Inc., to counter the National Association for the Advancement of Colored People (NAACP) and other civil rights groups.[83]

Sowell also praised *The Bell Curve* as "one of the most sober, responsible, thorough and thoughtful books to be published in years."[84] Demonstrating independence of mind, Sowell nevertheless takes issue with Herrnstein and Murray on one point. As he did earlier in *Race and Culture*, he maintains that not all of intelligence is fixed at birth and that improving social conditions will eventually narrow the gap between group differences in IQ.

Steele, an African American English professor at San Jose State University who might be said to have launched the opening salvo in the current debate on affirmative action, became a Research Fellow at the Hoover Institution in May 1995. Author of the 1990 best-seller *The Content of Our Character: A New Vision of Race in America*, in which he denounces affirmative action and charges that its supporters intentionally or not, have encouraged blacks to think of themselves as victims, Steele is at work on a sequel entitled *The End of Oppression*, which explores the paradoxes and ironies of civil rights and affirmative action.[85] Bunzel, another Hoover fellow, is a former president of San Jose State University and member of the U.S. Commission on Civil Rights under Reagan. The author of numerous articles attacking affirmative action, Bunzel frequently lectures on what he sees as the evils of multiculturalism and other dire threats to U.S. intellectual life.

Recently, the Hoover Institution expressed its support for the California Civil Rights Initiative, as well as a University of California Regents' measure prohibiting the use of race, religion, sex, color, ethnicity, or national origin as criteria in the University of California's admissions and hiring policies.[86] Hoover has received funding from the following foundations:

- William H. Donner Foundation—$125,000, 1992
- FMC Foundation—$30,000, 1992
- Jaquelin Hume Foundation—$75,000, 1993 (for grant made in form of stock)
- J M Foundation—$20,000, 1994 (toward research on how taxation affects economic growth and revenues)
- Ambrose Monell Foundation—$250,000, 1992 (for general support)
- Montgomery Street Foundation—$25,000, 1992 (for domestic and international research and studies program)
- J. P. Morgan Charitable Trust—$10,000, 1992 (for general support)
- John M. Olin Foundation
    - —$112,500, 1992 (for Russian Studies, American Institutions, and John M. Olin Media Fellows Programs)
    - —$84,000, 1992 (for Soviet Archives Project)
    - —$225,000, 1993 (for Russian Studies, American Institutions, and John M. Olin Media Fellows Programs)
    - —$225,000, 1993 (for Soviet Archives Project)
- Smith Richardson Foundation
    - —$25,000, 1992 (for competitiveness project)
    - —$25,000, 1992 (for research and writing on Congress, the judiciary, and regulatory policy)[87]

The Hoover Institution has also received funding from the Coors Foundation.[88]

Like Things Better the Way They Were in 1783? Try the Cato Institute

The Cato Institute, a libertarian think tank founded in 1977, has played a key role in forming the ideas and policies of the new Republican majority in Congress. In *The Cato Handbook for Congress*, the institute argues that the Commerce Clause of the U.S. Constitution should be restored to its original purpose, enabling Congress to guarantee the free flow of commerce among the states, and that the General Welfare Clause should never be exercised on behalf of particular persons, as in affirmative action and Aid to Families with Dependent Children. The institute proposes abolishing welfare, income tax, and regulations on business and industry, legalizing drugs, cutting the defense budget, and restraining the authority of law enforcement—all as part of its goal of enhancing individual liberty and reducing the scope of government. Cato believes that knowledgeable consumers control the market through their buying habits and provide checks against abuses; government's proper role is limited to providing police protection, enforcing contracts, and defending against invasions.[89]

Cato's emphasis on individual liberty is reflected in its opposition to affirmative action. In a *Heritage Foundation Policy Review* article entitled "The Terrible Ten: America's Worst Regulations," Cato Senior Fellow Doug Bandow cites Executive Order 11246, along with bilingual education, as one of America's worst programs. Bandow argues that affirmative action programs promote the idea of individual success based on membership in a group, rather than on personal achievement; those excluded lose benefits that are rightfully theirs, and those included, even if qualified, are diminished because others believe they have succeeded only because of their race.[90]

Former chair of the EEOC and now Supreme Court Justice Clarence Thomas wrote articles for and delivered speeches at the Cato Institute blasting affirmative action, including "Civil Rights as a Principle Versus Civil Rights as an Interest."[91] In a 1987 speech to Cato, Thomas praised Justice Scalia's dissent in *Johnson v. Transportation Agency*[92] in which the court upheld a voluntary affirmative action program even though no prior discrimination had been found. Thomas declared that Scalia's dissent would one day "provide guidance for lower courts and a possible majority for future decisions."[93] In a 1988 article for Cato, Thomas criticizes *Brown v. Board of Education*[94] for leading to a "disastrous series of cases requiring busing and other policies that were irrelevant to parents' concern for a decent education." He laments that the court in *Brown* and other cases was "more concerned with meeting the demands of groups than with protecting the rights of individuals."[95] It was undoubtedly views like this that prompted the institute to support Thomas wholeheartedly in his 1991 nomination to the Supreme Court. And in an astonishing coup, Roger Pilon, director of Cato's Constitutional Studies Center, convinced the American

Civil Liberties Union, Cato's sometime ally, to refrain from opposing Thomas.[96]

Cato is consistent—besides opposing Executive Order 11246, it has criticized the Americans with Disabilities Act, Title VII of the Civil Rights Act of 1964, the Civil Rights Act of 1991, the Equal Employment Opportunity Commission (EEOC) and the Justice Department for their policies and views on affirmative action. In regard to EEOC, Cato Institute policy analyst James Bovard, author of *Lost Rights: The Destruction of American Liberty*, argues that an employer anticipating a discrimination suit responds with an out-of-court settlement offer for several thousand dollars, because fighting it could be far more expensive. Bovard notes that EEOC cites such settlements as evidence of guilt, but what the settlements really reflect are the employer's dislike of nuisance lawsuits.[97]

Recently, Cato criticized the findings of the Federal Glass Ceiling Commission. Fellow Paul Craig Roberts argues in "Views Through the 'Glass Ceiling'" that the 1995 report, which finds that "prejudice against minorities and white women continues to be the single most important barrier to their advancement," is of questionable credibility because the commission is 75 percent female. Roberts also maintains that the commission got things radically wrong. The main legally sanctioned discrimination is today against white males, who are in effect second-class citizens—"stripped of the protection of the 1964 Civil Rights Act, and [with] inferior standing in law to 'protected minorities.'" He goes on to state that "the demise of equality before the law and the resurrection of status-based legal privileges is the most astounding development of the 20th Century."[98]

The Cato Institute has an annual budget of $6 million. Early on, Cato's bills were largely paid by the Koch family of Wichita, Kansas. Today it receives most of its financial support from entrepreneurs, securities and commodities traders, and corporations such as oil and gas companies, Federal Express, and Philip Morris that abhor government regulation. Although the institute also receives financial support from several private foundations, it no longer receives funding from Olin. Cato's position on foreign policy, specifically its opposition to all foreign military engagements, including the Persian Gulf War, moved former treasury secretary William Simon to withdraw his personal support from Cato as well as that of the John M. Olin Foundation, which he heads.[99] Because the institute favors reduced military spending, Scaife requires that its money be spent on economic studies only.[100]

The Cato Institute has received funding from the following foundations:

- Lynde and Harry Bradley Foundation—$25,000, 1992 (for publication of *Regulation* magazine)
- Jaquelin Hume Foundation—$50,000, 1993 (for grant made in form of stock)
- David H. Koch Charitable Foundation—$350,000, 1992
- Claude R. Lambe Charitable Foundation
    —$600,000, 1992 (for general support)
    —$200,000, 1992 (for program on Rules, Justice, and Orders)
- Montgomery Street Foundation—$12,500, 1992 (for program of public policy research)
- Sarah Scaife Foundation
    —$137,500, 1992 (for *Critical Review* and general operating support)
    —$125,000, 1993 (for Center for Constitutional Studies and for general operating support)
- Robert W. Wilson Foundation—$10,000, 1992[101]

Like Proving Things with Figures? Join the Rand Corporation

The Rand Corporation, a think tank based in Santa Monica, California, that specializes in national security problems and domestic affairs, has published several studies that seek to show that the economic progress blacks and women have made over the past thirty years is not attributable to affirmative action. In a 1978 study by economists James P. Smith and Finis R. Welch, Rand reported a narrowing of the wage gap between blacks and whites. Commissioned by the National Science Foundation, the study entitled *Race Differences in Earnings* found that in 1947 black men earned one-half the income of white men, while black women earned one-third that of white women; by 1975, black men earned three-fourths the income of white men, and the earnings of white and black women were nearly equal. The report argues that the improved income of blacks was due mostly to increased education and the industrialization of the South, which opened up higher-income jobs to blacks; affirmative action programs played a very minor role. While they acknowledge that affirmative action improved opportunities for black women "because hiring a black woman met both race and sex quotas set for employers," the authors found little evidence that it improved earnings for black men.[102]

In 1984, Rand released a second study, entitled *Women's Wages and Work in the Twentieth Century*, which reports a narrowing of the wage gap between men and women. It finds that women's pay rose from 60 percent of men's in 1980 to 64 percent three years later—the largest and swiftest gain of the century. The authors attributed the gains to women's improving job skills because of better opportunities for education and expanded work experience, rather than to affirmative action or other governmental efforts.[103]

Two years later, Rand released the results of a major study by Smith and Welch entitled *Closing the Gap: Forty Years of Economic Progress for Blacks*, which again finds that educational gains, rather than affirmative action, have been the main factor in the improved economic status of black men over the past forty years. Sponsored by the U.S. Department of Labor, it is arguably the most comprehensive examination of the economic status of blacks since Gunnar Myrdal's 1944 book *An American Dilemma*. Drawing on Census Bureau data, the study reports a dramatic increase in the size of the black middle class. The study also finds that the wage gap between blacks and whites narrowed as rapidly between 1940 and 1960, before affirmative action programs were adopted, as it did between 1960 and 1980, the heyday of affirmative action. This leads the authors to conclude that "the slowly evolving historical forces . . . that enhance the labor market skills of blacks—education and migration—were the primary determinants of long-term black improvement."[104]

But affirmative action, while resulting in "a radical reshuffling" of black jobs, in fact conferred no significant long-term economic benefit on the average African American. After passage of Title VII of the Civil Rights Act of 1964, black jobs simply shifted toward companies that were covered by EEOC and the Office of Federal Contract Compliance Programs (OFCCP). The study did find that affirmative action had a "significant, but short-lived positive effect" on the wages of younger blacks in the early years. For example, among recent college graduates, black men earned 75 percent as much as whites in 1966; by 1972 their earnings were equal. But the study found that once the firms reached their target number of black workers, the gains disappeared: Over the next five years, the wages of young black men dropped by nearly 10 percent in relation to those of whites. Smith and Welch also reported that affirmative action resulted in a "pro-skill bias." Because most blacks held low-skill jobs, employers took the easy route of increasing the number of minorities in higher-level jobs. Thus, young college-educated blacks benefited far more from affirmative action than did less well-educated ones.[105]

In 1993, *American Economic Review* published an article by Rand's economist James Smith entitled "Affirmative Action and the Racial Wage Gap," in which he seeks to explain why the gains made by blacks in the late 1960s and early 1970s reversed during the 1980s. Smith argues that although the Reagan administration sharply curtailed affirmative action enforcement in the 1980s, market forces were the prime reason for the stagnation in earnings among blacks. According to Smith, the slowdown began well before the Reagan administration's cuts in the resources of EEOC. Black men earned 45 percent less than white men in 1969. The gap narrowed to 29 percent by 1977 but froze at that level. Smith reports that while most blame the Reagan administration's cutbacks on affirmative action, this is unfair: The stagnation is attributable to a slowing in black educational gains, a sharp rise in income for increased education, and the rapid expansion of wage inequality for everyone.[106]

Rand has received funding from the following foundations:

- Lynde and Harry Bradley Foundation—$32,000, 1993 (for publication of book on crime and public policy)
- Ford Foundation—$250,000, 1993 (for project support for study of impact of immigration on California)
- William and Flora Hewlett Foundation—$270,000, 1993 (three-year grant; for general support of population research and training)
- Robert Wood Johnson Foundation
  —$1,366,610, 1993 (for analysis of options and implications of state health care reform)
  —$499,896, 1993 (three-year grant; for study of effects of changed Medicaid physician fees on access and costs)
  —$147,042, 1993 (for estimates of cost of insuring the uninsured)

- W. Alton Jones Foundation—$52,000, 1993 (to define advantages of mutual security arrangement between Russian and American militaries)
- Alfred P. Sloan Foundation
  - $200,000, 1993 (for research program, Effects of Liability on Business Decisions and the Economy)
  - $30,000, 1993 (for conference, Human Capital Investments and Economic Performance)
  - $30,000, 1994 (to disseminate findings of drug legalization study)[107]

Have Trouble Deciding Where You Stand on Affirmative Action? Join the Hudson Institute

The Hudson Institute, founded in 1961 by former Rand Corporation analyst Herman Kahn, has an annual budget of about $7 million and is headed by Leslie Lenkowsky. The institute is regarded as one of three think tanks, along with the Heritage Foundation and Cato Institute, responsible for generating many of the ideas held by the new Republican majority in Congress and is best known for its 1987 report *Workforce 2000*.[108] The report, commissioned by the United States Department of Labor as part of an ongoing project detailing shifts in the composition of the labor force, finds that by the year 2000 only 15 percent of new entrants into the work force will be white men, compared with nearly 50 percent in 1985; 29 percent will be minorities and 61 percent women.[109] Across the country this prediction galvanized corporations, which rushed to develop diversity courses and hire diversity consultants to sensitize employees to racial and gender differences. Shortly after the report was issued, R. Roosevelt Thomas Jr. labeled and launched diversity management training with his *Harvard Business Review* article, "From Affirmative Action to Affirming Diversity."[110]

Workforce 2000 was followed by other reports in a similar vein, including *Civil Service 2000* and *Opportunity 2000*, which highlight successful affirmative action strategies being used by government and private employers. Funded by a $160,000 grant, the latter report urges that companies recognize the "enriching influence" of a diverse work force and use affirmative action as "a vital human resources process that expands [productivity and] opportunities for everyone."[111] Written by Clint Bolick of the Institute for Justice (Justice Department nominee Lani Guinier's bête noir), the report features a variety of successful efforts by companies working alone or cooperatively with government, foundations, community colleges, or business groups. Bolick reports that corporations reached impressive results by treating minorities as individuals worthy of investment, rather than as mere numbers to be counted.[112]

Although much of Hudson's early work on affirmative action seems supportive of that policy, some of its recent publications have taken a different course. Over the past few years, Hudson Institute fellows such as William Bennett and Michael Horowitz have spoken out sharply on the travesties of racial preferences. Bennett has charged affirmative action with sparking anti-immigration sentiment in California.[113] Like Bennett, Michael Horowitz, director of the Hudson Institute's Commission on Social Justice and former general counsel for the Office of Management and Budget (OMB) under Reagan, asserts that affirmative action, despite its good intentions, has failed. He notes that only two groups have benefited from affirmative action: minority college graduates and "the lawyers and specialists who administer the affirmative-action industry."[114] In March 1995, Horowitz testified before the Senate Finance Committee that despite costing a reported $2 billion over the past twenty years, Section 1071 of the Federal Communication Commission's minority tax certificate program has done little to increase minority ownership in the communications industry. He also testified that while examining the results of the Labor Department's OFCCP program during his tenure as OMB general counsel, he observed that OFCCP-covered firms did not do any better and often did worse than non-OFCCP-covered firms in minority hiring and promotion. He also noticed that the program generates over $2 billion each year in legal fees, which go to white law firms to draft "safe harbor plans."[115]

The Olin Foundation has served as an important source of funding for the Hudson Institute, awarding grants worth $175,000 in both 1991 and 1992 to William Bennett, for example.[116] The Hudson Institute has received funding from the following foundations:

- Bodman Foundation — $20,000, 1992 (for efforts to preserve Western values, democracy, free enterprise, and individual liberty through academic curriculum)

- Lynde and Harry Bradley Foundation
    - $75,000, 1992 (for book project on Ethics and Government Act and Office of Independent Council)
    - $75,000, 1992 (for study on American labor movement)
    - $67,500, 1992 (for study of Latin American nationalism)
    - $44,850, 1992 (for study of Bush presidency)
    - $28,667, 1992 (for research project on classical political thought)
    - $198,750, 1993 (for study of national drug control policy)
    - $100,000, 1993 (for study of Robert McNamara and American liberalism)
    - $65,000, 1993 (for study of Latin American nationalism)
    - $60,000, 1993 (for study of American labor movement)
    - $34,000, 1993 (for study of school choice)
- Earhart Foundation — $10,000, 1992 (for Herman Kahn Fellowship in Political Science)
- JM Foundation — $35,000, 1994 (for *The American Dream: Renewing the Promise of American Life*)
- McCamish Foundation — $25,000, 1992
- Charles Stewart Mott Foundation — $100,000, 1994 (eighteen-month grant; for model state-based welfare reform providing recipients with access to paths out of both dependency and poverty)
- John M. Olin Foundation
    - $175,000, 1992 (for John M. Olin Fellowship)
    - $22,500, 1992 (for book on the American character)
    - $100,000, 1993 (for John M. Olin Fellowship)
    - $25,000, 1993 (for Competitiveness Center)
- Sarah Scaife Foundation
    - $50,000, 1992 (for research support)
    - $83,000, 1993 (for publication support)
    - $40,000, 1993 (for research support)
- Starr Foundation — $60,000, 1994 (two-year grant; for general support)
- Jay and Betty VanAndel Foundation — $15,000, 1992 (for general support)[117]

The Hudson Institute also receives funding from the Annie E. Casey Foundation.[118]

Not Yet Ready for the Big Leagues? Try a Think Tank on the Way Up

Perhaps spurred by the success of major institutes and think tanks like Heritage, AEI, and Hudson, dozens of small, regional think tanks have sprung up all over America, many of them anxious to get a foothold in the anti–affirmative action movement.

Heartland Institute

The Heartland Institute, an independent think tank located in Chicago, is directed by Lee Walker, who is also president of the New Coalition for Economic and Social Change, a black conservative think tank founded by Clarence Pendleton that focuses on personal responsibility and equality of opportunity. In 1989, Heartland released a fifty-eight-page report entitled "Disadvantaged Business Set-Aside Programs: An Evaluation." It examines set-aside programs adopted by the federal and Illinois state governments, finding that they failed to produce significant benefits while costing taxpayers millions of dollars each year in higher construction expenses. It also concludes that overly optimistic goals and vague language in defining minority businesses encouraged fraud, prevented benefits from reaching legitimate minority businesses, and adversely affected nonminority businesses.[119]

In 1991, Heartland released a report entitled "Beyond Affirmative Action," arguing that the civil rights establishment emphasizes collectivism, egalitarianism, and sociocultural determinism, all calculated to heighten racial tensions. According to the report, only "Social Spontaneity," a philosophy that incorporates individualism and individual liberty, reliance on private and voluntary institutions for the resolution of social problems, and reduced government intervention, can lead the United States beyond its current stalemate.[120] In 1994, Heartland author Steven Yates published a book entitled *Civil Wrongs: What Went Wrong with Affirmative Action*, which argues that affirmative action has harmed minorities and women by creating a "victim's mindset" and heightening racial tensions on campuses and in society at large. Yates maintains that the goals of President Kennedy's Executive Order 10925, which first ordered affirmative action, have been violated by court interpretations and administrative policies, and advocates social spontaneity as the alternative to affirmative action.[121]

Lee Walker, an African American, has written several articles lambasting affirmative action. In "Talking Politics: Life Will Go On Without Affirmative Action Plan," Walker argues that blacks (his kind, at least) do not need affirmative action to succeed.[122] In "Why It's Time to Reopen Affirmative Action Debate," Walker maintains that the program has run its course; minorities and women have been hired, but they have not moved up the ladder. He notes that the government has focused on hiring patterns rather than equal opportunity. Thus, "[it's] time to focus less on affirmative action and more on affirmative opportunity."[123]

The Heartland Institute has received $10,000 each from the Claude R. Lambe Charitable Foundation (in 1992, for a publication project), the John M. Olin Foundation (1993, for a new magazine, *Intellectual Ammunition*), and the JM Foundation (1994, to market *PolicyFax*). In 1992 the institute received $100,000 from the Sarah Scaife Foundation for general operating support.[124]

Black? Uncomfortable with Affirmative Action? Try the Lincoln Institute
The Lincoln Institute was founded in 1979 to study issues affecting middle-class blacks. Its founder, black conservative J. A. (Jay) Parker, became the first of his race to serve on the national board of Young Americans for Freedom in 1961. Parker was active in the Goldwater campaign, joined the ultra-right World Anti-Communist League in the 1970s, and worked with CAUSA, the self-styled educational arm of the Reverend Sun Myung Moon's Unification Church. In 1980, the institute had an annual budget of $100,000, receiving funding from Reader's Digest and Joseph Coors, among others. It opposes affirmative action programs, taking the view that minorities will advance only if expanding businesses produce more jobs.[125] The institute publishes its opinions in the *Lincoln Review*, a quarterly magazine Parker began editing in 1979. The reader might well imagine its content—pieces attacking abortion, praising capital punishment, and questioning the existence of discrimination. In addition to articles by Thomas Sowell of the Hoover Institution and Walter E. Williams of George Mason University, the review also has published three articles by Supreme Court Justice Clarence Thomas, including one in 1988 extolling the virtues of Sowell and placing him in the "pantheon of black Americans such as Frederick Douglass, Booker T. Washington, and Martin Luther King, Jr." Thomas, who served on the journal's editorial board for nearly ten years,

went on to express his own strong opposition to affirmative action and argued that racism will be overcome only by free enterprise.[126]

Institute for Justice

Another small think tank, the Institute for Justice, a libertarian organization founded in 1991 by two former Coloradans, William H. Mellor III and Clint Bolick, the institute's president and vice president, has an annual budget of $1.5 million and focuses on such issues as school choice, property rights, and affirmative action.[127] Bolick, a former assistant to Clarence Thomas at EEOC, today is one of affirmative action's most outspoken critics. At a 1991 forum, Bolick argued that instead of affirmative action programs that benefit "those who need the help the least," we should focus on improving the education of all job applicants regardless of race, raising the ability of people to compete rather than redistributing opportunity.[128] The institute has played an active role in helping the new Republican majority draft legislation to end affirmative action. In January 1995, it sponsored a briefing in which two House Republican committee chairmen, Representatives Bill Goodling (R-Pa.) and Henry J. Hyde (R-Ill.), announced that they would hold hearings on the Justice Department's civil rights agenda in an effort to eliminate quotas and racial preferences.[129]

The institute also urged Congress to "enact a Civil Rights Act of 1995, forbidding the federal government from engaging in racial or gender preferences in programs, contracts, or employment."[130] In February 1995, Bolick began working with Gingrich and Dole to eliminate funding for all affirmative action provisions in federal law. Bolick also helped Republicans draft legislation, recommended by the institute, that would replace affirmative action with a needs-based system in school admissions, federal contracting, and employment. He calls the current system trickle-down civil rights—"benefits are bestowed on those at the top in the name of those at the bottom." He reasons that benefits under a needs-based system would be distributed fairly to blacks and other minorities because they account for a disproportionate percentage of the poor.[131] Recently the institute helped Senators Bob Dole and Charles Canady draft legislation modeled after the California Civil Rights Initiative, which proposes an end to race and gender preferences. The main difference is that the federal version, entitled the Equal Opportunity Act of 1995, would allow for needs-based benefits by requiring that "individual merit or disadvantage," rather than race or gender, be the qualification for any affirmative action.[132] The bill would apply to all federal government employment, contracts, programs, and policies.

The Institute for Justice has received funding from the following foundations:

- Lynde and Harry Bradley Foundation
    - $35,000, 1992 (for general program activities)
    - $50,000, 1993 (for general program activities)
- Gilder Foundation — $15,000, 1992
- Jaquelin Hume Foundation — $20,000, 1993
- JM Foundation — $25,000, 1994 (for Operation Bootstraps, entrepreneurship program for low-income, inner-city residents)
- J. M. Kaplan Fund — $14,800, 1992 (for Empowerment, Self Sufficiency, and Community Program, which seeks to create greater economic opportunities and improved living conditions for inner-city residents)
- David H. Koch Charitable Foundation — $250,000, 1992 (for general support)
- Claude R. Lambe Charitable Foundation — $450,000, 1992 (for general support)
- John M. Olin Foundation — $25,000, 1993 (for litigation and education on legal rights issues)
- Sarah Scaife Foundation
    - $50,000, 1992 (for general operating support)
    - $60,000, 1993 (for general operating support)
- Robert W. Wilson Foundation — $25,000, 1992[133]

Independence Institute

The Independence Institute, a conservative think tank formed in 1985 and based in Golden, Colorado, has spearheaded the drafting of a Colorado measure modeled after the California Civil Rights Initiative. In January 1995, Tom Tancredo, a former Reagan-Bush bureaucrat and the institute's president, wrote an article entitled "Dr. King's Dream Didn't Include Quotas," praising the California initiative for proposing an end to "reverse discrimination" and declaring that he hopes "that support of the idea spreads quickly to other states, especially Colorado."[134] The institute has also touted ending affirmative action as a means for slowing immigration in Colorado.

Later that year, it released the results of a study that found that Coloradans pay $70 million a each year to educate and care for illegal immigrants, an effort that could end in cultural "meltdown." To slow this flood, the report proposes ending affirmative action, reforming welfare, and ending bilingual education.[135]

Independence has an annual budget of $300,000; 350 members each pay a minimum of $50 a year. Although the institute is often thought to be a conduit for Coors money, funding from Castle Rock, an Adolph Coors foundation, has never exceeded 10 percent of its budget, according to Tancredo; Jeff Coors, however, is a member of the board of trustees.[136] The Independence Institute has received $10,000 each from the El Pomar Foundation (in 1992, for general operating support) and the JM Foundation (1993, for state policy research program, AQA Project: Access, Quality, and Affordability regarding Colorado Health Policy) and $35,000 from the Adolph Coors Foundation (1993, for general support).[137]

Pacific Research Institute

The Pacific Research Institute for Public Policy, a San Francisco–based libertarian think tank, has sponsored books and conferences on affirmative action while taking an active role in promoting the California Civil Rights Initiative (CCRI). In 1990, the institute published Clint Bolick's book *Unfinished Business: A Civil Rights Strategy for America's Third Century*, in which he argues that quotas are immoral, counterproductive, and reward nonvictims at the expense of others who have done nothing wrong. Quotas, Bolick says, address only the symptoms of racial inequality, not the underlying causes—unequal education and entry-level job opportunities. Bolick's foreword was written by Charles Murray.[138] Sally Pipes, president of the Pacific Research Institute, is a member of the academic advisory board of the CCRI and has written articles in support of the initiative.

Recently, the institute caused a considerable stir with the release of a report by fellow Michael Lynch charging the California state system with using race as the sole factor in some medical school admissions. The report charges that, according to an analysis of admissions data from 1991 to 1993, African Americans, Mexican Americans, Puerto Ricans, and American Indians were admitted to University of California medical schools at rates two to four times higher than those for other minorities and whites with similar or better qualifications and that the chance of these minorities' being admitted at such high rates "without a preferential policy is less than one in a million." The report accuses the university of violating *Bakke*.[139]

Pacific has received funding from the following foundations: $25,000 from the Lynde and Harry Bradley Foundation in 1993 for general program activities; $15,000 from the Earhart Foundation in 1992 for general operating support; $30,000 from the Jaquelin Hume Foundation in 1993; $50,000 from the David H. Koch Charitable Foundation in 1992 for general support of Cutting Back, efficiency in government prize; $25,000 from the Claude R. Lambe Charitable Foundation in 1992 for general support; $100,000 from the Sarah Scaife Foundation in 1992 for general operating and special project support; and $28,500 from the E. L. Wiegand Foundation in 1993 for office equipment.[140]

Opponents of affirmative action repeat the themes of white innocence, the supremacy of Western ideas and books; and the weakness of black and other minority cultures. As one writer recently put it: "Scientific racism has made a major comeback, in its sociohistorical guise, with 'culture' as a stand-in for race. The step to biology is only a move within an evil framework that is already well established."[141]

All the social intervention in this country has been
done to make the intervener feel better and not the
recipient; caretaking is the ultimate form of racism.
—Morris R. Shechtman, psychotherapist and
consultant to the Republican Party

5

The Attack on Welfare

and the Poor

THREE DECADES AFTER President Lyndon Johnson launched the
"War on Poverty," Americans are rethinking their attitudes toward the
poor, calling for major overhauls of the welfare system and outright abolition of many of its components. During the Great Society period (the 1960s
and 1970s) public sentiment held that extrinsic forces are the cause of
much poverty and that government should take responsibility for assisting
those so afflicted. Shortly before his death, John Kennedy in a speech at
Amherst College spoke of inherited wealth and inherited poverty and
urged those better off in life to serve the community with compassion and
understanding. President Johnson sponsored an antipoverty bill in 1964
that provided for job training, part-time jobs for students, and antipoverty
projects of various kinds. Food Stamp and Medicaid programs were established during this period and Aid to Families with Dependent Children
(AFDC) benefits became more generous.

These programs caused the number of people receiving welfare benefits to grow. As inflation raged and the economy worsened, the public began calling for cutbacks. By 1973 Congress had enacted a "quality control" measure requiring states to make an effort to reduce overpayments in AFDC benefits or risk losing federal funding. From 1974 to 1975 stricter child support requirements were added so that mothers had to assist in finding the father of their children to be eligible for benefits.[1] Although both Presidents Richard Nixon and Jimmy Carter attempted to reform welfare, both failed to get their major proposals passed. Nixon's Family Assistance Plan (FAP) would have provided a minimum income to poor families, and money for job training and child care. Carter initiated the Program for Better Jobs and Income (PBJI), which included regulations and work incentives along with a program for public jobs.[2]

The conservative influence began in earnest during the 1980s, when the Reagan administration began waging a relentless attack on the poor, depicting them as deviants unwilling to fit into mainstream America.[3] Reagan enacted cuts in AFDC eligibility, tougher work requirements, and proposals to give states responsibility for welfare programs.[4] The most notable welfare legislation of this era was the Omnibus Budget Reconciliation Act of 1981 (OBRA), which lowered the earned income tax credit and monthly child care deductions and readdressed the eligibility of AFDC recipients. This legislation resulted in 408,000 families losing eligibility outright, and an additional 299,000 suffering substantial reductions of their benefits.[5]

Despite these cutbacks, expenditures on social welfare in 1981 were four times as great as they were in 1968, and with the budget crisis of the Reagan era caused by the inflation of the 1970s, something had to give.[6] The administration introduced supply-side economics—the idea that tax cuts for the rich will stimulate the economy and increase government revenue. The approach derives in part from the work of Arthur Laffer, professor of economics at the University of Southern California, who first urged that providing favorable treatment and reduced taxes for industrialists will cause wealth to "trickle-down" so that the poor will be better off than they would have been had the government merely given them handouts. Unfortunately, the Reagan era produced the highest federal debt in modern history, forcing supply-siders to change the focus of their theory from tax cuts to strengthen economic growth to heavy cuts in social programs.[7]

These cuts at first clashed with America's ingrained generosity. Thus, it was necessary for conservatives to prepare the way by the use of books, catch phrases, and media blitzes aimed at convincing the U.S. people that the poor deserved their plight and that social programs were dangerous for the national economy.

Want to Become Famous by Bashing the Poor? Write a Book

Central in disseminating the theory of the iniquity of the poor were conservative scholars Charles Murray, William Bennett, and Lawrence M. Mead. Charles Murray, at that time a senior fellow at the Heritage Foundation, was influenced by a period he had spent during the 1960s in Thai villages, where he saw the poor living in stability and harmony with little need for government intervention. In *Losing Ground*, perhaps the most influential work in the attack on welfare, he critiques the welfare state, suggesting that from 1964 to 1980 social policy in the United States "went from the dream of ending the dole to the institution of permanent income transfers."[8]

Murray proposes terminating the entire welfare system and indoctrinating children on welfare with middle-class values. He argues that welfare destroys human lives and incentives. He offers a "thought experiment," tracing the lives of a fictional couple named Phyllis and Harold after an accidental pregnancy and showing that in 1960, it was more rational for them to marry and for Harold to get a low-wage job, while by 1970 the rational decision would have been to stay single and have Phyllis collect welfare.[9]

Murray's premise is that single mothers with young children are neither a socially nor an economically feasible unit. They suffer from a high incidence of poverty, and government aid enables that condition to continue by reducing the need for a wage-earning father. He further argues that food stamps, welfare checks, and housing subsidies reduce the stigma that once accompanied out-of-wedlock births. Thus, by phasing out welfare and forcing pregnant women to rely on family, friends, and most important, the father of their child, everyone will be better off. In addition, he suggests that the government spend money on orphanages to care for the children that will inevitably be neglected and abandoned as a result of his proposal.

More recently, Murray has managed to shift the welfare debate even further by emphasizing the problem of illegitimacy. In an influential article in the *Wall Street Journal* in late 1993 entitled "The Coming White Underclass", Murray warned that rising illegitimacy rates among poor whites are creating a new white underclass. This article appeared just as welfare was coming up for debate on Capitol Hill. With Murray's neat side-step of racial issues, the media feasted on his proposal to reduce illegitimacy rates by ending all economic support for single mothers: no AFDC benefits, no food stamps, no subsidized housing.[10] In the following days, influential commentators like George F. Will, Charles Krauthammer, Michael Barone, John Leo, and Joe Klein wrote about the developing white underclass, and Murray was interviewed by David Brinkley, John Stossel, and Connie Chung. Murray's arguments have been so influential in the debate on welfare that Grover Norquist, president of Americans for Tax Reform, compares him to intellectuals like Darwin, Freud, and Marx. His linkage of welfare to rising illegitimacy rates was a brilliant stroke — it allowed the conservatives to take the moral high ground.[11]

Coming on Murray's heels, William Bennett wrote the best seller *The Book of Virtues*, a series of morality tales that echo the conservative attempt to re-moralize society and put an end to welfare dependency and illegitimacy. In this and other writings, Bennett challenges the perception that society is responsible for all social ills. Instead, he proposes to join social policy and moral principles and suggests that the government end welfare "cold turkey."[12]

Bennett seconded Murray's views on illegitimacy in opinion articles that ran in over twenty-six major newspapers and in numerous speeches and appearances on talk shows, including Rush Limbaugh's. Bennett and Murray's combined efforts were not lost on Washington. Representative Jim Talent (R-Mo.), who requires his interns to read *Losing Ground*, introduced an even harsher welfare reform bill early last year to compete with the Republicans' first bill sponsored by Senator Rick Santorum (R-Pa.) that most GOP legislators originally supported. Bennett and Murray backed Talent's bill, and Bennett condemned Santorum's version in a memorandum released by his conservative think tank, Empower America.[13]

Bennett also weighed in with his *Index of Leading Cultural Indicators*, released in March 1993. Consisting of data on nineteen social issues, including illegitimacy, divorce, and crime, complete with extensive graphs and charts; all profess to show an inverse relationship between government spending and results obtained. According to the statistics, since 1960 the number of illegitimate births has increased 400 percent, the number of single family homes 300 percent—all while social spending has risen sharply. To deal with these epidemics Bennett recommends personal responsibility as a theme in welfare reform, reduction of the economic penalties currently imposed on single mothers who marry, and a requirement of community service by welfare recipients.[14]

A third figure, Lawrence Mead of Princeton, in *Beyond Entitlement: The Social Obligations of Citizenship* also argues that poverty persists because government programs subsidize the poor without requiring them to work. Mead parts company with Murray by suggesting that merely cutting back welfare programs is not enough; the very nature of the welfare system must change. In particular, Mead wants able-bodied recipients to work for their benefits. "The most vulnerable Americans need obligations, as much as rights, if they are to move as equals on the stage of American life."[15] The impact of Mead's work is best seen in the Family Support Act of 1988, which compels recipients to perform work and requires states to establish Job Opportunities and Basic Skills Programs, with secondary educational instruction, job training and placement programs.

Mead also studied Wisconsin's work-based welfare system under the auspices of the Wisconsin Policy Research Institute, a conservative think tank. Mead noted that under Wisconsin's system, the number of welfare cases decreased by 3 percent from 1989 to 1993, while the number of cases nationwide increased by 29 percent. He pronounced paternalism the key to Wisconsin's success—caseworkers who require recipients to conform to social norms.[16] Inspired, perhaps, by Wisconsin's example, Mead wrote *The New Politics of Poverty: The Nonworking Poor in America*, in which he puts forward the thesis that with the right incentives, businesses could train and hire people on welfare, thereby decreasing their dependency on governmental assistance.

"Boob Bait for Bubba": Catch Phrases and Slogans in the War Against the Poor

Once books and essays made it intellectually permissible to attack welfare and blame the poor, the right used catch phrases and slogans to consolidate their gains and further inflame the public with the notion that the poor are getting away with something. Murray, for example, proposes allowing "100 flowers to bloom," in discussing his state and local alternatives to federal assistance.[17] Reagan coined the term "welfare queens" to drive home the view that women on welfare drive Cadillacs and spend their welfare checks on alcohol and cigarettes. The term rallied immense public support for cutting back welfare programs.[18] After the first one hundred days of the 104th Congress, Republican leaders urged congressmen to hold news conferences touting their success with chants of "promises made, promises kept," after nine out of the ten provisions of the Republicans' Contract with America were approved by the House, including two dealing with welfare.[19] Jack Kemp coined the term "ladder of opportunity" to advance his idea of replacing all cash payments with in-kind services.[20] Another catch phrase popular among conservatives is "little platoons," a term used by the eighteenth-century British political writer Edmund Burke and borrowed by William Kristol, chairman of Project for a Republican Future and former assistant professor at Harvard. Kristol uses the phrase to promote the idea that loose affiliations of individuals inevitably form to take care of one another when left to their own devices.[21]

Kristol is a favorite interviewee with such shows as CBS's *Face the Nation* and CNN's *Crossfire* and *Inside Politics*. He is the master of memorable quotations on welfare, whether in his speeches and interviews or in the memoranda he regularly sends to Republican leaders and three hundred media members. Kristol's comment in one such memorandum that welfare reform is the "boob bait for the bubbas" later appeared in headlines across the country, referring to the idea that President Clinton pulls welfare out of the bag only when he is falling in the polls.[22]

Conservatives also employ scare tactics and hyperbole to make the public believe the welfare system is a runaway threat. A press release by Simon and Schuster features the word "shocking" in bright red letters, followed by "chilling . . . raw . . . like a kick to the solar plexus"—a quotation from Rush Limbaugh's discussion of Bennett's *Index*. Robert Rector, senior policy analyst at the Heritage Foundation, in a paper entitled "America's Failed $5.4 Trillion War on Poverty," announced that in the past thirty years this country has spent that huge sum on welfare—70 percent more than the cost of defeating Germany and Japan in World War II and enough to purchase the nation's entire commercial infrastructure. In return, we have a system that makes it profitable to remain single and without a job, while continuing to procreate.

The problem with our welfare system, according to Rector, is "behavioral poverty," the decline in the morals of the poor, not "material poverty."[24]

Conservatives also use imagery strategically to attack welfare and enliven their theory of its moral wrongness with vivid stories of pregnant children, lazy welfare recipients, and drug-infested inner cities. Murray's thought experiment in *Losing Ground* is a prime example, as is Missouri Senator John Ashcroft's description during congressional hearings on welfare of the discovery in Chicago of the children of six families living in horrendous conditions, fighting over a chicken bone the dog had eaten, while the adults living in the home received a total of $65,000 in government support.[25] Such stories grab attention more effectively than do the endless lists of statistics recited by liberals.

Hollywood and the radio industry add to the antiwelfare message. *Forrest Gump,* with its up-by-one's-bootstrap moral, was the most successful movie of 1995, the year during which Speaker of the House Newt Gingrich suggested people watch the sentimental 1938 Spencer Tracy movie *Boys' Town* for proof of the merit of his proposal to have the government set up orphanages. Countless conservative radio talk show hosts fill the air with their strident rhetoric. Most notable is Rush Limbaugh, with his daily welfare-bashing reaching over 20 million listeners a week on over 660 stations. Larry Elder on KABC radio advocates abolishing welfare and preaches a black conservative Horatio Alger philosophy, Bob Grant on WABC in New York calls Martin Luther King Jr. a "scumbag" and Clinton the "sleazebag in the White House," and Bill Cunningham on WLW in Cincinnati calls liberals "loathsome dogs to be exterminated."[26]

Gingrich uses C-Span telecasts of welfare reform debates to exploit the public mood and further the conservative antiwelfare agenda. Over 60 million viewers across the country have seen conservatives berating welfare during debates over the subject in the House and Senate committees.[27]

Heavy Artillery: Conservative Organizations in the War on Welfare

In addition to expanding media attention through C-Span coverage of welfare debates, Gingrich spreads his influence through a broad network of organizations. In 1982, he joined with many young conservatives to form what he termed the "Conservative Opportunity Society" (COS), to contrast with the "liberal welfare state." This group adopted a deliberately confrontational stance in an attempt to attract media attention in the war against welfare. In addition to COS, Gingrich controls and influences a variety of conservative enterprises, including GOPAC which he took over from former Delaware governor Pete duPont, Renewing American Civilization, *Progress Report*, and the Progress and Freedom Foundation. A political action committee with an annual budget of $2 million, GOPAC trains candidates and spreads Gingrich's message. Renewing American Civilization, a Reinhardt College course transmitted by satellite to colleges and conservative groups, promulgates Gingrich's philosophy, including his antiwelfare stance, and recruits activists to work in the 1996 presidential elections. *Progress Report*, a talk show on Paul Weyrich's National Empowerment Television, features Gingrich-led discussions of political issues, including welfare reform.[28]

The Progress and Freedom Foundation, a think tank founded by Jeffrey Eisenach and staffed by Vin Weber and other conservative friends of Gingrich, promotes replacing the governmental welfare system with a private-sector version. It produced three policy papers in 1995, including one entitled "The People's Budget." With corporate donors like AT&T, Bell Atlantic, Bristol-Meyers Squibb, Coca-Cola, Eli Lilly, and Marion Merrell Dow, 1995 revenues are expected to reach $6 million.[29]

De-Funding the Left

Along with developing conservative networks such as Gingrich's, conservatives are attempting to trim down liberal groups, in a "De-Fund the Left" movement. Republicans are pressuring businesses, political action committees, and charitable foundations into withdrawing their support of the Democratic Party and of liberal causes generally. House Majority Leader Richard Armey (R-Tex.) sent a letter to eighty-two companies including Anheuser-Busch and May Department Stores warning that they are supporting interest groups that have expanded the welfare state. Capital Research Center, a conservative think tank in Washington, analyzed corporate donations and compiled the mailing list for Armey.[30] The National Alumni Forum writes to alumni of leading universities with scare stories of political correctness gone wild, urging that wealthy benefactors stop giving money to their schools or redirect their giving to programs they believe in. (See Chapter 7).

Meanwhile, corporate America continues to fund increasing numbers of conservative think tanks that are attacking the welfare system. The Adolph Coors Foundation, for example, donates to many conservative causes and think tanks across the country, supporting their stands on welfare reform, rising illegitimacy rates, and traditional values. The John M. Olin Foundation formed the Institute for Educational Affairs with the Sarah Scaife, JM, and Smith Richardson foundations to serve as a clearinghouse for corporate philanthropy, linking conservative scholars and thinkers seeking funding with corporations and foundations wishing to further a conservative public policy agenda.[31] This intricate network fulfills William E. Simon's strategy of organizing the conservative agenda promoted in his 1978 book *A Time for Truth.* The Heritage Foundation, the Hudson Institute, American Enterprise Institute, and Empower America have dominated the attack on welfare.

Heritage Foundation
Within a year of the formation of the Heritage Foundation in 1973 eighty-seven corporations were giving it financial support. These funds, supplemented by heavy contributions by six or seven major foundations (see Chapter 4), are now being used to support conservative Republicans and the attack on welfare. Heritage has been the forerunner in conservative thought since the Reagan era, when it presented the Reagan administration with *Mandate for Leadership,* a 1981 best seller. Heritage provided an equally influential plan for the Bush administration, with two thousand policy recommendations, including proposals to end AFDC after five years and to deny benefits under that plan to teenaged mothers who use them to live on their own.[32] In 1995, Heritage released a 260-page proposal on how to balance the budget entitled *Rolling Back Government: A Budget Plan to Rebuild America,* that would terminate most federal entitlements and provide block grants to states in order to balance the budget by the year 2000.[33]

Robert Rector has contributed heavily to the dissemination of Heritage's theory that welfare should be changed from a hand-out system to one of mutual responsibility. According to Heritage, it has been a mistake for the government to pay money to young girls on the condition that they have children and remain single. Rector impresses his views on Republicans, who then legislate accordingly. He has successfully changed the focus of the debate from work to wedlock. Rector helped draft the welfare bill passed by the House in 1995, a compromise between the proposal originally set forth by House Republicans, and Talent's alternative.[34]

In addition, when the Senate Finance Committee unveiled its proposal, Rector's editorial that appeared in newspapers nationwide on June 20, 1995, spurred conservative Senator Phil Gramm's alternative proposal. The editorial suggests that welfare be capped at 3 percent a year and that government limit benefits provided to unwed teenaged mothers, require mothers on AFDC to identify the fathers of their babies, and give tax credits for low-income couples with dependent children if one of the parents is employed.

Rector, who calls himself an "entrepreneur of ideas," believes his childhood influenced his theories on welfare. In the 1960s his family took care of a poor family, providing them with clothing, food, and toys. Nonetheless, Rector believes the aid did not help the poor family but instead created dependency.[35] He has written numerous welfare policy papers for Heritage in addition to "America's Failed $5.4 Trillion War on Poverty" and is the co-author with Michael McLaughlin of "A Conservative Guide to State Level Welfare Reform," suggesting that welfare erodes morality and leads to what Rector calls "behavioral poverty," a deterioration of social norms and ethics;[36] "Food Fight: How Hungry Are America's Children?" stating that children living in poverty are not malnourished but rather end up an inch taller and ten pounds heavier than an average child of the same age in the general population;[37] "President Clinton's Commitment to Welfare Reform: The Disturbing Record So Far," in which he claims Clinton is merely tinkering with welfare;[38] "How the Poor Really Live, Lessons for Welfare Reform";[39] "Combating Family Disintegration, Crime, and Dependence: Welfare Reform and Beyond";[40] and "How Clinton's Bill Extends Welfare."[41]

Heritage also funded Bennett's *Index of Leading Cultural Indicators* and sponsored the Third Generation, a program for young conservatives directed by Ben Hart, founder of the *Dartmouth Review*. (See Chapter 7.) Heritage holds monthly meetings at which over one hundred young conservative activists meet to discuss policy and network for job placement. Their goal is to cut back the liberal advances of the last several years, including welfare. Third Generation is closely associated with the Leadership Institute, directed by Morton Blackwell, which conducts seminars and helps young conservatives get placed in jobs.[42]

Heritage Budget Director Scott Hodge acknowledges that the organization helped identify liberal groups that are subsidized by federal money in an effort to disrupt the liberal infrastructure that supports welfare. The Child Welfare League, Planned Parenthood, and the Children's Defense Fund were among the groups targeted.[43] Representative David McIntosh (R-Ind.) responded by introducing a bill that would prohibit federal grants to groups that spend over 5 percent of their budget lobbying the government.[44]

Hudson Institute

The Hudson Institute has also played a large part in the attack on welfare. President Leslie Lenkowsky echoes the conservative theory that growth of welfare has played a large role in the rising teen pregnancy rates. He says society used to live by stricter codes of conduct. In previous times, violating social norms brought financial penalties; today welfare makes it easy to behave irresponsibly. Thus, Hudson supports doing away with the entire current welfare system and rebuilding it from scratch.

Michael Horowitz and Anna Kondratas, both senior fellows at Hudson, have influenced the current attack on welfare. Horowitz testified before the House Ways and Means Subcommittee on Human Resources. His testimony described the increasing dependency, illegitimacy, and hopelessness rampant in our cities, which conservatives believe is the direct result of the welfare system.[45] Horowitz also testified before the House Committee on Economic and Educational Opportunities.

Kondratas, administrator of food and nutrition service at the United States Department of Agriculture from 1987 to 1989 and assistant secretary of community planning and development from 1989 to 1992, testified before the House Committee on Agriculture, Department Operations, and Nutrition that poorly educated single mothers are more likely to be long-term welfare recipients than are married or divorced women. In her testimony, she proposed that welfare as we know it should be abolished and replaced with a completely different system. The current system, she said, was designed to help widows stay home with their children during a time when women's employment was low and divorce and illegitimacy were stigmatized. Today, both conditions have changed radically. Kondratas urges welfare reformers to focus on the family structure rather than the family income. She has also served on a variety of task forces on welfare and co-authored monographs on the "poverty trap."[46]

Hudson has sponsored several conferences on welfare, including a national policy forum in 1995 with the Progressive Policy Institute, entitled Putting Work First: Creating a Competitive Market for Moving Welfare Recipients into Work. In addition, Hudson is helping Wisconsin refine its welfare program. Wisconsin has been the forerunner in the reform effort, with time limits, family caps, and truancy penalties all prominent provisions of its system.[47] Hudson receives heavy contributions from the Bradley, Olin, and Sarah Scaife foundations and the liberal Mott foundations (see Chapter 4).

American Enterprise Institute

The American Enterprise Institute (AEI) has 120 employees, 45 resident scholars, and an annual budget of $12.6 million.[48] Along with Charles Murray, theologian Michael Novak is one of the think tank's premier voices on welfare. Novak believes welfare generates dishonesty, as recipients try to avoid the rules, and as taxpayers saddled with the cost of these programs engage in tax avoidance.

Novak directed a study by twenty scholars and concluded that the best way to avoid poverty is to finish high school, get and stay married, get a job and continue working, even at low wages.[49] Novak is also a member of the Welfare Crisis Group, consisting of eleven well-known conservative analysts, which proposes ending all cash benefits, food stamps, and housing subsidies in one year and using the money saved for the benefit of children.[50]

Among the seminars sponsored by AEI were "Ways Out of Poverty," in 1991; "Family and American Welfare Policy," in 1986," at which papers by Murray and Deborah Laren, with data concerning the age of AFDC recipients were presented; "Reducing Poverty in America" co-sponsored by UCLA in January 1993, featuring conservative speakers Murray, Douglas Besharov, Christopher Jencks, and Lawrence Mead; a seminar on illegitimacy in November of 1993 at which several conservatives presented papers, as did the neoliberal journalist Mickey Kaus, author of The End of Equality, proposing to replace welfare with a jobs program;[51] and the "Welfare Reform Breakfast," in January 1995, featuring William Bennett.[52]

AEI promulgates its viewpoints on welfare not only through these seminars, but also in its journals Public Opinion and This World, published jointly with the Institute for Educational Affairs, as well as in regular gatherings of welfare policy scholars. AEI is generously funded by a host of charitable trusts, foundations, and philanthropies. Bradley, Monell, Olin, Sarah Scaife, and Starr donate particularly lavishly (see Chapter 4).

Empower America

William Bennett formed Empower America with conservatives Jack Kemp, Jeane Kirkpatrick, and Vin Weber in 1993; Steve Forbes, editor and owner of *Forbes* magazine and 1996 presidential candidate, serves as chair. The organization's purpose is to provide fresh thinking for the Republican Party and rally Americans around conservative Republican proposals, including ones concerning welfare.[53] In December 1993 Empower America held a press conference with live C-Span coverage to assess Clinton's record up to that point and discuss the future of the conservative movement. Kemp, the featured speaker, told the audience that conservatives must learn not to impose their views and values on people.[54] Empower America joined with Heritage to sponsor a three-day conference for freshmen-elect with welfare one of the topics and a closing speech by Rush Limbaugh. Also addressing the newly elected Republicans was Ed Feulner of the Heritage Foundation, who told the legislators to look to Heritage for staff aides, guest speakers, bill drafting, and research papers.[55] Late in 1994 Empower America held another conference, which included a discussion titled "Give Welfare Back to the States."[56]

After President Bill Clinton unveiled his 1995 welfare reform proposal, Empower America ran a massive advertisement campaign denouncing it as cynical and deceptive, in part because it failed to cut off benefits to unmarried mothers under age twenty-one. Empower America also published a paper in response to Clinton's plan, and Bennett appeared on National Public Radio's *Morning Edition*, all in an attempt to shift the emphasis of welfare reform from employment to illegitimacy.[57] In addition Bennett, Kemp, and Weber wrote a commentary in the *Washington Times* on April 24, 1994, urging House Republicans to propose radical alternatives to the original House bill. The commentary criticized the House version, saying it had weak work requirements and inadequate measures on illegitimacy.

Other conservative organizations contributing to the attack on welfare include the Cato Institute and the Christian Coalition. Cato stands for limited government, individual liberty, and abolition of welfare. Its *Handbook for Congress* proposes cutting back the federal government by eliminating programs like Head Start and terminating all federal financing of welfare. In addition, congressional committee chairmen increasingly look to Cato scholars for testimony.[58] The Koch, Lambe, and Sarah Scaife foundations contribute the largest amounts of funding to Cato (see Chapter 4).

Pat Robertson's Christian Coalition has played a central role in the conservatives' attempt to improve the morals of America through legislation. Advancing the idea that personal responsibility should be a central theme in welfare reform, the Christian Coalition achieved its most prominent influence in the debate by expressing outrage over the original welfare reform bill introduced by the Senate Finance Committee. The coalition warned that it will not back a proposal that does not discourage pregnancies by unwed mothers. When Senator Phil Gramm proposed an alternative, the Christian Coalition was one of his main supporters.[59]

The attack on welfare is far from over. As it continues to advance through the legislative process, conservative figures and organizations are likely to continue to shape the direction of the debate. As one observer recently put it, "compassion is out, harshness is in."[60]

6

Tort Reform

IN CALIFORNIA a doctor's negligence in failing to discover an abscess in
a two-year-old child's brain led to the boy's blindness and permanent brain
damage. Instead of spending his youth playing with other children, the boy
will spend many years going to physical, speech, and occupational therapy
sessions. He was awarded $11.2 million; $7 million for pain and suffering
and the balance for the cost of continuing medical treatment and future
lost wages. The award for pain and suffering was quickly reduced to
$250,000, however, because of a cap placed on noneconomic injuries by
the California legislature in 1975. If the boy lives to age sixty his compensation for suffering will amount to around $4,000 a year.[1] (Because his le-
gal fees were $600,000, it could be argued that the recovery was a minus
number.)

Although liability caps run counter to a consumer's best interest, conservative think tanks, insurance companies, and trade organizations and coalitions, abetted by a few legal academics, have been highly successful in
changing the public's attitude toward the tort system (the body of law that
enables people to be made whole for injuries they suffer at the hands of others). Proponents of reform have succeeded in making citizens believe that

they are victims of high tort *costs* (mainly higher product and insurance costs and reduced availability of services) rather than (as they are) victims of tort *reform*. Employing television and radio commercials and bumper stickers, they make it appear that changes will stop tort victims from being unjustly enriched for feigned injuries—what they call "lawsuit abuse." Furthermore, proponents of reform have been able to portray themselves as underdogs up against greedy lawyers of the American Trial Lawyer's Association (ATLA), neatly concealing the way they themselves are backed by well-heeled think tanks, trade organizations, and coalitions funded by multi-billion-dollar corporations out to protect their own interests.

Even supporters of tort reform often will change their views when they become victims of a tort. For example, a lobbyist for the insurance industry was part of a successful fight to place a cap of $500,000 on awards for pain and suffering. Later, the lobbyist, a victim of medical malpractice, was confined to a wheelchair and hooked up to a morphine drip to control his constant pain. The man now opposes tort reform; ironically the promised reduction in insurance premiums did not materialize.[2]

What All the Shouting Is About

Tort reform has undergone three waves of change. The first wave started in the mid-1970s, when several states placed limits on medical malpractice judgments. A few years later, another set of legislative changes were instituted, ostensibly to control the liability insurance crisis, although it now appears that the crisis was due more to reduced profits throughout the insurance industry stemming from a sharp decline in interest rates than any radical increase in litigation. Today every state has limited medical malpractice liability. Forty-one have modified or abolished joint and several liability, which allows a plaintiff to collect the entire judgment from one negligent party if other defendants turn out to be insolvent. Thirty-one states have enacted various measures to restrict product liability claims—suits brought by consumers injured, for example, by defective pharmaceuticals. Twenty-seven have capped, prohibited, or made it more difficult to prove punitive damages (awards aimed at punishing or deterring potential offenders). Noneconomic damages (e.g., pain and suffering) have been capped in seventeen states. Eight have enacted legislation to reduce damages by reason of compensation received from other sources. A final wave of tort reform concerns recent congressional efforts to codify everything in the form of a uniform federal statute and to change the current contingent fee approach to a modified "loser pays" rule.[3]

The battle for federal tort reform legislation has raged for several years, but it has only recently received widespread attention because of the Republican control of Congress following the 1994 elections. In the prior Congress, product liability reform had twice failed to receive the necessary votes for cloture in the Senate. Before this time, tort reform measures had never been able to get out of committee.[4]

Both the House and the Senate have now passed bills. The House version puts a cap of $250,000 on noneconomic pain and suffering, and on punitive damages. It also eliminates joint and several liability in civil cases in both state and federal courts. A modified "loser pays" rule is applied in cases brought before federal courts, where a party must pay the other's legal fees if he or she rejects a settlement offer and the amount received is ultimately less than the offer. The Senate bill covers only product liability actions brought in state or federal courts, placing a cap of $250,000 on punitive damages, or twice the compensatory damages, whichever is greater. Under certain conditions, a judge can raise the cap. The bill also would eliminate joint and several liability in product liability actions.[5]

Because of the substantial differences between the bills, it is doubtful that a compromise version can pass both houses any time soon. A Democratic staffer speculates that Republicans may purposely avoid passing legislation to increase the chances of getting funding from the business community in the 1996 elections. Also, some advocates believe they can pass even more comprehensive measures if Republicans control the presidency as well. President Bill Clinton has implied that he will veto any bill containing a flat cap on punitive damages.[6]

Still, substantial changes have been made not only at the state level but also in softening the general public's views about tort reform. These changes are largely due to lobbying and advertising efforts made by trade organizations and coalitions financed by large corporations. These associations, in turn, rely heavily on conservative think tanks, which are funded by the same large corporations, for intellectual strategy and pseudoscientific support.

Think Tanks

Hate Being Sued? Try the Manhattan Institute

Of all of the conservative think tanks working in the area of tort reform, the Manhattan Institute has probably had the greatest impact. Originally called the International Center for Economic Policy Studies, in its early years it concentrated mostly on studies of global issues. When George Gilder, a well-known Reagan-era supply-side economist, joined the institute during the early 1980s he expanded the focus of issues the institute addressed. Today, aided by a huge staff and budget, the institute addresses a host of social issues, including affirmative action and tort reform.[7]

The institute's major impact has come from pamphlets, conferences, videos, and books they have sponsored, including, in the area of tort reform, two influential books written by senior fellow Peter Huber — *Liability: The Legal Revolution and Its Consequences* in 1988 and *Galileo's Revenge: Junk Science in the Courtroom* in 1991[8] — and a third, *The Litigation Explosion*, written in 1991 by senior fellow Walter K. Olson. Marketed as "objective research," the books popularized ideas later used by Dan Quayle during George Bush's 1992 reelection campaign and relied on by corporate trade organizations and coalitions during the current round of debates.

The institute's high point may have been the production of a pro–tort reform video in 1992 narrated by the much-revered Walter Cronkite. Costing $200,000 to produce, the video was largely financed by large corporate donations made to Manhattan. In it, a businessman tells about the calamitous effects his company experienced after a $5 million judgment was rendered against it. The video of course neglects to mention that the company was a subsidiary of Cooper Industries, Inc., which donated $50,000 toward its production.[10]

Most recently the institute has been instrumental in drafting a proposal to support a modified "loser pays" provision in the House bill. The original proposal was the brainchild of Manhattan Institute senior fellow Michael Horowitz (who has subsequently moved to the Hudson Institute) and tort scholars Jeffrey O'Connell of the University of Virginia Law School and Lester Brickman of Benjamin N. Cardozo School of Law. It provides that, after discoverable information is supplied, the defendant may make a settlement offer within sixty days, which need not include noneconomic injuries. If the offer is accepted, the plaintiff's attorney's legal fees are capped at his or her actual billable hours or 10 percent of the recovery up to $100,000 and 5 percent of recoveries over $100,000. If the offer is rejected, the attorney's contingency fee is limited to a percentage of the amount collected above the original offer. Supporters of the proposal ran the political gamut from Derek Bok, former president of Harvard and dean of its law school, to Norman Dorsen, former president of the American Civil Liberties Union.[11] The effort worked: The House bill ultimately contained a variation of the proposal.

Tired of Bashing Affirmative Action? Stick with the Washington Legal Foundation

Daniel J. Popeo, founder of the Washington Legal Foundation (WLF), is a former attorney for the Justice Department in the Nixon administration who disgustedly left government service after he successfully won a case for the government to close a one-man mining operation, a case that exemplified, in his view, government's excessive regulation. Popeo still runs WLF, which he describes as a "pro–free enterprise, public-interest law and policy center," somewhat like "a small business version of the American Civil Liberties Union" but with a focus on "economic civil liberties."[12] Also a principal player in the effort to roll back affirmative action (see Chapter 4), WLF has provided legal support for several important cases, including defense of the timber industry against environmental groups trying to limit logging to protect the spotted owl, a lawsuit by a Hispanic student for the right to compete for an academic scholarship regardless of race, and the right to display signs on private property. WLF also started a "Stop the Collapse of America's Legal Ethics" (SCALES) project, dealing with such subjects as tort reform, contingency fees, judicial ethics, attorney advertising, and what it regards as frivolous litigation. It has also supported the right to sue for injuries from illegal attorney solicitation.[13]

Enjoy Liberal Cachet but Hate Litigation and Lawyers? Try the Brookings Institution

The Brookings Institution, "the first private, nonprofit organization devoted to analysis of significant policy issues," has a staff of about two hundred, including fifty full-time scholars. Known for its objective scholarship, Brookings nevertheless has generated heated criticism for its recent research into civil justice reform, much of it directed by economist and lawyer Robert Litan.[14]

The criticism largely centers on three books, beginning with *Liability: Perspectives and Policy,* edited by Litan and senior fellow Clifford Winston in 1988. Contributing authors explore various dire trends, such as increased environmental consciousness and vigilance on the part of citizens and the bar, and the public's morbid fascination with avoiding the merest possibility of medical malpractice or unnecessary operations. The book concludes that the insurance industry should not be more highly regulated, but that tort law should be modified so that juries would apply cost-benefit analysis to the behavior of both plaintiffs and defendants to see who should bear the cost of accidents. The project was funded by Dow Chemical Company, Bell Atlantic, and the Alex C. Walker, Starr and Aetna foundations.[15]

A second book, *Justice for All*, reported the findings of a 1989 task force convened by Brookings on the problems of cost and delay in the federal justice system. Attorneys, house counsel, and former judges proposed ways to streamline civil justice. A short time later, Brookings published *The Liability Maze: The Impact of Liability Law on Safety and Innovation*, which extended the earlier research to five sectors of the economy where liability was thought to have inhibited enterprise: the automobile, chemical, health care, general aviation, and pharmaceutical industries. Litan and Peter Huber co-edited the book, which was funded by American Express, Xerox, Ford Motor Company, Chase Manhattan Bank, and the Prudential, Starr, Sloan, and Smith Richardson foundations among others. The book, which naturally found that being sued gave companies pause, was criticized by Ralph Nader for ignoring that sometimes the ability to achieve redress for citizens is a social good, not an evil. Nader charged that none of the book's participants considered the impact of tort reform on the ability of victims to receive compensation for injuries caused by defective products and presented a one-sided view of the so-called liability crisis. He also observed that the insurance crisis of the 1980s was more a result of poor underwriting and management practices than any sort of measurable litigation explosion.[16]

Want to Cut Out the Middle Man? Tired of Overly Intellectual Think Tanks? Form a Trade Association or Coalition

The Legal Reform Coalition
An umbrella organization for over twenty trade groups and product-liability associations, the Legal Reform Coalition was formed shortly before three tort reform bills were presented in the House of Representatives in

March 1995. The coalition is directed by conservative activist Dirk Van Dongen, president of the National Association of Wholesaler-Distributors, who raises between $500,000 and $1 million dollars a year for the Republican Party. The coalition primarily coordinates the lobbying efforts of other trade groups trying to pass product-liability tort reform.[17] It keeps them in line, attempts to avoid duplication of effort, and assures that the tort reform machine hums along smoothly. We discuss three such groups immediately following.

Product Liability Coordinating Committee

The Product Liability Coordinating Committee (PLCC) is a coalition of about a dozen trade organizations and their members. Their chief counsel is the well-known Washington lobbyist Victor Schwartz, who commanded a whopping salary of $18,000 a month during the tort reform debate in Congress. Other prominent members of PLCC who command high salaries are Nicholas Calio, of the Washington, D.C., law firm Calio & O'Brian, who was paid $20,000 a month during the debate. PLCC also paid the law firm of Hogan & Hartson $15,000 a month.[18]

In contrast to other groups, who until recently had concentrated most of their efforts at the state level, the PLCC for years has been fighting for tort reform changes on Capitol Hill. Its contributions to that debate included a $3 million fundraising effort for radio and television commercials used during the successful campaign to pass tort reform bills in the House and the Senate.[19]

Major representatives of PLCC's coalition include General Motors, Ford, Exxon, Aetna, TRW, Monsanto, and DuPont. Membership also includes such trade groups as the U.S. Chamber of Commerce, the National Association of Manufacturers, the National Federation of Independent Business, and the Chemical Manufacturers Association. The largest members of the Business Roundtable, a trade association of the largest companies in the United States, provide most of PLCC's funding.[20]

Have a Lot of Loose Cash? Try the Civil Justice Reform Group

The Civil Justice Reform Group (CJRG) operates on a yearly budget of $3 million to $4 million. CJRG has been nicknamed the $100,000 Club because that is the minimum cost to join. In contrast to other groups who try to stress their small-business membership, CJRG admits it has none. The group was formed in 1993 by the general counsels of seventeen Fortune 500 companies, many of which are also part of the Product Liability Coordinating Committee, including General Motors, Ford, Exxon, Aetna, Metropolitan Life, Johnson & Johnson, and DuPont. The head of CJRG is Ford's general counsel, John Manin.[21] Originally formed to focus on tort reform changes at the state level, to participate in public education efforts, and to assist court improvement projects,[22] CJRG recently expanded its scope to include federal reform.

Two members of CJRG's steering committee, George S. Frazza, general counsel of Johnson & Johnson, and Judith Pendell, vice president of law and regulatory affairs at Aetna, are also members of the Manhattan Institute's advisory board. The institute's one-time fellow Michael Horowitz is the author, along with Lester Brickman and Jeffrey O'Connell, of a pamphlet, "Rethinking Contingency Fees," circulated by CJRG to popularize the authors' contingent fee reform proposals during the tort reform debates in Congress in 1995.[23] CJRG raised between $3 million and $4 million for an advertising media campaign during the tort reform debates in Congress similar to that launched by PLCC.[24]

American Tort Reform Association

The American Tort Reform Association (ATRA) is a coalition of approximately four hundred members, including Fortune 500 companies, trade associations, and law, accounting, and insurance firms. ATRA, an acronym easily confused with ATLA (American Trial Lawyers Association—its rival), was founded in 1986 and currently operates with a permanent staff of eight and a yearly operating budget of about $2 million. ATRA concentrates mainly on tort reform advocacy and public education on legal issues. It has distributed several publications that deal with tort reform and sponsors a yearly conference in Washington, D.C., on that subject, as well as regional conferences dealing with civil justice reform issues.[25]

ATRA prides itself on having several small businesses as members, which it believes gives the association a more populist image. Most of its funding, however, comes from large corporations; a number of insurance companies contribute between $50,000 and $75,000 each. Its president is Sherman Joyce and one of its general counsels is Victor Schwartz, who also acts as the leader of the PLCC. ATRA joined PLCC and CJRG in the media blitz during the 1995 tort reform debates in Congress this year, producing many of the radio and television commercials used during the debates through its public relations firm, APCO Associates.[26]

Punting on Astroturf

As the Manhattan Institute discovered in 1992 after its release of the Cronkite video, slickly produced media advertising can get better results than traditional campaigns that rely on lobbying. The method that corporations have used to simulate grassroots movements has become known in the nation's capital as "Astroturf." In contrast to traditional lobbying in which lobbyists try to influence politicians directly through office visits and campaign contributions, Astroturfing tries to influence public opinion, usually by advertising on television.[27]

The reason for the increase in Astroturfing was the phenomenal success of the "Harry and Louise" commercials in helping defeat President Clinton's health care plan. The commercials showed a middle-class couple in their forties at a kitchen table discussing the dire effects that Clinton's health plan would have on their lives. Although the commercial portrayed middle-class people, the campaign was actually the carefully produced work of large, well-funded insurance companies. Several versions of the commercial were shot. In one, the two protagonists discussed health care problems in their living room, and in another with people around a table in a community center. It was only after test-marketing the different versions that the informal kitchen table setting was chosen as the most effective. The health insurance association that produced the ad spent between $300,000 and $400,000 on survey research alone—about what a major presidential candidate will spend on polling during the primaries. Altogether, $15 million was spent on the campaign.[28]

Astroturf advocacy advertising has the advantage over traditional lobbying efforts in that it is able to hide from the consumer the large companies that are actually sponsoring the advertisements and, in contrast to direct campaign contributions, lobbying advertising does not have to be reported. At the same time, the PLCC is trying to make the American Trial Lawyers Association look powerful by tracing contributions to political candidates by both individual ATLA members and ATLA as an organization. This way tort reform advocates hope to portray themselves as underdogs against the powerful lawyers' association.[29] Although political scientists suggest that advocacy advertising may have little effect on the public, the perception that it does influences politicians to think there is grassroots support for the advocacy's position.[30]

Tort reform proponents have initiated two themes in their advocacy advertising. First, they make people think they are victims of a litigation crisis by portraying the price tag of litigation as higher costs for products and a loss of services and jobs caused by the increased cost of insurance, if insurance is even available. Prominent ads that conveyed this message include one featuring a Little League ball player locked out of a baseball field because the team could no longer afford the insurance to continue playing. An announcer solemnly intones that Little League games are endangered because costs for insurance are higher than those of balls, bats, and uniforms.[31] Another ad features a Girl Scout saying that it takes 87,000 boxes of Girl Scout cookies to pay for liability insurance.[32] In another instance, Aetna Life and Casualty Company paid for an ad in the *Wall Street Journal* warning that "America's civil liability system has gone berserk. . . . [It] is no longer fair. . . . Americans must decide what kind of society they want in the years ahead. If we insist on living in a risk-free society, it's not just America's insurance that will be cancelled. Our hopes and dreams for ourselves, our children and our country will be cancelled."[33]

Second, reformers try to portray tort victims as unjustly enriched for their own negligence. Even before the recent advertising craze during the tort reform debates in Congress, ATRA used this approach to help pass tort reform legislation at the state level. ATRA featured an ad in Texas, Mississippi, and Louisiana that showed a man reaching to change a light bulb while standing on a ladder balanced on a chair, which in turn was balanced on a stack of phone books. As the man falls while lunging at the light bulb, a voice proclaims, "Some people misuse products and then look for someone to blame," then declares that 20 percent of the cost of a ladder goes to defend product liability lawsuits. The announcer concludes that "junk lawsuits" need to be stopped because they cost consumers "plenty."[34]

The most popular ad used by tort reform advocates during the congressional debates was the well-publicized McDonald's hot coffee case. ATRA produced a radio ad featuring a narrator who declares in a shocked voice: "A jury awarded a woman $2.9 million in a lawsuit against McDonald's. She spilled coffee on her lap and claimed it was too hot. . . . Every day there is another outrageous lawsuit. Who pays? You do." The ad did not mention that the woman suffered third-degree burns on her buttocks, thighs and groin or that McDonald's had refused to reduce their coffee's temperature for ten years, despite several lawsuits.[35] Referring to the McDonald's case, a Citizens for a Sound Economy radio ad preached, "Seems like every day you hear about so-and-so who does something dumb, sues the next guy over for it and then gets rich." The ad did not mention that the case was ultimately settled for an undisclosed amount after a judge reduced the award to less than $500,000.[36]

"Junk Science" and the Art of Statistical Information

The Manhattan Institute takes pride in promoting awareness of "junk science" to the general public. The term, used in Peter Huber's *Galileo's Revenge*, refers to questionable scientific evidence used in a legal proceeding. Manhattan sponsored senior fellows Huber and Olson and then sent their books free of charge to state and federal judges throughout the country. Memoranda from the institute give rave reviews of Huber's work, mention his many speaking tours, and even offer tapes of his appearances on talk shows.[37]

In *Galileo's Revenge*, Huber asserts that "junk science verdicts, once rare, are now common." Yet instead of providing statistical support, he relies on little more than anecdotes to make his point. In his first book, *Liability*, he announces that there existed a $300 *billion* tort tax, a figure that has been referred to as so serious a "factual distortion as to border on intellectual fraud."[38] Ironically, little of the research and statistics released by conservative think tanks would meet the standards they believe necessary in a courtroom. Law professor Marc Galanter, the leading civil justice system expert, traced the origin of the $300 billion figure to a guess of $80 billion by a corporate executive during a luncheon speech. Peter Huber then applied a "multiplier effect" to that figure to come up with the $300 billion. According to the Rand Corporation, the total payout to all plaintiffs each year is only $15 billion—an average of $15,000 a lawsuit. Even with defense and insurance administration costs added, the total reaches only $30 billion.[39]

Another figure tort reform advocates use to demonstrate the existence of a litigation crisis is that 20 million lawsuits are filed each year. In 1986 alone, the Insurance Information Institute spent $6.5 million to trumpet the "lawsuit crisis" to the American people. The campaign aimed to reach

90 percent of the American people through print and television, speaker packets, bumper stickers, and ads.[40] Yet all the campaigns rest on dubious facts, loudly proclaimed and repeated. The 20 million lawsuits, for example, include all civil suits, such as domestic relations, noise and nuisance complaints, and property disputes. Tort lawsuits comprise only 5 percent of the total civil docket. In fact, the fastest growing type of litigation consists of lawsuits in which businesses sue other businesses; tellingly, no reform has been proposed in that area.[41] As Second Circuit federal judge Jack Weinstein recently observed in *Pennsylvania Law Review*, "the truth about the litigation explosion is that it is a weapon of perception, not substance. If the public can be persuaded that there is a litigation crisis, it may support efforts to cut back on litigation access."[42]

The rationales for tort reform used by the corporations that fund the think tanks also do not ring true, as consumer advocate Ralph Nader has pointed out. Frank Popoff, CEO of Dow Chemical, has warned that product liability costs are "a killer for our global competitiveness." Yet in Dow's annual report to its investors it blandly declares, "It is the opinion of the company's management that the possibility that litigation of these [products liability] claims would materially impact the company's consolidated financial statements is remote."[43]

Monsanto's vice president for government affairs has charged that liability litigation "clogs our courts, curtails American innovation and creativity, drives up the costs of consumer products, and prevents some valuable products and services from ever coming to market." Yet in Monsanto's report to shareholders it concludes that "while the results of litigation cannot be predicted with certainty, Monsanto does not believe these matters or their ultimate disposition will have a material adverse effect on Monsanto's financial position."[44] Monsanto also sponsors lectures and symposiums at law schools on contingency fees, punitive damages, causation in science and the law, and even on the wisdom of the jury system itself.[45]

National Association of Manufacturers chairman Robert Dee decried the litigation crisis, likening U.S. lawyers to "a plague of locusts" bent on "suing the country out of business." He went on to warn that product liability awards are causing companies to go under every day. "Some avoid new product introduction [and] . . . people are throwing their hands up in despair."[46] Yet, Cornell law professors James Henderson and Theodore Eisenberg studied product liability cases, finding that "current trends favor defendants" and that industry leaders have been arguing from "question-able, if not false, premises."[47]

The debate over punitive damages also provides glaring proof that industry leaders' assertions about the tort and jury system are simply untrue, including the charge that punitive damages (meant to punish and deter repeated misconduct) are running wild and mainly enriching grasping lawyers. A 1992 study by two law professors of state and federal product liability cases found only 355 such awards in a twenty-five-year period. Most were reduced on appeal; in 38 percent of the cases the award was never paid at all.[48]

Score Card

The campaign against tort relief for consumers and patients injured by defective products and careless physicians has been effective. Many states have enacted measures to limit recovery for injuries. And a recent study by two University of Delaware sociologists shows that jurors are "suspicious of the legitimacy of plaintiffs' claims" (against corporate and insurance defendants) "and concerned about the personal and social costs of large jury awards." Basing their conclusions on interviews with 141 jurors from eighteen tort cases tried during a one-year period, the authors found that jurors are "generally favorable toward business, skeptical more about the profit motives of individual plaintiffs than of business defendants, and committed to holding down awards." The jurors interviewed also held strongly negative views about litigation and believed that most citizens "are too quick to sue."[49] The authors theorize that "concerted efforts of business and insurance companies to foster perceptions of a litigation explosion may have encouraged jurors to see plaintiffs critically" because their rhetoric was cleverly calculated to "resonate . . . strongly with preexisting cultural standards of responsibility."[50] Statements by the Insurance Information Institute also attribute tort reform measures to "the publicity surrounding passage of the reforms" that, in turn, created "a greater awareness on the part of the public, and hence of juries and judges, of what the reforms were designed to correct."[51]

A study by James Henderson shows that the publicity barrage has also affected judges' attitudes. "A day doesn't go by without seeing advertisements in this area," he said. "Judges read the papers as well as citizens and legislators."[52]

Sometimes, it seems, it pays to cry wolf.

Now that the threat of communism has receded and the Supreme Court is reformed . . . [i]t's time to make reform of our campuses a national priority. . . . The ideas and beliefs implanted in the three million seventeen and eighteen year olds entering college this year will influence our nation for decades to come. Let's make the 1990s the years that will be called the seedtime for the Conservative Movement.
—Ron Robinson, president of Young America's Foundation

7

Campus Wars

THE ATTACK ON MULTICULTURALISM has entered its second generation. Originally fought on the battleground of theory and curriculum and aimed at curing the supposed excesses of sixties-style liberal professors, efforts now focus on college and graduate students, as well as recent graduates and young professionals.[1] Leadership training helps shape career choices. Alternative student newspapers give voice to conservative points of view. Legal foundations defend transgressors of hated speech codes. New efforts are being made to target alumni giving. Perhaps believing that they have achieved all the gains that are possible by browbeating middle-aged academics and administrators, conservatives at think tanks and elsewhere are turning their attention to a younger group who will administer the final decisive coup de grace to multiculturalism in the years ahead.

Getting the Word Out: The Early Days

The Madison Center for Educational Affairs (MCEA), a conservative advocacy group, arose out of the merger of the Institute for Educational Affairs (IEA) and the Madison Center in 1990. The older of the two organizations, IEA was founded in 1978 by the neoconservative writer Irving Kristol and William Simon, Olin Foundation board president, to establish a network of conservative thinkers, scholars, corporations, and foundations and to finance conservative campus journalism. With money from the Olin, Sarah Scaife, Smith Richardson, and JM foundations,[2] it funded about thirty conservative campus newspapers, which later became known as the Collegiate Network. Grants of between $5,000 and $10,000 helped the papers get started; subsequent support was to be raised from alumni, subscriptions, and advertising. The student publications were seen as a vehicle to bring conservative political thought to college campuses under the thrall of liberalism.[3]

The papers were established at schools in all regions of the country — Harvard, Yale, Princeton, Stanford, the University of California, Duke, William and Mary, and Kenyon College, among others. They oppose multiculturalism, advocate eliminating affirmative action, and urge a return to Western values and tradition.[4] The *Dartmouth Review*, founded in 1980 with money from the Smith Richardson, Sarah Scaife, and Earhart foundations, was the first and most controversial of this group. During its first ten years, the *Review* received over $295,000 directly from the Olin Foundation and $15,000 from IEA.[5] Its parent organization, however, cut off funding in 1982 when the paper published "Dis Sho Ain't No Jive, Bro," an article written in "black English" insinuating that black students are illiterate.[6] Later, members of the review tore down shanties that had been erected on the campus to protest apartheid in South Africa; a few years later the paper published an excerpt from Adolf Hitler's *Mein Kampf* on a Jewish high holy day. Members of the review blandly answered their critics by pointing to the diversity on the staff — which includes women, blacks, Jews, and Asians[7] — and insisting that their actions are protected speech.

Several *Dartmouth Review* graduates have become important figures in the conservative world. Dinesh D'Souza, one-time editor-in-chief, went on to write *Illiberal Education* and *The End of Racism*, edit the Heritage Foundation's *Policy Review*, and serve as a fellow at the American Enterprise Institute. Others have found jobs at the White House and on the editorial staff of the *Wall Street Journal*.[8]

IEA also established the Federalist Society when, along with the Olin Foundation, it made available $24,000 to help fund travel and expenses for sixty law students and twenty legal scholars to attend the first nationwide symposium on federalism at Yale Law School in 1982. The conference drew two hundred and featured keynote speaker Judge Robert Bork.[9] Within three years the Federalist Society expanded to thirty chapters, many located at the top law schools. A symposium appears each year in the *Harvard Journal of Law and Public Policy*.

Cradle-to-Grave Conservatism: Starting Young

After clerking for conservative Reagan-appointed judges, a number of Federalist Society members took advantage of a placement service maintained by the Center for Judicial Studies (publisher of *Benchmark*) to secure jobs in the Justice Department and other legal offices of government. Morton Blackwell, president of the Leadership Institute, a leadership training organization, described the career placement process as "incremental, . . . not a great master stroke. Each young conservative you place is an incremental gain. . . . The next time we elect a conservative as president the administration will be much more homogeneous."[10]

MCEA's parent organization, the Madison Center, was founded in 1988 by William Bennett and Allan Bloom, author of *The Closing of the American Mind*, as a kind of Great Books program. It offered summer classes to fifty to one hundred selected undergraduates on the major works of Western civilization.[11] After merging with IEA in 1990, the center, in conjunction with the Hudson Institute and the National Association of Scholars, published the annual *Common Sense Guide to American Colleges*, which rates one hundred colleges and universities on how faithfully they adhere to a core curriculum and provide a congenial social and academic environment for young conservatives. Editors of Collegiate Network newspapers, as well as faculty and administrators, provide information on such issues as speech codes, diversity, admissions policies, and multiculturalism.[12]

Getting the Word Out in Earnest: Recent Efforts

MCEA continued funding the Collegiate Network, now consisting of over sixty conservative newspapers on seventy campuses, giving approximately $400,000 to the papers each year.[13] In 1989, $90,000 of that total came from the Olin Foundation.[14] About half of the Collegiate Network papers receive grants from MCEA averaging $3,200 a year that must be used for operating and production costs.[15] MCEA insists it must support these papers because student governments classify them as political organizations unqualified for campus funding. The papers and the center reason that if they are political, then so are the myriad feminist, minority, and other groups that do receive funding. A number of the papers have "Review" in their name, after the conservative *National Review,* while others emulate the *American Spectator* with "Spectator" in their title.[16] Not all conservative campus papers are funded by MCEA; the *Stanford Review,* for example, is backed by the Hoover Institution, which is located on the Stanford campus.[17] No black college, as yet, boasts a MCEA-funded newspaper.

Nearly all of the papers are available at a Madison Center site on the Internet, as are most of the publications of the Center's European Journalism Network. Students and editors can e-mail the Madison Center, participate in electronic discussions on political issues, post notices, and exchange and trade articles.

Readers who have toiled in a crowded, underfunded student newspaper office will be interested to know that MCEA provides the Collegiate Network

- a toll-free hotline for writing, editing, or business advice
- Newslink, a monthly newsletter featuring articles about educational issues and tips for running a student newspaper
- "Collegiate Times," a nationally syndicated column
- CN Friends, a news service from magazines like *The New Republic* and think tanks such as the Heritage Foundation
- a book-of-the-month club
- national editors conferences
- site visits by Madison Center program officers for junior staff
- internships at *The New Republic, Roll Call,* and NBC News
- summer programs in Washington, D.C.
- a clearing house for potential advertisers
- annual publications awards[18]

Other MCEA projects include support of *Diversity and Division,* billed as a quarterly journal of race and culture, and the European Journalism

Program. *Diversity* is aimed at college students and recent graduates assumed to be disillusioned by a too liberal education. It was first published in 1991 and now has a circulation of about ten thousand.[19] The European Journalism Program, established by former Collegiate Network program officer Jonathan Bacal, aims to bring the conservative message to the new democracies of Eastern Europe, starting with two Czech universities in 1991. MCEA helped find office space, provided computers, and taught the new members how to write editorials, organize, and manage. Expansion is planned into Slovakia, Hungary, and Russia. The Network hopes that the young editors will have a large impact on public opinion, as they graduate and become future leaders of their countries.[20]

In 1992 MCEA received support from the following foundations:

- Bradley Foundation — $150,396 (including $83,745 for the student journalism program)
- JM Foundation — $25,000 (toward educational activities and publications for college and university students)
- F. M. Kirby Foundation: $17,500
- John M. Olin Foundation — $220,600 (including $174,000 for the Collegiate Network)
- Smith Richardson Foundation — $195,000 (including $120,000 for the Collegiate Network)
- Sarah Scaife Foundation — $100,000 (for general operating support and student journalism program)
- Walton Family Foundation: $15,000[21]

The Olin Foundation has continued its support with a grant of $100,000 in 1993.[22]

Although conservative students complain that most campus papers are liberal, no known network among them is financed in such a lavish or organized way. Liberation News Service (LNS) (the wire service of the underground press of the 1960s and 1970s) supplies reprints of leftist writings, photographs, and artwork to about 160 liberal publications that it considers understaffed and short of funds.[23] LNS has clients in Canada and Asia, as well as the United States, but has little contact in Eastern Europe. "At this point, the left hasn't gotten around to funding its youth programs as well as the right," explains Jason Ramsas, LNS staff person, "but we do the best we can."[24]

Training the Next Generation: The Leadership Institute

Leadership Institute (LI) offers seminars to young conservatives on the way up. Among LI's accomplishments it lists training students working at half the conservative alternative student newspapers that were established by the MCEA, according to Morton Blackwell, institute president. Blackwell was the youngest Barry Goldwater delegate to the 1964 Republican convention and later served in the Reagan administration as liaison to all religious, conservative, and veterans groups.[25] He now serves as executive director of the Council for National Policy, the five-hundred-member, by-invitation-only mother of all conservative strategy groups. (See Chapter 1.) The Contract with America is said to have been drafted in his Madison County, Virginia cabin.[26]

Founded in 1979 with Coors family money, the institute was established to instruct conservative youth and young professionals on issues of public policy. To achieve this goal, LI offers nine different programs. Gov. Terry Bransted (Iowa) and Senator Mitch McConnell (R-Ky.) were among the first and most successful graduates of the institute's flagship Youth Leadership School, billed as a "crash course on how to win." Beginning in 1983, the Student Publications School (SPS) has trained seven hundred conservative journalists in intensive weekend seminars offered five times a year in Washington, D.C. It teaches students how to "beat speech codes, multiculturalism and political correctness," using the *Dartmouth Review* as a model.

Other schools offer opportunities to learn broadcast journalism, campaign leadership, public relations, rhetoric and campaign skills, as well as candidate development and Capitol Hill staff training. The Foreign Service Opportunity School boasts it can help "beat the rigorous Foreign Service entrance process." LI also provides intern and employment placement programs. A speakers bureau offers a slate of fifty well-known conservatives ready to appear at a moment's notice.[27]

Funding comes from appeals to prominent wealthy conservatives. Direct mail solicitations on behalf of one of the institute's programs (SPS) included urgent pleas from Holly Coors and Representative Dick Armey (R-Tex.), avid supporters of the movement. Coors and Armey believe that many college papers "are hostile to religion and blame America for everything." "While you read this letter," they warn, "left-wing journalism professors are preparing their new crop of media radicals." In support of his view that the media have a liberal bias, Armey cites a poll conducted by S. Robert Lichter and Stanley Rothman in which 85 percent of journalism students described themselves as liberal.[28] Liberals have no organization comparable to the Leadership Institute. Smaller groups such as Midwest Academy, founded by Heather Booth, former Mississippi Freedom Summer activist, teach grassroots community organizing to groups like Ralph Nader's Public Citizen and the Union of Concerned Scientists, as well as to liberal social activists from around the country.[29] The Center for National Policy, headed by former Secretary of State Edmund Muskie, hoped to raise $50,000 for the liberal student press. In 1988, however, only $10,000 had been given to about twenty liberal and progressive publications at leading campuses. No grants were offered during the following two years because the center was not able to raise the money.[30]

Blackwell attributes his successful fund-raising to the direct-mail skills he picked up while working with Richard Viguerie years earlier. The institute's revenue recently rose from $1.2 million in 1992 to about $4.2 million in 1994, and it has graduated its ten thousandth student.[31] In 1992 the M. J. Murdock Charitable Trust gave the institute $115,000 for Youth Leadership Schools and Job and Talent Bank Placement Services. The Salvatori Foundation granted $28,500 for college campus lectures on American values. Substantial support was also given by the Carthage Foundation: $65,000; McCamish Foundation: $25,000; Kirby Foundation: $20,000; and DeVos Foundation: $10,000.[32] The Coors Foundation, instrumental in the institute's creation, no longer provides it with funds.[33]

The "incremental gain" Blackwell hoped for paid off even earlier than expected. And, it turned out to be more than incremental. When Republicans swept to victory in Congress in the November 1994 election, a cadre of young conservative professionals stood at the ready to fill a myriad of jobs. The Leadership Institute, along with the Heritage Foundation and the GOP study committee, reviewed thousands of resumés to fill hundreds of junior legislative staff positions. Using a "public policy preference" questionnaire, the institute asked applicants to indicate the degree to which they agreed with a list of issues, groups, and noted public figures. Although there were no right or wrong answers, LI officials declared, the tests were meant to screen for ideological compatibility.[34]

Back to the Middle Ages (We're Not Making This Up): National Journalism Center

The National Journalism Center (NJC), operating under the auspices of the Education and Research Institute (ERI), has been in existence for sixteen years. NJC's program is similar to the Leadership Institute's Student Publications School, offering media training to students with traditional values.[35] M. Stanton Evans, director of ERI and NJC, has been a forceful activist and journalist for the right for over thirty years. His recent book, *The Theme Is Freedom: Religion, Politics, and the American Tradition*, argues that the foundation of American political and economic freedom lies, not in the Enlightenment, but in the medieval heritage of the Roman Catholic Church and the feudal barons who produced the Magna Carta.[36] Stanton, the former editor of the Quayle family-owned *Indianapolis News*, serves as a trustee to the Intercollegiate Studies Institute and as a commentator for Voice of America.

By the end of 1993, NJC had placed over eight hundred graduates at over fifty media outlets, including The *Wall Street Journal,* CNN, C-SPAN, The *Washington Post,* and AP and UPI. NJC graduates, many still in the early phases of their careers, have written or edited eighteen books on such issues as the First Amendment, AIDS, Grenada, and South Africa. Some are published by conservative presses, others by general trade publishers. NJC's and ERI's seventy-five annual seminars, lectures, and special events feature representatives from conservative and business-oriented publications and organizations such as journalist Robert Novak, and Peter Ferrara and Scott Hodge of the Heritage Foundation.[37]

In 1992 the Education and Research Institute received grants of $35,000 each from the Olin Foundation and the Bradley Foundation.[38] Olin continued its support in 1993 with a grant of $25,000.[39]

God and Man Today: Intercollegiate Studies Institute

William F. Buckley Jr., Yale alumnus and author of *God and Man at Yale,* served as the first president of the Intercollegiate Studies Institute (ISI) when it was founded in 1953. By 1990, secular humanism had given way to multiculturalism as the number one hobgoblin, and so the institute followed suit. In the following five years, membership doubled to about fifty-five thousand on eleven hundred campuses.[40] Convinced that colleges and universities are the last bastion of the radical left, ISI mobilized a battalion of campus-directed programs. It now publishes *The Intercollegiate Review* and *CAMPUS*, many of whose contributors are the same students who write for the Collegiate Network newspapers. *CAMPUS* is distributed free to students and faculty at eleven hundred schools, featuring stories like "The Feminist Assault on the University." The institute also publishes *Modern Age* and the *Political Science Reviewer*, as well as books, bibliographies, and audio and video tapes all spelling out the articles of conservative faith. Over forty conferences annually offer small group seminars and leadership training. ISI earmarks at least $125,000 a year to fellowships for graduate students planning to teach.[41] Its national speakers program sponsors over three hundred lecturers a year at universities, colleges, and prep schools; it paid *Illiberal Education* author Dinesh D'Souza $174,000 in speaker fees in 1993.[42]

In 1992, the largest funders for ISI were the Salvatori Foundation, which provided $390,000 for teacher training to promote American values; the Allegheny Foundation, which designated $300,000 for the prep school lecture program; and the Sarah Scaife Foundation, which granted $300,000 for general operating, project, and publication support. Other contributing foundations included Bradley, DeVos, Earhart, Gilder, Kirby, Lilly, McKenna, Montgomery Street, Olin, Stranahan, and Wiegand. The Olin Foundation continued its support in 1993, increasing its contribution to $125,000; one grant of $75,000 went to support *CAMPUS* and a lecture series on multiculturalism, a second of $50,000 to support a special project on multiculturalism.[43]

Like the Madison Center, ISI is preparing a college directory for parents, including information on grade inflation. It has targeted secondary education as well. Gripped by the fear that faculty and lecture programs at elite preparatory schools are covertly leftist, the institute developed a program to bring conservative speakers to prep schools. When William Bennett spoke at Phillips Exeter in 1994, the students, more pleased than the faculty, gave him a rousing standing ovation.[44]

The institute's most visible, and perhaps most effective venture, however, is the Forum for University Stewardship. ISI selects campuses that are "extremely politically correct" and encourages alumni to withhold contributions. It has committed $200,000 to targeting six of these schools: Stanford, Vassar, Duke, Yale, Washington and Lee, and Converse College, where it took credit for helping oust the first female president in 1993 because of her positions on diversity issues. ISI spreads the word to alumni by sending them copies of student articles from conservative campus newspapers written about speech codes, gay student groups, women's studies programs, and multicultural curricula.[45]

At Stanford, ISI and the *Stanford Review* established Winds of Freedom, a conservative alumni-student group that sponsored its first conference featuring former National Endowment for the Humanities chair Lynne Cheney as the keynote speaker at a $100-a-plate dinner, and panel discussions by Hoover Institution members. The group has signed up fourteen hundred members and, according to ISI, is the largest, richest alumni-student organization to date. It has received financing from David Packard, cofounder of Hewlett-Packard, and Charles Schwab, of the stock brokerage company. Winds of Freedom is currently performing a study of undergraduate education at Stanford, largely paid for by ISI, to monitor "the direction of Stanford's curriculum." The effort parallels that of a curriculum revision commission begun by President Gerhard Casper but uses Hoover Fellows and well-known alumni to perform the study. The group encourages alums to withhold donations and write letters supporting conservative candidates for Stanford's board of trustees.[46]

In another battle, ISI became embroiled in a bitter fight over a $20 million gift to Yale University by Texas philanthropist and Yale alumnus Lee M. Bass, who gave the money in 1991 to create a program in Western civilization. As of fall 1994, the program had not yet been started, and in March 1995, Yale returned the money to Mr. Bass. The story came to public attention in "The $20 Million Dollar Deception," an article by Yale undergraduate Pat Collins in *Light and Truth*, a conservative Yale paper funded by ISI, which mailed five thousand copies of the issue to Yale alums. The article blamed failure to implement the program on liberal faculty and students who saw the gift as a threat to Yale's multicultural curriculum. University officials responded that delays were due to Yale's $12 million budget deficit, which had imposed a freeze on faculty hiring for Bass's or any other program.[47]

Pat Collins researched and wrote the article while attending a summer program at the National Journalism Center in 1994. M. Stanton Evans, NJC director and trustee of ISI, denied that there was any input from the institute regarding the article, nor that he knew that ISI would eventually publish it. The NJC approved the project, Evans declared, because he is an alumnus of Yale and believed the issue significant.[48]

Want to Hassle Your Professor? Try Young America's Foundation

Young America's Foundation traces its origins to Vanderbilt University, where, in 1969, a group of students formed University Information Service (UIS). Alarmed by their perception that their campus was dominated by radical leftists, the students set out to provide a philosophical alternative by bringing conservative speakers to campus. The movement went national in the early 1970s with a new name—Young America's Foundation (YAF), echoing an older right-wing organization, Young Americans for Freedom.[49]

The Speakers Program remains at the core of the organization's project of rebalancing what it sees as the left-wing bias of most campuses. Complaining that most campuses spend little money on speakers who present the conservative point of view, YAF funds nationally known figures to promote that message. Its twenty fifth Anniversary Report and publicity brochures feature an extensive list of names, including Patrick Buchanan, Fred Barnes, George Will, Robert Novak, Jeane Kirkpatrick, Jack Kemp, Michael Medved, Caspar Weinberger, Christina Hoff Sommers, Michael Williams, Richard Ebeling, Phyllis Schlafly, Ronald Reagan, Norman Schwarzkopf, Russell Kirk, Barry Goldwater, Phil Gramm, Elliott Abrams, Milton Friedman, J. A. Parker, and David Horowitz.[50]

Highly prominent conservative leaders tour the campus lecture circuit every year under the auspices of named lectureships endowed by successful entrepreneurs (Henry Salvatori, William Howard Flowers Jr., and Grover Hermann). Among recent circuit-riders YAF counts Edwin Meese III, William F. Buckley Jr., William Bennett, Oliver North, Walter Williams, Angela "Bay" Buchanan, and the indefatigable Dinesh D'Souza.[51] YAF also hosts a number of student conferences, the cornerstone of which is an annual National Conservative Leadership Conference in Washington, D.C. First held in summer 1979, it attracted thirty students. In the last sixteen years, over twenty-two hundred students have been trained "to anticipate leftist positions and to respond to them." In addition to instruction about free market economics, foreign policy, cultural values, and the media, as well as discussions with well-known conservatives including Jesse Helms, John O'Sullivan, Ralph Reed, and Ronald Reagan, students also participate in congressional briefings with lawmakers such as Robert Dole, Newt Gingrich, Dick Armey, and Robert Dornan. Originally intended to "prepare students for survival in the hostile atmosphere of left-dominated colleges and universities," the foundation believes that the most important effect of the conferences has been the infusion of young dedicated "spokesmen for conservatism" into colleges and universities. It continues support of student activities directly on campus as well. During the Persian Gulf War, for example, YAF helped students sponsor panel discussions and organize rallies in support of the U.S. position.[52]

YAF's latest approach to countering what they consider ever-present liberal bias takes the form of targeting liberal arts colleges known for their progressive bent. The "crusade carried out at Swarthmore College has proven to be one of the Foundation's most successful and high-profile projects to date," proclaims its twenty-fifth Anniversary Report. After Dinesh D'Souza's talk raised conservative consciousness at Swarthmore in spring 1993, YAF brought six student leaders to its headquarters to plan a year-long speakers program for the following year. The E. L. Wiegand Foundation granted $37,000, most of which paid for Phyllis Schlafly, William F. Buckley Jr., Walter E. Williams, Edwin Meese III, Michael Medved, David Horowitz, and Christina Hoff Sommers (as well as a return visit by D'Souza) to speak to standing-room-only crowds.[53]

By spring 1994, the Swarthmore Conservative Union had grown from six members to seventy-five and a campus newspaper, *Common Sense*, had been started. "The goal," explains YAF executive director James B. Taylor, a Swarthmore alumnus, "was to select a small liberal arts college and concentrate programs and resources in such a way as to permanently change that campus."[54] Heartened by the success of its effort, the foundation plans to establish versions of the Swarthmore Project at five more colleges, as well as use it as a model in a handbook for student activists.[55]

YAF makes available reprints of traditional conservative classics as well as influential new works at discounted prices. Publications include Barry Goldwater's *The Conscience of a Conservative*, Henry Regnery's *Memoirs of a Dissident Publisher*, and a new edition of Russell Kirk's *The Roots of American Order*. Students may also purchase *The Conservative Guide to*

Campus Activism; Continuity, allegedly the only conservative journal of history; *The Myth of the Robber Barons,* by Burton W. Folsom Jr., portraying a positive view of the industrial revolution; and Robert Royal's *Columbus on Trial.*

Among its board of directors the foundation counts many prominent leaders from other conservative organizations. President Ron Robinson and four of the current seven directors have served as officers of Young Americans for Freedom. James B. Taylor and T. Kenneth Cribb Jr. have held prominent positions in the Intercollegiate Studies Institute, of which Cribb is president. All held posts in the Reagan administration.[56] Grants to YAF in 1992 included $80,000 for lectures on America's founding values from the Salvatori Foundation and $37,300 from the E. L. Wiegand Foundation for a general lecture series. Stranahan Foundation gave $30,000; the Kirby Foundation, $20,000.[57] Unlike many other conservative groups, however, YAF does not depend solely on yearly grants, thanks to a recent bequest from the estate of John and Virginia Engalitcheff of $8 million. John Engalitcheff escaped from the Soviet Union at the age of ten. The bequest is used in part to fund the $10,000 Engalitcheff Award, given periodically to faculty members who "demonstrate courage in defending the ideals of free expression and academic standards in the university."[58] In 1994, YAF named the University of Pennsylvania professor Alan Kors winner of the award for defending Eden Jacobowitz, the student accused of racial harassment for calling a group of female black students water buffaloes.

A lifelong campaigner for the conservative movement, president Ron Robinson warns grimly, "a young person can become a liberal by picking up ideas in our popular culture with little thought. This should alarm every conservative, indeed every citizen, concerned about the future of our society. . . . The Foundation reports on the Left's activities on campus and we act to eliminate or overcome them."[59]

How to Really Hassle Your Professor: Accuracy in Academia

Founded in 1985 as a student-oriented spin-off of Reed Irvine's Accuracy in Media (AIM), Accuracy in Academia (AIA) was created to counter the supposed liberal bias of American universities. Student volunteers, recruited mostly though college Republican clubs, monitor classes and report back to AIA if professors fail to include the conservative point of view, or if they demonstrate what the monitors judge to be Marxist leanings.[60] To support their claims, the students are urged to send course catalogs and descriptions, syllabi, reading lists, and other materials in which they see examples of bias — especially direct quotations from class notes. AIA tells the students that "classroom indoctrination is intended to leave you angry about America's alleged crimes and injustices," and its "fail[ure] to meet an unnatural standard of [racial] equality." The stories are published in AIA's monthly newspaper, *Campus Report*, which is distributed free to about fifteen hundred colleges and high schools. AIA also sponsors Freedom Network, a computer bulletin board to connect students, professors and "other interested parties."[61]

Reaction from educators and civil libertarians to the watchdog group's agenda was sharp and swift. Leading academics charged that AIA threatens academic freedom. The American Association of University Professors warned that the secret surveillance and note-taking could discourage classroom debate and inhibit faculty from discussing unpopular theories. Conservatives William Bennett and Irving Kristol distanced themselves, criticizing AIA's tactics. Nevertheless, within its first three months, AIA claimed to have student monitors at 150 colleges and chapters at Brown and Wisconsin.[62] "Black headed pins [on a map of the United States] marked each campus where AIA had a contact," writes James Ledbetter in an article in which he describes the way he infiltrated AIA in fall 1985. Teachers at Arizona State University (ASU) were the first to be targeted, one accused of peace mongering because much of his political survey class dealt with the nuclear freeze. The campaign began when a student named Matthew Scully sat in on the professor's class and wrote a series of critical articles for an ASU student newspaper. Scully was one of the first two staffers to be hired at AIA the following year.[63]

The other, Laszlo "Les" Csorba III, was a student at the University of California at Davis at about the same time. During academic year 1984–85, Csorba, head of Students for a Better America, targeted Saul Landau, a visiting professor of Latin American history. In a letter to the editor of a campus newspaper, Csorba denounced Landau as a Marxist with close ties to Fidel Castro. His proof? Sources at the Council for Inter-American Security (CIAS), a conservative organization dedicated to fighting left-wing movements in Latin America[64] and whose secretary was none other than

Lawrence Pratt, president of English First. At the time, members of CIAS were heavily engaged in defining a conservative foreign policy agenda; some became advisors to incoming-president Ronald Reagan on the Panama Canal and Nicaragua. At a meeting in New Mexico in 1980, the council's Committee of Santa Fe declared that Central American conflicts were the third phase of World War III—a war in which the United States was already engaged.[65]

Landau later learned that Csorba had been one of three students to tour Latin America in 1984 on behalf of the CIAS. He traveled to El Salvador where he posed with government soldiers and praised Roberto D'Aubuisson, right-wing Salvadoran major presidential candidate and alleged architect of the assassination of Salvadoran archbishop Oscar Romero. Students for a Better America, founded by Reed Irvine, director of Accuracy in Media, had received support from Heritage Foundation members and occupied temporary national office space in the Reverend Sun Myung Moon's *Washington Times* offices.[66]

Upon graduation, Csorba became the first executive director of Accuracy in Academia. He explained to a Heritage Foundation interviewer that AIA started because of Irvine's conviction that the media were more critical of the United States than of its enemies; therefore, he concluded, journalists were trained incorrectly in colleges and universities. The remedy, Irvine proclaimed, was to expose radical faculty members and organizations.[67] To do so, AIA started with a one-thousand-name "secret target list" of professors who had endorsed a rally opposing U.S. engagement in Central America and relied on a cadre of student volunteers to report additional names of teachers they perceived as intolerant and hostile toward conservative ideas. The tactics echo Csorba's earlier treatment of Landau at U.C. Davis. Landau reported that information in Csorba's accusatory letter to the student newspaper closely paralleled materials in a file he later obtained from the FBI under the Freedom of Information Act, which led Landau to conclude that Csorba had ties with the U.S. intelligence community.[68] AIA continued to rely on tips from students, professors, and groups, such as University Professors for Academic Order, sympathetic to its cause.[69] After the Reagan-Bush era, AIA's focus shifted away from student and faculty opposition to U.S. policies in Central America; it joined other conservative student groups in monitoring "political correctness" and multiculturalism on campuses.

In June 1994, *Campus Report* named the twelve universities judged to be "consistent offenders of free speech and academic freedom": Harvard, Yale, University of California at Irvine and at Los Angeles, University of Texas, Cornell, Dartmouth, University of Michigan, Antioch, Occidental, University of Pennsylvania, and Wisconsin. The freshman English program at Texas, which had recently been revamped to include more readings by and about minorities, was cited as an example of outlandish liberal bias. Mark Draper, AIA's executive director, declared, "These are the colleges, other than the University of Rwanda or Haiti Tech, where you would least want to send your younger sister to school."[70]

AIA receives material and moral support from several conservative groups. Its speakers program functions in conjunction with Accuracy in Media/Allied Educational Speakers Bureau. The College Republicans provide AIA with mailing lists and services; its president has endorsed AIA. Daniel J. Flynn, a program officer at YAF, wrote the lead article of the May 1995 *Campus Report.*[71] Accolades in AIA's information brochure come from Thomas Sowell of the Hoover Institution and John W. Howard, president of the Individual Rights Foundation. In 1992, Accuracy in Media received money from the Carthage Foundation — $100,000; the Stranahan Foundation — $25,000; and the Kirby Foundation — $25,000.[72] The organization also receives income from contributions for a one-year subscription to *Campus Report*. Reed Irvine has denied persistent rumors of funding from CAUSA, an arm of the Reverend Sun Myung Moon's Unification Church, which for years channeled millions of dollars into anti-Communist efforts in Central and South America. Irvine admits that Unification Church members work for him. CAUSA's offices are located on the floor above the Council for Inter-American Security in a Capitol Hill office building.[73]

Too Much New Reading? Join the National Association of Scholars

An organization of over thirty-five hundred professors, college administrators, and graduate students opposed to campus multiculturalism, diversity, and "political correctness," the National Association of Scholars (NAS) was founded in 1987. NAS sprang from a small group of like-minded academics in the New York City area who began meeting in 1982 under the title Campus Coalition for Democracy.[74] The group's credo: "Only through an informed understanding of the Western intellectual heritage and the realities of the contemporary world can citizen and scholar be equipped to sustain our civilization's achievements."[75] Believing that traditional intellectual values are at stake, Stephen Balch, president, argues that the academic left intends to turn the university curriculum into "oppression studies."[76] "The rigor of the curriculum is diluted as politicized or frivolous subject matter invades and displaces serious study," he writes. "Ancestry and group membership are given precedence over intellectual merit."[77]

The NAS attempts to reverse these alarming trends it sees through a multi-faceted attack. It publishes a quarterly journal entitled *Academic Questions*, and a newsletter called *NAS Update*, operates a speakers bureau, placement service, fellowships, and research center, and holds annual conferences. Its thirty-nine local affiliates in thirty-six states and Guam[78] maintain high profiles and provide scholarly legitimacy to attacks on the left.

At its 1988 annual meeting entitled "Reclaiming the Academy: Responses to the Radicalization of the University," keynote speaker Jeane Kirkpatrick, former U.S. ambassador to the United Nations, called NAS enemies "the fascist left." Herbert London, co-founder of NAS and dean at New York University and sometime columnist for the conservative *New York City Tribune*, railed against inclusion of literature by women and non-whites in the core curriculum, because "it does not lead us toward our true humanity." At the same meeting, Alan Kors, the professor who later was to attract national attention for his defense of student Eden Jacobowitz, used even blunter language. He denounced racial awareness programs as attempts at "thought control" and urged members to "use ridicule against blacks, feminists, and gays" — remarks that most of the audience, composed mainly of older men in tweed jackets, a few women, and a single black, cheered.[79]

In early 1992 the NAS attempted to create a new accrediting organization for higher education. The effort was motivated by the Middle States Association of Colleges and Schools' practice of taking diversity into consideration in its accreditation process. Middle States denied reaccreditation to Baruch College of City University of New York (CUNY) because it did not have enough black administrators. Bush administration education secretary Lamar Alexander, who controlled renewal of accrediting boards, delayed Middle States' renewal for over a year, eventually approving it for four years instead of the customary five. Alexander also made it easier for new accrediting associations to get approval, declaring that "if a group of universities . . . don't want to be quizzed about their diversity standards and think that's their own business, they can form a different accrediting association that focuses on academic quality rather than issues like diversity." NAS did not wait long to act on Alexander's invitation, forming its own advisory accrediting organization, American Academy for Liberal Education, funded by the Olin Foundation with $100,000 in seed money.[80]

NAS prepares position papers on issues such as academic freedom and sexual harassment. One, on multiculturalism and entitled "Is the Curriculum Biased?" declares that "an examination of many women's studies and minority studies courses and programs discloses little study of other cultures and much excoriation of our society for its alleged oppression of women, blacks and others." Another, "The Wrong Way to Reduce Campus Tensions," argues that policies such as affirmative action programs in admissions, hiring, and financial aid result in "application of a double standard or the repudiation of appropriate intellectual criteria." As Jeffrey Hart, NAS member and retired professor of English at Dartmouth put it, offering everyone a college education merely leads to the "dumbing down" of the university.[81] Most NAS members would describe themselves as politically conservative, according to the late Barry Gross, former NAS national program director and professor of philosophy at CUNY-Queens. But Glenn Ricketts, NAS research director, observes that "a lot of [NAS] members are liberals who've been mugged."[82]

Funding for NAS comes from several sources. Graduate students pay yearly dues of $18, professors and administrators $36. The larger portion of NAS support, however, comes from conservative foundations. In 1992 the organization received $375,000 from the Sarah Scaife Foundation for general operating expenses and support of the Accreditation Program; $125,000 from the Olin Foundation for publication and conferences; $100,000 from the Smith Richardson Foundation for the publication of *Academic Questions* and $25,000 for the California Association of Scholars; $72,500 from the Bradley Foundation for general programming activities; and $11,300 from the E. L. Wiegand Foundation for office equipment.[83] In 1993, Olin gave $110,000.[84]

Members of the NAS Board of Advisors serve on other conservative advocacy groups and think tanks as well. Chester Finn Jr. served as president of the Madison Center for Educational Affairs, as board member for the National Alumni Forum, and as Olin Fellow at the Hudson Institute. Irving Kristol co-founded the Institute for Educational Affairs; Leslie Lenkowsky served as president. John Agresto served as first president of the Madison Center, and Richard D. Lamm is co-chair of the National Alumni Forum. Shelby Steele and John Bunzel are both Hoover fellows.

Don't Like Where Your Money Goes? Consider the National Alumni Forum

"Higher education reform," writes NAS president Steven Balch, "has two essential components: ideas and money." "Reform," he argues, "ultimately means curricular reconstruction," but even the best ideas will come to nothing without the funding required to put new programs or keep old ones in place. In announcing the formation of the National Alumni Forum (NAF), NAS declared that it is "proud of the significant role it played in creating the Forum and looks forward to working closely with it."[85]

The Forum is the first organization dedicated entirely to enlisting alumni, trustees, and philanthropists in the battle over ideas. Launched the same week Yale returned Lee Bass's $20 million gift, the forum is headed by Richard Lamm, NAS board member and former Colorado governor, and Lynne Cheney, former chairperson of the National Endowment for the Humanities and current Bradley Fellow at American Enterprise Institute. At its opening press conference, Cheney announced the group's goal: to alert alumni to actions it deems politically intolerant and that threaten academic freedom on campuses, such as speech codes and erosion of the Western civilization–oriented curriculum. It charges that public confidence in higher education has dropped from 61 percent to 25 percent in the past twenty-five years.

NAF encourages alumni to use the power of their financial support— $2.9 billion dollars annually—to influence the direction of colleges and universities. It suggests they do this by participating in governance, serving on committees and boards, and targeting or withholding gifts according to what they see going on on campus. It contacts alumni nationwide by newsletter, fax, telephone, and computer; it reaches them through news conferences as well as at regional chapter meetings, conferences, homecomings, graduations, and special events and supplies them with "documented studies" and reports about academic freedom.[86]

Ten NAS Board members sit on various councils of the National Alumni Forum: John Agresto, president, St. John's College, Santa Fe; Edwin J. Delattre, former president St. John's College, Annapolis; Chester Finn, Olin Fellow, Hudson Institute; Eugene Genovese, University of Georgia; Gertrude Himmelfarb, CUNY; Donald Kagan, Yale; Irving Kristol, cofounder of IEA and co-editor of *The Public Interest*; Richard Lamm, former governor of Colorado; Leslie Lenkowsky, president, Hudson Institute; and James Q. Wilson, UCLA. Other NAS members active in NAF include Elizabeth Fox-Genovese of Emory; Alan Kors of the University of Pennsylvania; and Herbert London, founder of NAS and Olin Professor at NYU. Martin Peretz, editor-in-chief of *The New Republic*, also serves on NAF's National Council; Ward Connerly, regent of the University of California and recent drafter of the university's anti–affirmative action policy, serves as trustee.[87]

The philosophy and thrust of the National Alumni Forum parallel those of the Intercollegiate Studies Institute's Forum for University Stewardship program, which was successful in establishing the Winds of Freedom alumni group at Stanford. As Chairperson Lynne Cheney puts it, "It comes down to the question of who owns the university."[88] American Council on Education spokesperson David Merkowitz interprets the NAF and ISI agendas as an attack on the recent democratization of higher education, formerly seen as a bastion of privilege.[89] Foundations rallying to support the National Alumni Forum during its first year include the Lynde and Harry Bradley, William H. Donner, Earhart, Jewish Community, John M. Olin, John William Pope, and Smith Richardson foundations. Individual contributions totaled about $13,000.[90]

Don't Like the Way Things Are Going?
Sue Somebody! Center for Individual Rights

The Center for Individual Rights (CIR) was founded to provide litigation services in the areas of property rights and anti-regulation but quickly became known for challenging campus speech codes and affirmative action programs, as well as defending persons accused of discrimination against minorities and women. "We saw a vacuum there,' said co-founder Michael Greve. "Nobody was going to bat for these people who are screaming reverse discrimination."[91] The center originally relied on referrals from the National Association of Scholars, from which it still receives glowing endorsements. NAS President Stephen Balch touts CIR as "the legal arm of the higher-education reform fight."[92] That it is, and more. Greve warns universities who crack down on sexual harassers and utterers of hate speech: "We'll sue you for punitive damages. We will attack your integrity. We will nail you to the wall."[93]

Greve, a German-born baby-boomer, came to the United States in 1981 to earn a Ph.D. in political science, specializing in environmental regulation. Trained in German law, he is not qualified to practice in the United States, holding solely the American LL.M. degree from Cornell. He came, in his words, as "a refugee from the German welfare state," and though he would like to practice conservative public interest law in what used to be East Germany, he believes there is little market for it.[94] More reason, then, that Greve is proud to have written the amicus brief the center filed on behalf of the defendants in *R.A.V. v. City of St. Paul* (the "cross-burning" case), which Justice Antonin Scalia used in writing the Supreme Court opinion. That Greve, a privileged German immigrant, played such a major role in affecting the quality of life of American blacks is an irony that has not been lost on his detractors.

Michael McDonald, co-founder with Greve, made his reputation as a conservative expert on libel law. Known as an astute litigator, he serves as co-counsel in many of the center's cases. He recently argued and earned a Supreme Court victory in CIR's "Wide Awake" case (invalidating the exclusion of a Christian student magazine from university funding because of its religious content and viewpoint).[95] Both men have been criticized for caustic comments and "consistently dismissive, haughty, and puerile" attitudes.[96] But, says McDonald, "litigation . . . is hand-to-hand combat. It is to 'academic freedom' what mud-wrestling is to classical ballet."[97] McDonald serves as president and general counsel of the center, while Greve functions as executive director.

CIR has become known as the conservative's ACLU, with which it has been allied on a number of freedom-of-expression cases. According to its annual report, it focuses primarily on two areas: "the defense of free speech

. . . and the promotion of government neutrality in matters of race."[98] Although Greve opposes affirmative action programs pure and simple, he seems to agree with the need for at least one kind of diversity. In his work with Cornell University's Telluride Association, a summer program for gifted high school students, he allows that if merit were the only criterion for scholarships, "we'd have 18 very, very smart Jews from Brooklyn."[99]

CIR's most renowned case is that of Donald Silva, who claimed he was wronged when a group of students filed a sexual harassment complaint against him at the University of New Hampshire. They objected to examples Silva employed to teach writing concepts as inappropriately sexually suggestive; one illustrated the meaning of simile by describing belly dancing as somewhat like Jell-O on a plate with a vibrator under it. Silva, a tenured professor and also a minister at a local Congregational Church, said he had not been challenged for using these examples in the twenty years he has been teaching writing.[100]

CIR's Academic Freedom Defense Fund paid for Silva's legal defense when he filed a civil rights suit against the university in reaction to his suspension and the order that he seek counseling. In September 1994, Silva won a temporary injunction and was reinstated to his position. Shortly thereafter the university, in response to the judge's indication that Silva would win at trial, officially reinstated him, granting him $60,000 in back wages, benefits, and damages, and the center $170,000 in legal fees.[101]

CIR created the Academic Freedom Defense Fund in 1991 with money from four major sources[102] and later received grants specifically earmarked for the fund from the Carthage, Bradley, and Olin foundations.[103] Since 1989 the center itself has received $570,000 from Smith Richardson, $450,000 from Carthage and Bradley, and $385,000 from Olin.[104] Olin, however, in 1993 significantly reduced its giving to CIR, providing only $25,000 in grant money, which was earmarked to support litigation programs on property rights, civil rights, and the First Amendment.[105] The Adolph Coors, de Tocqueville, JM, Scaife, and Wiegand foundations have contributed lesser amounts. (Smith Richardson's generous support should not be surprising since Greve once worked as a program officer for the foundation.)

The center also has received money from the controversial Pioneer Fund. But it coyly listed the $30,000 gift as coming not from Pioneer but rather from Harry F. Weyher, president of the fund. Pioneer is known for supporting research that shows ties between race and intelligence. (See Chapter 3.) When this was called to his attention, Greve replied: "The omission of the foundation's name was an oversight, and not an effort to hide anything." Greve was true to his word. Next year's 1994–95 annual report does not mention Weyher's name but does indicate an anonymous gift in the exact alphabetical place Pioneer would be had it continued its funding.[106]

Perhaps invigorated by gifts such as Weyher's CIR defended Michael Levin, a professor at CUNY who believes that blacks as a group are genetically inferior to whites. CIR won the lawsuit in which Levin was charged by his university with "conduct unbecoming of a scholar" and therefore subject to tenure revocation. CIR also represented Linda Gottfredson in her suit against the University of Delaware to allow her to accept a grant from the Pioneer Fund to continue her research on race and intelligence.[107]

Large grants have helped CIR attain a phenomenal record of success in a short period. But the numerous victories in its six-year history would not have been possible without the $1 million dollars' worth of pro bono assistance contributed by the thirty-six law firms listed in its latest annual report. Taking a lesson from his liberal counterparts, McDonald made a concerted effort to engage experienced attorneys to work with him on high-profile, precedent-setting cases. In addition, McDonald and Greve are skilled at engaging the media. Both make frequent radio talk show and television appearances, and Greve regularly addresses chapters of the Federalist Society at law schools around the country.[108]

Want Your Own "Drive-By Shooting"? Join the Center for the Study of Popular Culture

Whereas nailing recalcitrant universities to the wall delights Michael Greve, Peter Collier loves publishing because, he says, "it gives me the opportunity to kick the power structure in the shins and watch them squeal." Collier was speaking not of *Ramparts*, the New Left periodical he co-edited with David Horowitz during the sixties and early seventies but of their new publication, *Heterodoxy*, which they dub "the cultural equivalent of a drive-by shooting." Savagely critical of "political correctness" on campuses, *Heterodoxy* is published by the Center for the Study of Popular Culture, which the two founded in 1988.

Horowitz and Collier, known also as "Collierwitz" because of their long association extending over several decades, are consummate muckrakers endowed with irreverent wit and eyes and ears for vivid anecdotes and cutting gossip. They belong to the small generation born at the beginning of World War II; neither Depression-era children nor baby boomers. Collier came from a working-class family in California, while Horowitz was a red-diaper baby from Brooklyn. They met in Berkeley in 1960 when Horowitz served as teaching assistant in a Shakespeare class Collier was taking. Their lives sent them in different directions—Collier to the South for civil rights work and Horowitz to London to write a book of Marxist analysis. After their paths intersected again in the mid-sixties, they began publishing *Ramparts*, one of the most radical New Left periodicals. In it they promoted the Black Panthers and decried the Vietnam War—positions they later repented.[109]

In a public apologia in the *Washington Post* in 1985, they explained why they had voted for Ronald Reagan in the previous presidential election: It was a "way of saying good-bye to all that—to the self-aggrandizing romance with corrupt Third Worldism; to the casual indulgence of Soviet totalitarianism; to the hypocritical and self-dramatizing anti-Americanism which is the New Left's bequest to mainstream politics."[110] Shortly thereafter, they convened a meeting in Washington, D.C., for repentant former liberals, which they called the Second Thoughts Conference. Sponsored by the National Forum Foundation, Second Thoughts was generously supported with gifts totaling $450,000 by several major conservative foundations: Smith Richardson, Coors, Olin, JM, Murdoch Trust, Scaife, and Bradley. A "panel of elders," neoconservatives who had had similar conversion experiences decades earlier, sat through the day's confessionals and appeared on a program in the evening. Among them were Irving Kristol, Norman Podhoretz, Nathan Glazer, William Phillips, and Hilton Kramer.[111]

Horowitz and Collier used the conference as a springboard to found the Center for the Study of Popular Culture the following year. The culture they profess to study includes universities, the public media, and the legal system. Three periodicals focus on these respective areas. *Heterodoxy*, launched with $40,000 from the Olin and Bradley foundations, skewers campus culture with derisive stories about speech codes, diversity training, multiculturalism, date rape, and AIDS. Funded by the Bradley, Scaife, JM, and Olin foundations, *COMINT* monitors left/right balance in public broadcasting, as well as in the programs of the National Endowment for the Arts and the National Endowment for the Humanities. *The Defender* focuses on First Amendment issues and is published by the Individual Rights Foundation (IRF), the center's legal arm.[112]

Horowitz and Collier arouse passionate reactions from former colleagues. Says Dougald Stermer, who worked with them on *Ramparts,* "They're back stabbers. They're political opportunists. They haven't just changed their views politically. They feel a need to trash everyone ever associated with those views." Collier counters that the world has turned upside down, insisting, "We are the counterculture. We're the people in opposition to what Orwell called the smelly little orthodoxies. We've got the underground press now in *Heterodoxy.*"[113] Michael Lerner, editor of the progressive Jewish monthly *Tikkun,* attributes their turnabout to their complete commitment to their former cause: "They were responsible for the most bizarre orthodoxies of the New Left." Lerner, a former editor at *Ramparts,* says that few on the left embraced the Black Panthers so unquestioningly. "David became a Black Panther cheerleader," Lerner says; Horowitz and Collier uncritically championed every group that claimed to be oppressed. "They became camp followers of political correctness." Now he sees them as equally predictable opportunists of the opposite kind: "Wherever the bandwagon goes, they jump on." Horowitz replies, "We remain as always rebels, and rebels in defense of what's right and what's just!"[114]

The Center for the Study of Popular Culture created the Individual Rights Foundation (IRF) in 1992 to challenge campus speech codes. Although the foundation and center are California-based, over two hundred lawyers across the country serve as affiliates in litigation. Adamant that individual rights should never be sacrificed to group rights, IRF pursues cases that they say even the ACLU has declined to handle.[115] John Howard, president of IRF, disagrees with campus policies that send the message, "If you are favored because of some past wrongs committed against you, you can do what you want."[116] The foundation's success is due in large part to passage, in 1992, of California's Leonard law, which provides students at private universities with the same First Amendment rights as those at public ones. In its first two years IRF won more than forty cases dealing with First Amendment rights.[117]

You, Too, Can Grow Up to Be Like David Horowitz: The First Amendment Coalition

A spin-off of Horowitz and Collier's group, the First Amendment Coalition (FAC) was founded at the University of Florida in November 1992 by David Gentry, a graduate student at the university, in response to a takeover of the student government by the Black Student Union. FAC opposes multicultural course requirements, mandatory sensitivity training, and speech codes. To address these issues FAC presents forums on the role of the university, publicizes reports of "political correctness" on campus to the press and interested alumni, and lobbies state legislatures for laws giving students free speech protection. FAC spread rapidly, now boasting chapters at thirty campuses, including the University of Texas, Indiana University, the University of Pennsylvania, and Swarthmore, and endorsements by the National Association of Scholars, Young America's Foundation, and the Center for the Study of Popular Culture.[118]

FAC's strong suit is the mega-conference. In April 1994 it convened a meeting at Harvard entitled "The First Amendment and the Western Tradition." The conference was co-sponsored by two groups having goals similar to those of FAC—the National Association of Scholars and the Individual Rights Foundation. Students from dozens of universities thrilled to speeches denouncing multiculturalism, oversensitive minorities, and other declared outrages. At the conference's conclusion, FAC issued a document entitled the "Cambridge Declaration," calling on universities to "reaffirm their commitment, in word and deed, to intellectual diversity, universal standards and academic freedom." Speaker David Horowitz likened the conference to the Port Huron of the 1990s, referring to a meeting convened by SDS (Students for a Democratic Society)—a radical student group—in the 1960s. National Association of Scholars president Stephen Balch, a speaker at the meeting, must have smiled.[119]

During the conference, the FAC was attacked by a left-wing group called the University Conversion Project as being a "well-heeled front for conservative foundations seeking to turn the clock back on gains made on campus by blacks, women, and homosexuals." Rich Cowan, a researcher for UCP said, "The biggest problem is that the people supplying the money are connected to organizations with an anti-democratic agenda." FAC admits to having a 1993 budget of $20,000 and expenditures of "a couple hundred thousand." It received start-up funds from some corporate sources as well as from the NAS and IRF, which in turn are funded by conservative foundations. David Horowitz dismissed the UCP as "attack dogs" who merely were raising the funding issue as a smoke screen for their own agenda.[120] FAC has been described as the "student arm" of the Individual Rights Foundation.[121]

At a follow-up conference held at Columbia University in October 1994, hundreds of students from fifty colleges and universities agreed to circulate petitions for a National Free Speech Bill. This legislation would allow challenges to speech codes at private colleges and universities receiving federal funding.[122] Representative Henry Hyde (R-Ill.), three years earlier, introduced such a bill known as the Collegiate Speech Protection Act. Although endorsed by the ACLU and other free speech absolutists, the bill died a quiet death. Hyde welcomed the opportunity to try again, and the First Amendment Coalition and Individual Rights Foundation are poised for the effort.

Business and the enterprise system are in deep trouble. It's time for American business . . . to apply their great talents vigorously to the preservation of the system itself. . . . The judiciary may be the most important instrument for social, economic, and political change.
—Lewis F. Powell Jr., in a confidential memorandum to a U.S. Chamber of Commerce chair in 1971. (Quoted in Nancy Blodgett, "The Ralph Naders of the Right," *American Bar Association Journal*, May 1984.)

How It Happened and What

to Do About It

HOW SHOULD WE SEE the extraordinary successes of the New Right in the last decade and a half? Many liberals profess astonishment, as though the string of victories happened by some sort of magic trick: "They stole our country." But it was not a trick. Conservatives deployed a series of shrewd moves, orchestrating one campaign after another with the aid of money and brains. Here, we summarize the principal tools and strategies conservatives used to effect their revolution of the eighties and early nineties. We then offer an explanation of why it proved so easy — why conservative change (in our era, at least) is easier to bring about than the liberal variety. Finally we predict what will happen if the left continues paralyzed and ineffectual, draw a few lessons that progressives and liberals should glean from this book, and offer suggestions for the kind of effort that can bring the country back into better balance. As we say in our Introduction, a guiding premise of this book is that American society functions best when it receives a roughly equal infusion of ideas from the left and the right. Currently, the balance is seriously out of kilter. This concluding chapter highlights how this happened and what must be done to set things right.

How They Did It: Techniques and Strategies the Right Used to Turn the Country Around

What, then, have been the principal techniques the right deployed in changing the country's social and economic agenda over the past fifteen years? None of what follows will be new to the reader who has come this far. Each of the campaigns presented in the preceding chapters (official English, immigration reform, race-IQ and eugenics, affirmative action, welfare reform, tort revisionism, and campus wars) saw most, if not all, of these strategies in action.

Greater Focus on a Small Number of Issues

In contrast to liberal foundations and think tanks, which back a wide variety of studies and good works, ranging from poverty to cultural activities, to advocacy on behalf of political prisoners and refugees, food production in Third World countries, and early childhood education, the right's efforts are narrowly focused. Only two or three issues are on the front burner at a given time. Although there are differences among the right—neoconservatives, cultural conservatives, and traditional, Buckley-style conservatives have somewhat different agendas, as do the more individualistic libertarians—the right seems always to tackle only a relatively small number of targets at a time, moving on to new ones when victory is accomplished.[1] In this book, we see how conservatives backed English-only, first at the state, then the federal level. Much of the momentum for a national English-only bill comes from victories in states where the Hispanic immigrant population is large and perceived as a threat.[2] Then, many of the same people who backed English-only moved over to immigration reform.[3] Much the same happened on the nation's campuses. At first, right-wingers targeted speech codes and multicultural curricula and theme houses. After rolling back these liberal features, they moved on to attack affirmative action itself. Now that that campaign is nearing completion, conservatives are intensifying their campus efforts on training young conservatives who, in turn, will lead government and society into the twenty-first century.[4]

Careful Selection of Issues: The Multiplier Effect

Not only does the right focus on a smaller number of issues than does the more diffuse left, it chooses them carefully. Conservatives seem better able than liberals to select issues that will pay off in the future—by bringing benefits, not so much to humanity at large, but to the conservative movement itself, strengthening it in preparation for the next campaign. Recall, for example, how much effort the conservative movement has invested in leadership courses and other opportunities for young conservatives.[5] This investment is beginning to pay off: Trained undergraduates have been able to throw aging liberal professors on the defensive, so that they do not respond so forcefully to the establishment of a conservative newspaper or cutbacks for ethnic studies departments. Graduates of these early campus programs (like Dinesh D'Souza) are finding work for Republican congresspersons, writing conservative books, gaining fellowships in conservative think tanks. Soon they will move on to become newspaper editors, heads of new think tanks, directors of foundations. Within a few years, they will be in Congress and perhaps the presidency.

Conservatives seem to have a gift for thematic coherence as well. Consider the campaign for immigration reform. More stringent rules kept out immigrants, of course. Most immigrants join the Democratic Party. Immigration reform thus immediately benefits Republicans vis-à-vis Democrats. And the very *campaign* against immigrants draws on middle- and working-class people's fears, painting foreigners and immigrants as the source of their economic ills and uncertainties. This splits the working class, neatly deflecting attention from what is going on at the top—the tax cuts, mutual favors, tort revisionism, and corporate maneuvering that drastically affect the lives of working-class people by closing factories, sending jobs overseas, reducing worker-safety regulations, union-busting, and sacrificing research and development in favor of corporate raids and takeovers. It also prepares the public for other conservative efforts that tap many of the same fears, such as the drive to reduce affirmative action.[6] This seamless quality, with issues reinforcing and dovetailing with each other, characterizes much of the right's agenda. Everything works together in a flawless design.

Money

Conservatives tend to have more money than liberals. (This is in the nature of capitalism.) But they also raise it more effectively and spend it more wisely than their counterparts on the left.[7] They know how to tap corporate coffers for tort reform, but an entirely different set of constituents for immigration reform or English-only.[8] They thus not only target issues intelligently, they raise money for those issues shrewdly and professionally. And the money they do spend goes to good effect. Recall, for example, how the Pioneer Fund supports a single issue: the link between race and intelligence. It selects the best proposals from the best scholars and funds them amply; grants of $200,000 and more are not rare. Known as the preeminent sponsor of research in this area, it is spending so lavishly that it appears to be depleting its capital so that it may eventually disappear. But before this happens, it will have achieved a remarkable record. Much of the research relied on in the influential book by Richard Herrnstein and Charles Murray, *The Bell Curve*, for example, was financed by the fund.[9] As the Chronicle of Higher Education recently put it, "Whether people revere, revile, or review the Pioneer Fund from a safe distance, most say that it has successfully stretched [its] dollars a long way."[10] According to Barry Mehler, a historian who has been studying them for nearly two decades, "The Pioneer Fund has been able to direct its resources like a laser beam."[11]

Use of the Media

The right also are far more adroit than the left in their use of the media. Indeed, making the most of their opportunities with the popular press seems to have been a conscious policy of the right since the mid-1970s.[12] Recall, for example, how FAIR and other immigration-reform organizations used talk shows, direct-mail campaigns, newspaper ads, and skewed scholarship to persuade the public that immigrants (who, according to most economists represent a net gain to the economy) are actually a drain on government and the taxpayer. Recall how these organizations mobilized sentiment among the elderly and retired with scare messages implying that the high cost of services for the families of immigrants will endanger Social Security.[13] (Of course, the opposite is true: Most immigrants are young, vigorous, and employed. They contribute much more to the Social Security system than they are ever likely to take out.) Tort reformists used many of the same methods plus slick television commercials like "Harry and Louise."

Recall, too, the media blitzes, information packets sent to members of Congress, and the press conferences and speaking tours that launched books like *Illiberal Education, Losing Ground,* and *The Bell Curve* toward best-sellerdom.[14] Recall the catchy phrases that conservative publicists and media experts have coined: "reverse discrimination," "political correctness," "innocent white male," "immigrant horde," "balkanization," "Tower of Babel." "When the Zulus produce a Tolstoy, I'll read him." The reader is invited to ask himself or herself: When, in recent memory, has the left coined even one such memorable phrase?

Conservatives established programs for young journalists to counteract what they believe is the liberal bias of the nation's journalism schools. Recall how organizations such as M. Stanton Evans's National Journalism Center and Morton Blackwell's Leadership Institute have trained a cadre of conservative students to enter the print and broadcast media. Recall, as well, how Reed Irvine created Accuracy in Academia, a junior version of Accuracy in Media, to show students how to monitor faculty they suspect of liberal bias and expose their slips in AIA's monthly newspaper distributed free to hundreds of colleges and high schools across the land.

The right also capitalizes, consciously or not, on double or even triple feedback loops that give its media efforts even greater success than they would otherwise command. For example, in marketing an idea, a conservative group such as the Heritage Foundation will often send a report or position paper to Congress and to leading newspapers simultaneously.[15] Then, as a major newspaper "bites" and publishes a story featuring the proposal or idea, the organization will photocopy the story and mail it to the same sources in Congress it targeted earlier. The result is that a busy congressperson will get the idea that the proposal is beginning to be backed by a growing consensus across the nation.[16] As we write, major newspapers have just broken the story that a poll, stage-managed by Newt Gingrich to show widespread public support for his Contract with America, was fabricated. Many members of Congress apparently voted for measures out of the mistaken belief that they were what the American people wanted, although the real level of support was much lower.[17] The same targeting and phasing of appeals is visible in the direct-mail campaigns described in several chapters of this book. The busy fax machines in conservative offices and think tanks churn out letters and requests to the faithful, alerting them to the need to send money, write letters to editors, make telephone calls to their member of Congress, and so on. The right's complexes contain thousands of journalists, congresspersons, and other opinion makers on their rolodexes—individuals known to be receptive to conservative ideas and swayable by a letter or telephone campaign.[18] They also have handy a list of 133 labels prepared by GOPAC, the Republican advocacy group headed by Gingrich, to praise each other or put down liberals—terms such as sick, pathetic, incompetent—or confident, moral, candid.[19]

Conservative public relations machines and fund-raisers work hand in glove. The more the right is able to get media attention directed to an issue, the more money rolls in. And with more money, the propaganda machine is able to conduct even more effective media blitzes, and so on in a self-reinforcing cycle. People read; people give; capitalism gains; corporate money flows into the coffers; Congress votes according to what it sees as the new consensus; tax proposals and deregulation favor the rich; more money flows; culture changes; momentum builds. And the whole country moves further to the right.

Better Use of Brains, Authority, and Expertise

Not only does the right make better use of money, it makes better use of brains. On college campuses—where most scientific and social science expertise is located in our society—the prevailing orientation is liberal. Yet, expertise is essential to any campaign to change social policy: One needs facts, evidence, analyses, arguments, expert opinion. Precisely because most of the leading social scientists in the United States are liberal, conservatives have neatly circumvented this difficulty in three ways. First, they have channeled lavish amounts of support on scholars willing to orient their research in directions conservatives hold dear, such as defending the Western canon, tracing the race-IQ connection, or demonstrating the biological impossibility of feminism.[20] Second, conservatives have adopted a grow-your-own approach, funding law students, student editors, and campus leaders with scholarships, leadership training, and law-and-economics classes aimed at ensuring that the next generation of academic leaders has an even more conservative cast than the current one.[21]

Third, conservatives have "cut out the middle man" (so to speak) by setting up their own mini-college campuses in the form of think tanks and institutes.[22] These organizations provide support staff, access to the like-minded, prestige, and in many cases handsome stipends. A fellow in one of these institutes has many of the perks of academia without the messy business of teaching classes, grading bluebooks, or undergoing peer review. Many conservatives—Dinesh D'Souza and Charles Murray are examples—have never taught a class, suffered the anxieties of a tenure review, or sat on an admissions committee reviewing hundreds of files of would-be law or graduate students. Yet, to a busy congressperson or news editor, a report or book issued by the Heritage Foundation looks as authoritative as one authored by a busy academic squeezing time in between other duties, agonized over for five years, and published by a university press. Liberal think tanks do exist, of course. But they are not nearly so well funded or numerous as their conservative counterparts. A hypothetical young scholar weighing the option of spending time at the American Enterprise Institute or at the liberal Joint Center for Political and Economic Studies, and deciding purely on the basis of prestige and material support, would surely choose the former.

Recall, as well, how right-wing legal foundations, with the aid of conservative funding and lavish pro bono help from prestigious law firms, have sued, threatened to sue, and pressured campus administrators to further the conservative agenda. Not only have they circulated legal reports and opinions widely to policymakers, judges, legal scholars, and university presidents, they have litigated selected issues intelligently and with precise focus and timing. In some respects, their approach to rolling back affirmative action, hate-speech codes, and other liberal measures is reminiscent of the campaign the NAACP Legal Defense Fund waged on behalf of school desegregation, culminating in *Brown v. Board of Education* fifty years earlier—but, of course, in reverse.

Finally, consider how the right shuttles key players from issue to issue as the need arises, making the best possible use of the available talent. A liberal scholar is likely to spend an entire career on one issue—for example, world hunger, voting rights for blacks, or low cost housing. Conservatives have no such limitation. Quite the contrary, conservatives expect to *win* on the issues they are currently working on; thus, the idea that they will move on to another one next year, and another the year after that is not at all strange to them. Moving from one issue to the other has a further advantage: It reminds the key player that he or she is part of a larger conservative agenda. A liberal working on a single issue (say, low cost housing) is likely to view himself or herself more in terms of that issue than of liberalism as a whole. If conditions change so that the worker is needed more urgently on a different campaign, he or she may decline, preferring to continue to work in a familiar laboratory or office on the issue he or she knows well.

The reader is urged to recall how many conservative figures—Irving Kristol, Lawrence Pratt, Linda Chavez, William Simon, David Horowitz, William Bennett—have woven their way through this book, playing leading roles in one conservative campaign, then another. We met Lawrence Pratt, for example, in Chapter 1, where he was instrumental in orchestrating the campaign for official English as well as funding anti-abortion efforts. He reappeared in chapter 7 opposing Latin American liberation movements and supporting Oliver North's gun-running escapades in Nicaragua. Recently he gained the limelight as executive director of Gun Owners of America. Or consider the ubiquitous John Tanton, who first appeared as a conservationist, then prominent spokesperson for population control. After wearing out his welcome with those movements, he went on to form a leading organization waging war against immigration—FAIR. When that organization refused to jump aboard the English-only bandwagon, he simply switched causes, establishing U.S. English. Or, on a different level, consider the scholarly career of Charles Murray, author of the leading tract advocating elimination of welfare for the poor. After completing his 1984 Manhattan Institute book *Losing Ground*, Murray produced a number of minor reports and monographs, then resurfaced ten years later at the American Enterprise Institute as co-author of an audacious volume, *The Bell Curve*, that has proven as instrumental in the race-IQ/eugenics debate as his earlier volume was in the war against the poor. The left boasts very few such all-stars.

Cradle to-Grave Job Security
As was mentioned earlier, the right takes pains to inculcate youth with conservative values and to promote and train those who show particular promise. The effort begins early in life. Conservative money pays for training in the principles of freemarket economics as early as high school. And we have seen how right-wing foundations fund conservative campus newspapers like the

Dartmouth Review, where Dinesh D'Souza cut his teeth. These newspapers not only serve to raise issues on campus, they provide fertile training grounds for young writers who later will staff conservative think tanks and begin to take over the nation's major news rooms.[23] Conservatives have established programs for young journalists to counteract what they regard as liberal bias in the nation's newspapers. A number of conservative philanthropies fund leadership programs in which conservative college students learn how to take notes, hassle a progressive professor, write a letter to the campus newspaper complaining of liberal bias in the classroom, and establish conservative forums, speaker series, and support groups. These camps, often conducted during the summer, provide the skills their graduates will need to become congressional interns and junior fellows at conservative think tanks following graduation. The liberal reader is invited to consider whether he or she knows of a single program (since the virtual demise of the Peace Corps) that serves a comparable function for young progressives.

Why It Was So Easy

One reason why the right has been ascendant over the last two decades is that they are simply shrewder. They use resources more precisely, concentrate their efforts on a few targets at a time, and make sure various campaigns reinforce and dovetail with one another. They move personnel from one front to another and train the young to take their places in a future conservative regime.

Could the left emulate these features and techniques? Of course, and it should. Unfortunately, we believe that even doing so may not be enough: The left must try even harder than the right, for a number of features of American society suggest the country finds conservative change easier and more congenial than the liberal version. We set out several below; and the next section predicts what will happen if the country remains, as it is now, seriously dominated by just one faction.

Better Narratives
Not only do conservatives have more money to spend (and the determination to spend it well), the nature of their rhetoric, slogans, metaphors, heroes, myths, rallying cries, and stirring causes is more calculated to rally

support among the uncommitted than those the liberals have to offer. As everyone knows, our country is based on a free market tradition. Many of the things we are proudest about have to do with inventors, railroad builders, lunar explorers, pilgrims, frontier settlers, and others who took chances and achieved breakthroughs. Most Americans subscribe to the Judeo-Christian ethic and so do give lip service to the ideals of altruism, public service, selfless giving, and aid to the poor and defenseless. But the deeds that really move us are individualistic acts of bravery, resourcefulness, intelligence. We thrill to the exploits of John F. Kennedy, the P.T. boat commander and president who called Fidel Castro's bluff. Of course, we also believe that Mother Theresa's work with the poor is commendable. Still, there is little question that more Americans would like their children to grow up to be like JFK or J. P. Morgan than like Mother Theresa or Mahatma Gandhi. A host of tales, narratives, scripts, stories, and movies extol the hero or heroine who fights off danger, saves another, or accomplishes some similar feat. Very few celebrate someone who gives away half of his or her wealth or spends a lifetime working with the poor. Indeed Newt Gingrich and others are trying to convince the American people that compassion is oppressive and a form of racism.[24]

We think there is something bracing, manly almost, about the conservative ethic of hard work, competition, and succeeding by one's own merits. Liberal ideals of sharing and public service are fine aspirationally or on Sunday, but are likely to strike us as cloying, a little too self-effacing for our dog-eat-dog lives. Without a change in the way we think about self, productivity, and sharing, the conservatives' ideals and stories will simply carry more weight than the liberal ones, at least in the short term.

Conservatives, then, are able to tap the powerful narrative of manliness, in contrast to which liberals can easily be made to seem weak and ineffectual. But there are other narratives that aid the conservative cause. A second is pride: America is "the best"—a narrative that resonates more soundly with (and is more readily captured by) the conservative tradition. The "we-are-best" narrative reminds the hearer or reader of exactly what the conservatives wish to highlight—the idea that competition (not compassion), merit (not special treatment) made this country great. It is easier to be proud of one's exalted station or standard of living if one can believe that one has won it fair and square.[25] The conservative narrative of America-the-best, then, lends itself to nativism, English-only, the defeat of affirmative action, and many of the other campaigns so successfully waged by conservatives and discussed in this book.

A third narrative the conservatives are better situated than the liberals to marshal is that of threat. The notion that we are under attack, played out, for example, in the campaign against immigration, is calculated to manipulate fear and insecurity.[26] During times of fear and threat, people tend to come together to defend the old ways. They look for differences: Is this outsider, unlike us, likely to add to the threat we feel? The sense of endangerment contributes to a we-they attitude and a need to hold onto what one has—a leading conservative impulse. The reader is urged to recall slogans like: "brown horde," "wave of immigrants," "balkanization," "loss of our Western heritage," "our country's deteriorating gene pool" and notice the extent to which many of them play on such fears.[27]

Right-wingers are always ready to tell the story of someone they heard of, usually a white male, turned down for a job because an affirmative action program awarded it to a less-qualified minority. Liberals, by contrast, base their arguments on statistics, which are of course less emotive and rhetorically effective. The conservative's anecdote capitalizes on the listener's fears that the outrageous event—the discrimination suffered by the innocent, highly qualified white—will generalize so that one day he or she, too, will be a victim. The liberal's statistics showing that very few whites are displaced by unqualified minorities under affirmative action programs are cold comfort when the conservative is able to tell "I heard of a case . . ." and the listener thinks, "The next case could be me."[28]

Use of Memory: The Past's Rosy Glow

Although intelligent spending, careful choice of images and narratives and clever use of the media account for much of the right's recent success, the role of memory may play an equally central part. Liberals are urging society to step off into the unknown, into a place where we have never been. Naturally, this meets resistance—how do we know this will not lead to disaster? We think, if we let them tinker with this one thing, might not the whole system fail in some unexpected way? We want to know who will bear the costs of the liberals' reform. Will it be us? How great will it be? Those of us who lead comfortable lives may be disconcerted by the prospect of change unless we can be sure our status will improve, or at least not worsen. Often the liberal cannot offer these guarantees.

Conservatives, by contrast, are urging that we remain true to some past vision, or even return to a regime we remember from former times.[29] Many of us remember the past fondly. Roles were clearer, people knew their places. Children were obedient. Workers did what they were told. Families ate dinner together, went to church on Sunday, knew their neighbors. Immigrants assimilated quickly. Everyone subscribed to a common morality, spoke a common language, lived their lives in one town or neighborhood. Technological changes came at a slower pace. Life seemed simpler. It is easy to blame the liberals, who press for innovation, for the confusing and stressful aspects of our current state.

The positive feeling–tone many associate with the past thus gives the conservatives an edge. But a second feature also favors them: Because the past is known and fixed, a conservative is able easily to see how the pieces of a plan or program fit together. Piecemeal change is likely to fail, however, because the new rule or practice slips back, is swallowed up by surrounding practices that remain unchanged, is interpreted in dozens of administrative and private decisions against a background of meanings and beliefs that vitiate the new regime. That is why law reform strategies—even ones that result in a "breakthrough" like *Brown v. Board of Education*[30]— end up changing things very little. A conservative can tell you exactly how to change the school system to strengthen the values conservatives hold dear: Reinstate religion and neighborhood control; resist busing; set up differential merit tracks; insist on teacher examinations; and allow school attendance boundaries to reflect neighborhood and housing preferences. Ask a liberal exactly what changes he or she would institute to improve academic performance on the part of minority students, and the answer is likely to be vaguer and more circumspect—he or she really does not know, and the reason is simply that unfortunately we have never experienced a regime in which minorities have achieved great success in school. The coherence of the conservative vision gives it a further edge over its liberal counterparts.

If one doubts this, think how quickly and easily conservative spokespersons like Richard Brookhiser are able to enumerate the six key Anglo traits of conscience, anti-sensuality, perseverance, and so on.[31] What are the six key liberal traits? The upshot is that conservatives find it easier to visualize and replace elements in larger swatches. Their changes end up being structural because memory and coherence of vision give them an edge. They confront no *reconstructive paradox*. And the reason is that they are not in the reconstruction business at all. They want to resurrect old foundations, not build a new edifice from scratch.

The Reconstructive Paradox: Why It Is Easier to Pull Things Back Than to Push Them Forward

Liberal reform is hard to bring about and even harder to maintain in place. Liberal reformers tend to take one step and then stop, believing the task finished. The culture then swallows the gain up. Things slip away, successively interpreted against a background of the old meanings and assumptions. Liberals often place great faith in the judicial system as an instrument of progress. Therefore, consider briefly the most famous law case in recent history, *Brown v. Board of Education*.[32] *Brown* was the culmination of a long and gallant campaign by the NAACP and its liberal supporters to bring about the end of segregated public education. The talented litigators of the NAACP Legal Defense Fund hoped not only to end a long-standing system of separate schools but to put in its place one in which children of all races would meet and learn on equal terms.

Unfortunately, as everyone knows, the landmark opinion has not brought about those gains. School officials resisted, interpreting the decision's mandate in the light of their own experience and sense of social reality. In most cases, teachers and administrators, curriculum, and discipline remained the same. White families moved to the suburbs. Black children were expelled or consigned to educationally disadvantaged classes and tracks in disproportionate numbers. Private schools were not subject to *Brown*'s mandate. As the result, the nation's schools are nearly as segregated today as they were in the time of *Brown*.[33]

Despite this lack of palpable results, few liberals today are marching in the streets for school reform. They believe that battle ended in 1954 with the *Brown* decision. A radical program of school reform could easily be imagined, but it would go much further than a simple prohibition against deliberate, state-supported segregation of the races. Such a program would need to change many things at once—early childhood education, teaching methods, curriculum, and approaches to discipline, just to name a few. There would need to be many more black teachers, administrators, and aides. The cost of such a program would be much greater, the amount of perseverance necessary to effectuate it higher, and the social costs steeper. It would require the kind of staying power—even ideological quality of motivation—that one associates with conservatives.[34] As we explain more fully in the following section, liberals lack the kind of concrete and vivid goals, doggedly pursued, that characterize conservatives. The reason is simple: They have not experienced the state of affairs they are trying to bring about. There is no template. They want to move society to a place where it has never been. Is it any surprise their efforts and programs have a tentative, incremental, cautious quality?

In our society, progressive change is an aberration. Society's natural condition is to slip back rather than to progress onward in an unending line. The whole picture must change, otherwise cultural interpretations and undertows will exert their inexorable drag. The net effect of the hurdles and headwinds we have identified for liberal change may, for convenience, be labeled the "reconstructive paradox."[35] The paradox can be boiled down to six steps:

1. The greater the social evil (for example, black subordination) the more it is likely to be entrenched in our national life.
2. The more entrenched the evil, the more massive the social effort necessary to eradicate it.
3. An entrenched evil will be invisible to many, because embedded and ordinary, requiring little attention.
4. The massive social effort will inevitably collide with other social values and things we hold dear (for example, settled expectations, religion, the family, privacy, the Southern way of life). This will entail dislocations, shifts in spending priorities, new taxes, changes in the way we speak and relate to one another.
5. These efforts will be highly visible—by contrast with the evil—and will spark resistance and accusations that the backers are engaging in totalitarian tactics, siding with big government, dislodging innocent whites, operating in derogation of the merit principle, elevating group relief over individualism, reviving old grudges, whipping up division where none existed before, and so on.
6. Resisting all these unprincipled things will feel right, for one's adversary (liberals) will appear to be callously sacrificing real liberty, real security, real resources for a nebulous goal.

Therefore, reconstruction will always strike many in a society as unprincipled, unwarranted, and wrong. Little surprise, then, that few take up its cause, persist for long in the face of resistance, or even frame their programs and objectives broadly enough so that if they are adopted they have a chance of remaining in place and achieving real effects.

Dogmatism and Refusal to Enter the Arena of Dialogic Politics
A final reason why conservatives have managed to change the nation's consciousness so swiftly and effectively has to do with the intensely ideological nature of much of their program. Many conservatives pride themselves on being "principled," one aspect of which is a refusal to compromise. For example, a conservative who detests crime will often vote with others as a bloc in favor of more and harsher prisons, refusing to balance this need against other things a rational citizen might want: rehabilitation for criminals, better schools, Head Start programs for the poor, parks, roads, and support for the arts. Crime is bad; criminals deserve to be punished; therefore, society must have more prisons regardless of the expense.

Politics, as it is ordinarily understood, entails trade-offs. These, in turn, require deliberation about the various ends and goals a society might want. Conservatives behave, superficially, like anyone else engaging in politics: They vote, run for office, mail letters and position papers, and so on. But, as with children one discovers were not playing after all, it turns out that on many issues conservatives are not really engaged in deliberative politics; rather, they are doggedly pursuing an agenda. (Consider, for example, how the early William Simon call to arms, written in 1978, formed the near-perfect blueprint which conservatives have been following for nearly two decades.)[36] This gives them an enormous advantage over the more tolerant, open-ended liberals who can always see that a goal they would like to accomplish would, under certain conditions, need to be subordinated in favor of another, more urgent, one, at least for now.

The conservatives' refusal to compromise thus weakens deliberative democracy, because their intransigence removes certain items from the realm of ends or teleology—goods to be promoted if possible (i.e., along with others). Rather, the goals become Kantian imperatives, matters that must be seen to, with any money or energy left over then distributed according to what the people want. Their basic program turns out to be beyond discussion because it is ordained by a higher authority, a higher principle.

This sort of intransigence can, in time, change the very character of the community itself. It maintains huge prison systems, for example, as a matter of course: with a sense neither of resignation nor of pride but because that is the way things are. We no longer deliberate about that particular feature because it is relegated to the realm of presupposition. As with the religious custom of tithing, one does not even consider the possibility of not maintaining a large prison system. One simply makes allowance for its cost, then turns to the question of how the community should vote with respect to other expenditures. This is why slavery, Jim Crow laws, and separate-but-equal schools persisted for so long: They became second nature. And it is why affirmative action, once society jettisons it, will not return for a very long time.

There is no zero-based politics, no neutral starting point; every position adversely affects some segment of the community. But intensely ideological conservatives are in a better position to ensure that their zero-state becomes the starting point for discussion. A conservative victory becomes forever — unlike a liberal one, which can always be changed back. The most unalterable feature about a society is one that is internalized, that is inside everyone's heads, that is never questioned because it seems that it has always been there. Imagine a group of villagers who have for generations followed a certain path from point A to point B. A huge boulder rolls down a mountain, blocking the path and forcing a detour. In time a new path is formed. The new path now becomes "the road to point B." In similar fashion, one might imagine a liberal American discussing his or her country with a progressive Italian counterpart. The Italian asks the American to explain the country's high incarceration rate or restrictive immigration laws. The American shrugs and says, "That's just the way things are. We've always been that way. I know it seems strange, but . . ." Like the villager with the boulder, the American has accepted the conservative feature as normal, as part of reality. And part of the reason is that those who put it in place have succeeded in declaring it beyond discussion. As with a tithe, the society learns to live without.

What Will Happen If the Left Does Not Mount More Resistance? Suggestions for Reformers and Progressives

American society functions best if the left and the right have roughly equal power and influence. Currently, however the right is in full cry, the left demoralized. Things are more out of balance than they have been for quite some time.

As with a pendulum, will society achieve a balance between conservative and liberal programs and platforms? There is room for doubt. The right has perfected its techniques—for organizing, publicizing itself, controlling the media, and manipulating slogans, myths, and fears—to a high art. It is aided, as we have seen, by a host of forces that render society highly receptive to its message; conservative change is almost always easier to bring about than the liberal version. And, once things are institutionalized, they come to seem normal. As with tithing, the country accepts the conservative state of affairs. And because conservatives often regard their agenda as dictated by principle, they rarely succumb to introspection or enter into dialogue with the other side. Irrespective of who wins the presidential election of 1996, conservatives have been successful in reframing the debate. Even Clinton has moved to the right.

There are measures that liberals can, and should, take, before it is too late. But it is worth reflecting, first, on what American society will likely look like in the years ahead if conservatives meet (as they have in the recent past) little effective resistance. Black misery will increase. The gap between the rich and the poor (already the highest in the Western world) will widen. Women's gains will be rolled back, foreigners will be excluded, English-speaking enforced, campus orthodoxy rigidly enforced. Conservative judges, appointed by conservative presidents with the encouragement of a conservative Congress, will repeal prisoners' and children's rights, and narrow women's procreative liberties. Unregulated industries will require employees to work in increasingly unsafe workplaces, pollute the air and water, and set aside less and less money for workers' health benefits and retirement. Tort reform will ensure that consumers and medical patients injured by defective products, medical devices, and careless physicians will be unable to obtain compensation. Children will be required to pray in schools, absorb conservative principles of freemarket economics, salute the flag, and learn in English whether they know that language or not. College students will read conservative newspapers edited by conservative student editors trained at conservative leadership institutes and funded by conservative foundations. Editors, legislators, and authors of leading books will, in the main, be conservative. Affirmative action will disappear, as will ethnic studies and multicultural programs on the nation's campuses. Foreign enclaves like Chinatown will shrink; there will be fewer ethnic restaurants and shops. One will hear fewer foreign languages as one walks down the street. The nation will retain a large military establishment even in peacetime. The safety net for the poor will weaken or be abolished outright. Homelessness will increase. Wealthy people will live in locked enclaves behind security gates watched by twenty-four-hour guards. The prison industry will grow, constituting the only form of public service that is fully and willingly funded. Police will be able to search one's home on less and less of a showing of cause. Liberal professors will be fired or denied tenure. Books like this will be hard to find.

What can the left do to slow down the right-wing juggernaut that is well on its way to institutionalizing an America like the one described above? Liberals must learn from the successful tactics and strategies of the right. They must learn how to raise money, to manipulate the media in the interest of causes they hold dear. For example, why could not progressive publicists make capital at the expense of Republican deregulators under a motto like, "Why are they trying to poison your water?" Or, why could not civil rights organizations coin slogans like, "Newt Gingrich's party wants you back where you belong—in chains." Liberals could take a leaf from the deadly serious operatives of the right and establish single-issue think tanks aimed at funding, for example, books, papers, and conferences showing that immigration benefits a region's economy, that affirmative action improves, not weakens, the quality of goods and services available to all Americans, and so on.

Liberals can try to "flip" the debate and portray liberalism as the usual state of affairs, harkening back to the country's revolutionary past and to spokespersons like Thomas Jefferson, John Stuart Mill, Frederick Douglass, and Franklin Roosevelt, while depicting conservatism as an aberrant, pinched deviation from the country's norm. They could show how measures like tort reform, tax cuts for the wealthy, and draconian crime control measures endanger everyone's well-being and liberty. They can train promising young liberal intellectuals, giving them opportunities to acquire the skills and experience necessary for careers in government and public service. They can tap moderate and liberal corporations and foundations, pointing out how a highly stratified society with a growing underclass can never be really secure or productive. They can make ties with progressive leadership in other countries, so that potential trade partners insist on immigration reform and civil rights progress as conditions of dealing with us.

Can liberals do these things without taking on the hyper-organized, regimented, and narrowly result-driven orientation that characterize much of the right? Can they counter the conservative blitz that we have been describing without forfeiting cherished liberal ideals of autonomy, openness, and a broad social concern—without, in effect, becoming their opponent, the right? We think they can, and must. The left does not need a czar. It does not need, even, an ironclad master plan, although some degree of coherence and prioritizing of programs would help. It does need to raise more money. Progressive corporations and individuals must be asked, often and insistently, to back liberal causes. They must be given many more options than they have now. They must be assured that their money will go to causes that count: that will not only help make the world a better place but counter the conservative juggernaut and strengthen liberal institutions into the future.

The left also needs to set up think tanks and special-interest litigation and defense funds. There is no reason why the right should be miles ahead on this score. Intelligent scholars and policy experts producing scores of highly focused monographs, articles, and books, for example, debunking the IQ-race connection or challenging the premises of nativist anti-immigration policy, all in readily readable prose and with a quick turn-around, would surely draw financial support from both individuals and progressive businesses. They can fund and help start up serious left-wing journals, comparable to the right's *American Spectator, Commentary,* and *New Criterion.* Liberals can help the young avoid the crushing debt and dismally constrained career choices that force many to make compromises that prevent them from following their social consciences. They can provide leadership training so that college students can learn how to defend key liberal programs, such as affirmative action and non-Western literature, from the predictable, but often effective, conservative arguments they hear on campuses. They can borrow a leaf from the right and begin using the press and broadcast media to get their ideas out. They can heed friendly critique, both from the far left and from writers like ourselves. None of these measures entails any sort of compromise with liberal principle. If anything, attending to these pragmatic features will ensure a more dynamic left, constantly generating new ideas and producing new faces in a way that will galvanize leftism and give it new life.

Conservatives have no monopoly on brains or money. With effort, progressive people can get the country back on course from the sharp veer it has taken to the right. No society does well when it is out of balance. It is time for a little ingenuity, planning, and hard work from the left.

Appendix

Table 1
Think Tanks, Related Organizations, and the Issues They Support

	English Only	Proposition 187	Affirmative Action	Welfare	Tort Reform	Campus Wars
Accuracy in Academia						X
American Enterprise Institute			X	X		
American Immigration Control Foundation		X				
Americans Against Illegal Immigration		X				
Brookings Institution					X	
California Coalition for Immigration Reform		X				
Cato Institute			X			
Center for Equal Opportunity			X			
Center for Individual Rights			X			X
Center for the Study of Popular Culture						X
Empower America				X		
English First	X					
English Language Advocates	X					
Federation for American Immigration Reform		X				
Heartland Institute			X			
Heritage Foundation			X	X		X
Hoover Institution			X			X
Hudson Institute			X	X		
Independence Institute		X	X			
Institute for Justice			X			
Intercollegiate Studies Institute						X
Leadership Institute						X
Lincoln Institute			X			
Madison Center for Educational Affairs						X
Manhattan Institute			X		X	
Mountain States Legal Foundation			X			
National Alumni Forum						X
National Association of Scholars						X
National Journalism Center						X
Pacific Research Institute			X			
Rand Corporation			X			
U.S. English	X					
Washington Legal Foundation		X	X		X	
Young America's Foundation						X

Table 2
Funding of Think Tanks and Similar Organizations

	U.S. English	AAII	FAIR	AICF	WLF	CIR	MSLF	Heri-tage	Man-hattan	CEO
Alcoa Foundation								X		
Allegheny Foundation		X								
Armstrong Foundation										
Bodman Foundation										
Boettcher Foundation							X			
Lynde and Harry Bradley Foundation						X		X	X	
Butcher, Forde, and Mollrich		X								
Carthage Foundation			X		X	X		X	X	
Commonwealth Foundation									X	
Adolph Coors Foundation†					X	X	X	X		
S. H. Cowell Foundation			X							
Shelby Cullom Davis Foundation								X		
de Tocqueville Foundation						X				
DeVos Foundation										
William H. Donner Foundation									X	
Earhart Foundation										
FMC Foundation								X		
William Stamps Farrish Foundation								X		
Leland Fikes Foundation			X							
Ford Foundation										
Gates Foundation							X			
Rollin M. Gerstacker Foundation								X		
Gilder Foundation									X	
William Randolph Hearst Foundation								X		
Grover M. Hermann Foundation								X		
Herrick Foundation								X		
William and Flora Hewlett Foundation										
Conrad L. Hilton Foundation								X		
Jacquelin Hume Foundation								X		
JM Foundation					X	X			X	
Howard Jarvis Taxpayers Association		X								
Jewish Community Foundation										
Robert Wood Johnson Foundation										
W. Alton Jones Foundation										
J. M. Kaplan Fund									X	
F. M. Kirby Foundation						X		X		
David H. Koch Charitable Foundation										
Claude R. Lambe Charitable Foundation										
Laurel Foundation	X									
Thomas and Dorothy Leavey Foundation					X					
Lilly Foundation										
Henry Luce Foundation			X							

AEI	Hoover	Cato	Rand	Hudson	Heart-land	IJ	II	PRI	MCEA	LI	NJC	ISI	YAF	NAS	NAF	CSPS
X												X				
X				X												
X		X	X	X		X		X		X		X	X	X	X	X
												X				
	X							X				X				
										X		X				
X	X													X		
X				X				X				X			X	
X	X															
			X													
X																
						X						X				
		X														
	X	X				X	X									
X	X			X		X	X	X	X							X
															X	
			X													
			X													
					X											
											X	X	X	X		
		X				X	X									
		X			X	X	X									
											X					

Table 2
continued

	U.S. English	AAII	FAIR	AICF	WLF	CIR	MSLF	Heritage	Manhattan	CEO
John and Mary R. Markle Foundation									X	
McCamish Foundation								X		
Philip M. McKenna Foundation								X		
Ambrose Monell Foundation										
Montgomery Street Foundation								X		
J. P. Morgan Charitable Trust										
Charles Stewart Mott Foundation										
M. J. Murdock Charitable Trust					X			X		
Foundation for the National Capital Region										
Samuel Roberts Noble Foundation					X			X		
John M. Olin Foundation					X	X		X	X	X
Pioneer Fund			X	X	X					
El Pomar Foundation										
John William Pope Foundation										
Randolph Foundation										
Reader's Digest Association								X		
Philip D. Reed Foundation										
Roberts Foundation										
Billy Rose Foundation										
Frederick P. and Sandra P. Rose Foundation									X	
Henry Salvatori Foundation					X			X		
Scaife Foundation‡					X	X		X	X	
Alfred P. Sloan Foundation										
Smith Richardson Foundation						X			X	
Starr Foundation								X	X	
Stranahan Foundation						X		X		
Ruth and Vernon Taylor Foundation							X	X		
Jay and Betty VanAndel Foundation								X		
Walton Family Foundation										
Weeden Foundation			X							
E. L. Wiegand Foundation					X	X		X		
Matilda R. Wilson Foundation										
Robert W. Wilson Foundation									X	

†Includes large contributions by individual family members
‡Includes both Scaife foundations and large contributions by individual family members

AAII = Americans Against Illegal Immigration
FAIR = Federation for American Immigration Reform
AICF = American Immigration Control Foundation

WLF = Washington Legal Foundation
CIR = Center for Individual Rights
MSLF = Mountain States Legal Foundation
CEO = Center for Equal Opportunity
AEI = American Enterprise Institute
IJ = Institute for Justice
II = Independence Institute
PRI = Pacific Research Institute

MCEA = Madison Center for Educational Affairs
LI = Leadership Institute
NJC = National Journalism Center
ISI = Intercollegiate Studies Institute
YAF = Young America's Foundation
NAS = National Association of Scholars
NAF = National Alumni Forum
CSPS = Center for the Study of Popular Culture

AEI	Hoover	Cato	Rand	Hudson	Heart-land	IJ	II	PRI	MCEA	LI	NJC	ISI	YAF	NAS	NAF	CSPS
X																
				X							X					
X												X				
	X	X										X				
X	X															
				X												
											X					
X																
X	X			X	X	X			X		X	X		X	X	X
							X									
															X	
X																
											X					
X																
X																
X																
X										X		X	X			
X		X		X		X	X	X	X			X		X		X
			X						X					X	X	
X				X								X	X			
												X	X			
				X												
								X								
							X					X	X	X		
X																
		X				X										

Table 3
Pioneer Fund: Where the Money Goes

Recipients	Amount	Issues
Americans for Immigration Control Foundation	$200,000	Immigration reform
Thomas Bouchard (University of Minnesota)	$1,300,000	Twins study linking intelligence with heredity
Center for Individual Rights	$30,000[‡]	Hate speech litigation
Coalition for Freedom	$10,000	Established Jesse Helms Institute; conservative television programs; political candidates campaigns
Federation for American Immigration Reform	$1,100,000	Immigration reform
Robert Gordon (Johns Hopkins University)[†]	$214,000	Research linking race to intelligence, juvenile delinquency, and criminality
Linda Gottfredson (University of Delaware)	$335,000	Race norming
Garrett Hardin (University of California at Santa Barbara emeritus)[†]	$29,000	Proposing restriction of non-European immigration because of population growth and limited resources
Seymour Itzkoff (Smith College)[†]	$60,000	Arguing that declining average IQ of racial minorities contributes to downfall of U.S.
Arthur Jensen (University of California at Berkeley)[†]	$1,096,094	Blacks genetically inferior to whites
Michael Levin (City College of New York)[†]	$124,500	Black inferiority, not white neglect, responsible for blacks' predicament
Richard Lynn (University of Ulster, Northern Ireland)[†]	$325,000	"Caucasoids and Mongoloids" migration to harsher climates explains their higher intelligence than "Negroids," who stayed in Africa
R. Travis Osborne (University of Georgia emeritus)[†]	$386,900	Intellectual deficit of blacks
Roger Pearson (English anthropologist)[†]	$787,400	Advocating "supergeneration" of whites
J. Philippe Rushton (University of Western Ontario)[†]	$770,788	Reproductive strategies developed by three major racial groups affect intelligence and brain size
Ralph Scott (University of Northern Iowa)[†]	$36,500	Campaign against busing
William Shockley (Stanford University)	$200,000	Bonus sterilization plan for low-IQ people
Donald Swan (University of Southern Mississippi)[†]	$147,700	Research on Anglo-Saxon intelligence
Daniel Vining Jr. (University of Pennsylvania)[†]	$187,750	Dilution of intelligence due to higher birth rates of low-IQ people

[†]Adam Miller, "Professors of Hate," *Rolling Stone*, October 20, 1994, p. 114.
[‡]Contribution from Harry Weyher of the Pioneer Fund.

Notes

Chapter 1

1. Jerry Moskal, *Making English Official Stirs Strong Emotions*, GANNETT NEWS SERVICE, Aug. 24, 1993, available in LEXIS, NEXIS Library.

2. Gail Diane Cox, *"English Only": A Legal Polyglot*, NAT'L L.J., Oct. 26, 1987, at 1.

3. Letta Tayler, States News Service, Dec. 9, 1987, available in LEXIS, NEXIS Library.

4. Cox, *"English Only."*

5. Tayler, STATES NEWS SERVICE.

6. James Crawford, HOLD YOUR TONGUE (Reading, Mass.: Addison-Wesley, 1992), at 153.

7. *Maryland Governor's Veto of State Language Bill Called "Political Cowardice,"* U.S. NEWSWIRE, May 24, 1995, available in LEXIS, NEXIS Library.

8. U.S. ENGLISH FOUNDATION, INC., AND AFFILIATE, *Financial Statements*, 5 (1993).

9. *English-Only Rules Are Increasing, as Critics, Backers Debate Legality*, BNA DAILY LAB. REP. No. 12, Jan. 19, 1994, at D23.

10. Crawford, TONGUE, at 154.

11. John Tanton, WITAN IV Memo, Oct. 10, 1986. Copies of the memo can be obtained from People for the American Way (202) 467–4999.

12. *People For/U.S. English; People For Calls for Resignations from U.S. English Board; Members Include Walter Annenberg, Arnold Schwarzenegger, Saul Bellow,* BUSINESS WIRE, Oct. 19, 1988, available in LEXIS, NEXIS Library.

13. Ibid.

14. Dick Kirschten, *Alistair Cooke; Defending the Primacy of the English Language,* NAT'L. J., Apr. 29, 1989, at 1064.

15. Norman D. Shumway, *English Primarily,* L.A. *Times,* Jan. 17, 1993. Book Review at 13.

16. *U.S. English Slams Bustamante Proposal for Government Operations in Spanish,* U.S. NEWSWIRE, Oct. 17, 1991, available in LEXIS, NEXIS Library.

17. Ruth Conniff, *The War on Aliens: The Right Calls the Shots,* THE PROGRESSIVE, Oct. 1993, at 22.

18. Crawford, TONGUE, at 170–73; U.S. English, *Financial,* at 3.

19. *Poll Shows Americans Overwhelmingly Support Official English,* BUSINESS WIRE, Feb. 5, 1991, available in LEXIS, NEXIS Library.

20. Katherine Ely, *Common Language Supporters Rally at U.S. Capitol,* U.S. NEWSWIRE, Sept. 17, 1991, available in LEXIS, NEXIS Library.

21. U.S. English, *Financial,* at 3. The annual report does not disclose the sources of U.S. English's funding.

22. Crawford, TONGUE, at 157–58; Conniff, *War on Aliens.*

23. Michael Pye, THE SCOTSMAN, Oct. 17, 1994; Salim Muwakkil, *The Ugly Revival of Genetic Determinism,* S.F. *Examiner,* Dec. 6, 1994, at A14; Michael Lind, *Brave New Right,* NEW REPUB., Oct. 31, 1994, at 24.

24. Crawford, TONGUE, at 157–58, 267n. 2.

25. Ibid. at 158; Conniff, *War on Aliens.*

26. Alexander Cockburn, *Follow the Money; Environmental Politics; Beat the Devil,* THE NATION, Sept. 5, 1994, at 225.

27. Patrick J. McDonnell and Paul Jacobs, *FAIR at Forefront of Push to Reduce Immigration; Population: Group's Roots Are in the Environmental Movement. It Is Now an Influential Player in Border Issues,* L.A. TIMES, Nov. 24, 1993, at A1.

28. Cockburn, *Follow the Money.*

29. Arthur Brice and Don Melvin, *"Bell Curve" Research Tied to Supremacist Group,* ATLANTA J. & CONST., Nov. 23, 1994, at A1.

30. Wendy Lin, *Choosing the Right Language of Learning,* NEWSDAY, Oct. 16, 1991, News at 26.

31. Richard Colvin, *A Lead Role in Bilingual Controversy,* L.A. TIMES, June 18, 1989, Metro, Part 2 at 1.

32. Marilyn Elias, *The LEAD Driver to Put English First*, USA TODAY, July 21, 1993, at 7D.

33. Crawford, TONGUE, at 228, 275n. 16.

34. Carol Innerst, *Studies Hit Native-Language Education; Bilingual Program Reported Failing*, WASH. TIMES, Mar. 9, 1995, at A6.

35. Crawford, TONGUE, at 170–73, 269nn.15, 16.

36. Ibid. at 268n. 13.

37. ENGLISH FIRST, *Does America Need Official English?*

38. Ibid.

39. Cox, *"English Only."*

40. ENGLISH FIRST, *Does America Need.*

41. *English-Only Rules Are Increasing.*

42. *Letters*, ATLANTA J. & CONST., Apr. 6, 1995, at A15.

43. *Georgia Governor's Veto of Official English Called "Political Cowardice,"* BUSINESS WIRE, May 15, 1995, available in LEXIS, NEXIS Library.

44. Dan Fricker, *English First Asks Voters to Pick Tropiano, Frey*, THE MORNING CALL, May 14, 1995, at B5.

45. Peter Brimelow, *The Immigration Invasion*, NAT'L REV., Oct. 24, 1994, at 64.

46. *English Language Advocates Move Swiftly to Defend Arizona "Official English" Amendment*, PR NEWSWIRE, Dec. 12, 1994, available in LEXIS, NEXIS Library.

47. Tayler, STATES NEWS SERVICE.

48. Russ Bellant, THE COORS CONNECTION: HOW COORS FAMILY PHILANTHROPY UNDERMINES DEMOCRATIC PLURALISM (Boston: South End Press, 1991), at 74.

49. Leonard Zeskind, *Armed and Dangerous: The NRA, Militias and White Supremacists Are Fostering a Network of Right Wing Warriors*, ROLLING STONE, Nov. 2, 1995, at 86.

50. Ibid.

51. Ibid., at 55, 61. See also James Ridgeway, *The Posse Goes to Washington: How the Militia and the Far Right Got a Foothold on Capitol Hill*, VILLAGE VOICE, May 23, 1995, at 17.

52. Bellant, COORS CONNECTION, at 36–46; Jean Otto, *Readers Don't Know What They're Missing*, ROCKY MTN. NEWS, May 7, 1995, at 103A; Sidney Blumenthal, *Reagan Doctrine's Passionate Advocate; North, Rallying the Right, Forged a Political Base for Contra Aid*, WASH. POST, Dec. 17, 1986, at A1.

53. *Buchanan Denies Aide Racist*, DENVER POST, Feb. 16, 1996, at A24; Frank Rich, *The Pratt Fall*, N.Y. TIMES, FEB. 17, 1996, SEC. 1, AT 23.

Chapter 2

1. Gebe Martinez and Doreen Carvajal, *Prop. 187 Creators Come Under Closer Scrutiny; Initiative: From Secret Location, Political Veterans and Novices Lead the Campaign Against Illegal Immigration*, L.A. TIMES, Sept. 4, 1994, at A1.

2. Paul Feldman, *Figures Behind Prop. 187 Look at Its Creation*, L.A. TIMES, Dec. 14, 1994, at A3.

3. Ed Mendel, *Immigration Control Could Zoom Into Law—If Its Time Has Come*, S.D. UNION-TRIBUNE, Aug. 1, 1994, at A-3.

4. Martinez and Carvajal, *Prop. 187 Creators*.

5. Pamela Burdman, *Closing the Door on Illegal Immigrants*, S.F. CHRONICLE, Oct. 23, 1994, at 11/Z1; *Decision '94*, L.A. TIMES, Oct. 30, 1994, at W9.

6. Burdman, *Closing*.

7. Mendel, *Immigration Control*. Joe Maliniak, spokesperson for Taxpayers Against 187, declared: "Sure there's an immigration problem. But the answer is to strictly patrol the border and strictly enforce laws about hiring illegals, not throw kids out of school and their parents out of health clinics." B. Drummond Ayres Jr., *The 1994 Campaign: In California*, N.Y. TIMES, Sept. 25, 1994, at sec. 1–24.

8. Burdman, *Closing; Decision '94.*

9. Morton M. Kondracke, *Prop. 187 Is Sinking; Immigrant-Bashing to Collapse With It?* ROLL CALL, Nov. 3, 1994; John Wildermuth, *Unz Preaches Conservative Gospel in Bid to Oust Wilson*, S.F. CHRONICLE, May 31, 1994, at A3.

10. *Press Conference*, FEDERAL NEWS SERVICE, Nov. 21, 1994, available in LEXIS, NEXIS Library.

11. James E. Garcia, *Kemp, Bennett Unlikely Allies with Proposition 187*, AUSTIN AMERICAN STATESMAN, Nov. 20, 1994, at E1.

12. Kondracke, *Immigrant-Bashing.*

13. Paul Feldman, *Proposition 187, Measures Foes Try to Shift Focus from Walkouts to Issues*, L.A. TIMES, Nov. 4, 1994, at A3.

14. Susan Ferriss, *Elderly Ante Up Most Donations for Prop. 187; But Anti-Immigrant Initiative's Opponents Raise More Funds Overall*, S.F. EXAMINER, Oct. 16, 1994, at A-1; Pamela J. Podger, *Ballot Measures Attract Big Money*, THE FRESNO BEE, Oct. 17, 1994, at B3.

15. Martinez and Carvajal, *Prop. 187 Creators*.

16. Pamela Burdman, *Campaign Watch*, S.F. CHRONICLE, Sept. 10, 1994, at A4.

17. Ferriss, *Elderly*.

18. Podger, *Ballot Measures; Ferriss Elderly*.

19. Brad Hayward, *Immigration Measure Foes Level Charge*, SACRAMENTO BEE, Sept. 10, 1994, at A6. The year he co-authored Proposition 187 he was paid $70,000 by FAIR, his only client. Alexander Cockburn, *In Honor of Charlatans and Racists;*

"The Bell Curve" Pays Tribute to Some of History's Most Notorious Pseudoscientific Hatemongers, L.A. TIMES, Nov. 3, 1994, at B7.

20. For an excellent history of the eugenics movement in the United States and its relationship with that in Germany prior to World War II, describing the role of members of the Pioneer Fund, see Stefan Kuhl, THE NAZI CONNECTION (New York: Oxford University Press, 1994). For articles on the recent activities of the Pioneer Fund, see Adam Miller, *Professors of Hate*, ROLLING STONE, Oct. 20, 1994, at 106; *About the "Bell Curve"-Footnotes from Hell*, NEWSDAY, Nov. 9, 1994, at A42; John Sedgwick, *The Mentality Bunker*, GQ, Nov. 1994, at 228; Michael Lind, *Brave New Right*, NEW REPUB., Oct. 31, 1994, at 24.

21. Ed Mendel, *Prop. 187 Opponents Question FAIR Funding*, S.D. UNION TRIBUNE, Sept. 8, 1994, at A-4.

22. Hayward, *Immigration Measure*.

23. Cockburn, *Charlatans and Racists*.

24. Mendel, *Prop. 187*; THE FOUNDATION GRANTS INDEX 1995 (Ruth Kovacs ed., 1994).

25. Miller, *About the "Bell Curve."*

26. Ruth Conniff, *The War on Aliens: The Right Calls the Shots*, THE PROGRESSIVE, Oct. 1993, at 22.

27. Marc Cooper, *The War Against Illegal Immigrants Heats Up*, VILLAGE VOICE, Oct. 4, 1994, at 28.

28. Ibid.

29. Ibid.

30. *Immigration Drains California*, ARIZONA REPUBLIC, Oct. 1, 1994, at B7. Tessie Borden, *Rice Professor Criticizes LULAC Official's Remarks*, HOUSTON POST, May 5, 1994, at A29.

31. *Health Care: California Votes to Deny Health Care to Illegal Immigrants*, BNA 34 DAILY REPORT FOR EXECUTIVES, No. 34, Nov. 10, 1994, at A216, available in LEXIS, NEXIS Library.

32. Stanley Mailman, *California's Proposition 187 and Its Lessons*, N.Y.L.J., Jan. 3, 1995, at 3. (On Nov. 20, 1995, Judge Pfaelzer struck down as unconstitutional the parts of the proposition that would impair programs funded by the federal government and asked state officials to submit a list of state-funded programs that they believed could be denied to illegal immigrants.)

33. *Proposition 187 'Save Our State' Sweeps to Victory in California Election; State Volunteers Show the Power of the People*, PR NEWSWIRE, Nov. 10, 1994, available in LEXIS, NEXIS Library.

34. Ronald Brownstein, *Wilson Proposes U.S. Version of Prop. 187*, L.A. TIMES, Nov. 19, 1994, at A1.

35. David Andrew Price, *But Who Should Pay?* Wash. Post, Nov. 13, 1994, at C7.

36. Mark S. Pulliam, *Judicial Activists Subvert Will of Majority on Proposition 187*, 5 Legal Opinion Letter No. 10, Apr. 28, 1995, available in LEXIS, NEXIS Library.

37. Isabel Alegria, *California's Proposition 187 May Start New Trend*, Morning Edition, Nat'l Pub. Radio, Nov. 11, 1994, Transcript #1475-9, available in LEXIS, NEXIS Library.

38. Reena Shah Stamets, *Fla. Hears Calls to Get Tough on Immigrants*, ST. PE-TERSBURG TIMES, Nov. 16, 1994, at 1A.

39. *Anti-Immigrant Plan Unveiled*, ST. PETERSBURG TIMES, May 5, 1995, at 7B; Rick Barry, *Immigration Problem? Blame Ohio, Alabama*, TAMPA TRIB., May 14, 1995, at 1.

40. Patrick J. McDonnell, *For Them, Prop. 187 Is Just the Beginning; Flush with Victory, Groups That Launched the Initiative are Widening Their Reach*, L.A. TIMES, Jan. 28, 1995, at A1.

41. Stephen Chapman, *Do We Truly Want to Get Rid of Our Illegal Immigrants?* CHICAGO TRIB., Apr. 6, 1995, at 31.

42. Maureen Harrington, *Coalition Protests "Racist" Measure Coloradans Out-raged by Calif. Proposition*, DENVER POST, Nov. 11, 1994, at B-1.

43. Brian Weber, *Prop. 187 Stirs Passions in Colorado; Should the State Join California Crackdown on Illegal Immigrants? Study, Debate Fire Up*, ROCKY MTN. NEWS, Nov. 12, 1994, at 4A.

44. Reuben S. Villegas, *Recapping Busy Week in Latino Community*, ROCKY MTN. NEWS, Nov. 28, 1994, at 3N.

45. Tom Tancredo, *Make a Candidate Sweat—Ask About Illegal Immigrants*, DENVER POST, Apr. 30, 1995, at E-1 (quoting Independence Institute study, "Compassion or Compulsion: The Immigration Debate and Proposition 187").

46. *Press Conference*, FEDERAL NEWS SERVICE, Nov. 21, 1994, available in LEXIS, NEXIS Library.

47. Michael Doyle, *Wilson Lashed on Immigration*, SACRAMENTO BEE, Nov. 22, 1994, at A1.

48. Carlos Guerra, *Immigration Policy Dividing Republican Party*, AUSTIN AMERICAN STATESMAN, Nov. 26, 1994, at A15.

49. Marc Sandalow, *Republicans Battle over Immigration for "Soul of Party,"* S.F. CHRONICLE, Nov. 22, 1994, at A3; Roberto Suro, *Kemp Camp vs. Proposition 187; Immigration Issue Splitting the GOP*, THE RECORD, Nov. 22, 1994, at A18.

50. Suro, *Kemp Camp.*

51. Sandalow, *Republicans Battle.*

52. Roberto Suro, *GOP Would Deny Legal Immigrants Many U.S. Benefits*, WASH. POST, Dec. 24, 1994, at A1.

53. *Senator Shelby Introduces an Immigration Moratorium Bill; Growing Public*

Sentiment Demands Real Reform, PR NEWSWIRE, Jan. 6, 1995, available in LEXIS, NEXIS Library.

54. Mike Miller, *Immigration Overhaul Bill Called "Disaster,"* DENVER POST, Nov. 29, 1995, at 6A.

Chapter 3

1. Richard J. Herrnstein and Charles Murray, THE BELL CURVE: INTELLIGENCE AND CLASS STRUCTURE IN AMERICAN LIFE (New York: Free Press, 1994).

2. Leon J. Kamin, *IQ, Race, and Heredity; Reactions to Charles Murray's "The Bell Curve" and Its Critics*, COMMENTARY, Aug. 1995, at 15. See Irene Sege, *"The Bell Curve": The Other Author*, BOSTON GLOBE, Nov. 10, 1994, at 91; *Heavy N.Y. Times Coverage Aids Launch of "Racist I.Q. Book,"* PR NEWSWIRE, Dec. 1994, available in LEXIS, NEXIS Library. See also Chuck Lane, *The Manhattan Project; Manhattan Institute*, NEW REPUB., Mar. 25, 1985, at 14 (role of Manhattan Institute in touting Murray's earlier work).

3. Daniel J. Kevles, IN THE NAME OF EUGENICS: GENETICS AND THE USES OF HUMAN HEREDITY (New York: Knopf, 1985), at ix, 3–19.

4. 163 U.S. 537 (1896).

5. Stanley Fish, THERE'S NO SUCH THING AS FREE SPEECH AND IT'S A GOOD THING, TOO (New York: Oxford University Press, 1994), at 80–86. See also Richard Delgado, *Rodrigo's Tenth Chronicle: Merit and Affirmative Action*, 83 Geo. L.J. 1711 (1995); Leslie Camhi, *A Family Affair: The Museum of Natural History Redesigns the Past*, VILLAGE VOICE, July 26, 1994, at 15; Vernon Jarrett, *Beyondism Has Roots in Racism*, CHICAGO SUN-TIMES, Dec. 21, 1993, at 25.

6. Kevles, NAME OF EUGENICS, at 96–112 (on these and other events); Stephen Hume, *A Brief History of the Idea of the Master Race*, VANCOUVER SUN, Jan. 6, 1995, at A-15.

7. Ibid. See Buck v. Bell, 274 U.S. 200 (1927).

8. Adam Miller, *About "The Bell Curve": Footnotes from Hell*, NEWSDAY, Nov. 9, 1994, at A-42; Alexander Cockburn, *In Honor of Charlatans and Racists*, L.A. TIMES, Nov. 3, 1994, at B7; Stefan Kuhl, THE NAZI CONNECTION (New York: Oxford University Press, 1994), at 48, 86–88.

9. Judith Colp, *Pioneering Research or Racist Campaigns?* WASH. TIMES, July 3, 1991, at E-2; Kuhl, NAZI CONNECTION, at 5–10; Adam Miller, *Professors of Hate*, ROLLING STONE, Oct. 20, 1994, at 106; John Sedgwick, *The Mentality Bunker*, GQ, Nov. 1994, at 228.

10. Adrian Wooldridge, *"Bell Curve" Liberals; How the Left Betrayed IQ*, NEW REPUB., Feb. 27, 1995, at 22.

11. Ibid. For praise of Cattell's work, see THE BELL CURVE at 15, 345–46, 366.

12. On the Fund generally, see Miller, *Professors of Hate*; Michael Dye, THE SCOTSMAN, Oct. 17, 1994; Sedgwick, *Bunker*; Colp, *Pioneering Research*; Hume, *Brief History*. On the propaganda film and repatriation idea, see Kuhl, NAZI CONNECTION, at 6, 48–50; Miller, *Professors of Hate*, at 112; Michael Pye, THE SCOTSMAN, Oct. 17, 1994.

13. Sedgwick, *Bunker*, at 230,232, 234; Tim Kelsey and Trevor Row, *Academics Were Funded by Racist American Trust*, INDEPENDENT, Mar. 4, 1990, Home News Page, at 4.

14. Miller, *Professors of Hate*, at 111–12; Miller, *Footnotes from Hell*.

15. Miller, *Professor of Hate* at 112; Sedgwick, *Bunker*, at 231; Thomas B. Edsall and David A. Vise, *CBS Fights a Litmus Test for Conservatives*, WASH. POST, Mar. 31, 1985, at A1; David A. Vise and Thomas B. Edsall, *Battle for CBS Takes on Air of Mudslinging Contest*, WASH. POST, Mar. 31, 1985, at A16.

16. *Fund Stays Totally Hands Off*, Toronto Star, Apr. 23, 1995, at A-22; Sedgwick, *Bunker*, at 231.

17. Arthur Jensen, *How Much Can We Boost IQ and Scholastic Achievement*, 39 HARV. ED. REV. 1 (1969). Sedgwick, *Bunker*, at 230; Miller, *Professors of Hate*, at 112; Shelley Page, *Philippe Rushton*, OTTAWA CITIZEN, Jan. 8, 1995, at B-1.

18. Miller, *Footnotes from Hell*; Sedgwick, *Bunker*, at 230–31; Charlotte Allen, *Gray Matter, Black-and-White Controversy*, WASH. TIMES, Jan. 13, 1992, at 4.

19. Adolph Reed Jr., *The Bell Curve*, THE NATION, Nov. 28, 1994, at 654; Sedgwick, *Bunker*, at 231; Sumiko Tan, *Intelligence: Is it 70% Nature and 30% Nurture?* STRAITS TIMES (Singapore), Sept. 17, 1994, at 32.

20. Joye Mercer, *A Fascination with Genetics*, CHRON. HIGHER ED., Dec. 7, 1994, at A28. On the Human Genome Project, see Sedgwick, *Bunker*, at 231. Colp, *Racist Campaigns*.

21. Arthur Brice and Don Melvin, *"Bell Curve" Research Tied to Supremacist Group*, ATLANTA J. & CONST., Nov. 23, 1994, at A-1.

22. Michael P. McDonald, *Defending Academic Freedoms*, Heritage Foundation Rep., No. 371, Nov. 21, 1991; Miller, *Professor of Hate*, at 108.

23. Miller, *Professors of Hate*, at 108, 114.

24. Allen, *Gray Matter*.

25. Miller, *Professors of Hate*, at 108, 110.

26. Sedgwick, *Bunker*, at 251; McDonald, *Defending Academic Freedoms*.

27. Mercer, *Fascination*; Miller, *Professors of Hate*, at 114. On the National Alliance's bid, see Courtland Milloy, *AT&T: A Long Distance to Go*, WASH. POST, Mar. 27, 1988, at B3.

28. Miller, *Professors of Hate*, at 110, 114; Shelley Page, *Nurture or Nature, Science or Racism*, CALGARY HERALD, Jan. 14, 1995, at B-4.

29. Sedgwick, *Bunker*, at 234.

30. Ibid., at 235.

31. Miller, *Professors of Hate*, at 111.

32. On Rushton's ranking of the races, see Page, *Nurture or Nature*.

33. Miller, *Professors of Hate*, at 110–11.

34. MANKIND Q. 31:254–96; Jeffrey Rosen and Charles Lane, *Neo-Nazis! Race, IQ, and Genetics in the Charles Murray, Richard J. Herrnstein Book, "The Bell Curve,"* NEW REPUB., Oct. 31, 1994, at 14.

35. Miller, *Professors of Hate*, at 114. On migration patterns and race, see Fox Butterfield, *Why Asians Are Going to the Head of the Class*, N.Y. TIMES, Aug. 3, 1986, at Sec. 12, p. 18.

36. Tim Kelsey, *Ulster University Took Grant From Fund Backing Whites*, INDEPENDENT, Jan. 9, 1994, Home News Page at 2; Kelsey and Rowe, *Racist American Trust*.

37. Rosen and Lane, *Neo-Nazis*.

38. Sedgwick, *Bunker*, at 233.

39. Colp, *Racist Campaigns?* Miller, *Professors of Hate*, at 112; Sedgwick, *Bunker*, at 233.

40. Miller, *Professors of Hate*, at 112; Barry Mehler, *Ralph Scott's Curious Career*, THE NATION, May 7, 1988, at 640.

41. John Connelly, *Of Race and Right*, IRISH TIMES, Dec. 6, 1994, Ed. & Living Supp., at 6; Rosen and Lane, *Neo-Nazis*; Kelsey and Rowe, *Racist American Trust*; Mehler, *Curious Career*.

42. Sedgwick, *Bunker*, at 230.

43. Charles Lane, *The Tainted Sources of "The Bell Curve,"* N.Y. REV. OF BOOKS, Dec. 1, 1994, 14. See also Charles Murray, *"The Bell Curve" and Its Critics*, COMMENTARY, May 1995, at 23.

44. Sege, *"The Bell Curve."*

45. Sedgwick, *Bunker*, at 251.

Chapter 4

1. Dina Bunn, *A White Hot Controversy; Angry White Male Claims Affirmative Action Works Too Well, Provides Unequal Opportunities*, ROCKY MTN. NEWS, May 21, 1995, at 12R; Charles Oliver, *Next Hot Button in California*, INVESTOR'S BUS. DAILY, May 9, 1995, at A1; Robert A. Rankin, *Foes of Affirmative Action Can Almost Taste Victory; GOP Looking Beyond the Contract*, RECORD, Feb. 26, 1995, at A19; Steven V. Roberts, *Resentment over Preference May Be Political Time Bomb; Affirmative Action Comes Under Siege*, ROCKY MTN. NEWS, Feb. 12, 1995, at 4A; Patrick J. McDonnell, *For Them, Proposition 187 Is Just the Beginning; Flush with Victory,*

Groups That Launched the Initiative Are Widening Their Reach. They Are Targeting Aid to Mexico, Affirmative Action and Other Issues, L.A. TIMES, Jan. 28, 1995, at A1.

2. Paul D. Kamenar, *Revising Executive Order 11246: Fulfilling the Promise of Affirmative Action,* Heritage Foundation Rep., No. 121, Nov. 13, 1985.

3. 497 U.S. 547 (1990).

4. *Washington Legal Foundation v. Alexander,* 778 F. Supp. 67, *aff'd,* 984 F.2d 483, 299 U.S. App. D.C. 353 (1991) (district court granted government's motion to dismiss and appellate court affirmed); Ken Myers, *Conservative Group Sets Sights on Scholarships for Minorities,* NAT'L L.J., Apr. 15, 1991, at 4.

5. 38 F.3d 147 (4th Cir. 1994).

6. 115 S. Ct. 2097 (1995).

7. Marcia Coyle, *Supreme Court Ponders Racial Set-Aside Case; New Era or Step Backward?* NAT'L L.J., Jan. 23, 1995, at A1; Sam Skolnik, *Ralph Neas' Last Stand? Activists Gird for Battle After Adarand,* LEGAL TIMES, June 19, 1995, at 16.

8. *Briefing on the Nomination of Clarence Thomas by the Washington Legal Foundation, Legal Studies Division,* FEDERAL NEWS SERVICE, Sept. 3, 1991; *Subject: The Nomination of Clarence Thomas to the Supreme Court,* FEDERAL NEWS SERVICE, Sept. 20, 1991, both available in LEXIS, NEXIS Library.

9. James W. Singer, *Liberal Public Interest Firms Face Budgetary, Ideological Challenges,* NAT'L J., Dec. 8, 1979, at 2052.

10. William G. Castagnoli, *What Is the WLF and Why Is It Challenging the FDA? Washington Legal Foundation,* MED. MARKETING & MEDIA, Apr. 1995, at 26; James Andrews, *Conservative Law Groups Adopt Liberals' Model,* CHRISTIAN SCI. MON., Oct. 3, 1994, at 13.

11. *Do Major Corporations Know That Their Philanthropy Is Supporting Efforts to Abolish Affirmative Action and Black Scholarships?* J. BLACKS HIGHER EDUC. (1994), at 28.

12. THE FOUNDATIONS GRANTS INDEX 1995 (Ruth Kovacs ed., 1994); THE FNAS. SEE NATIONAL ASSOCIATION OF SCHOLARS FOUNDATIONS GRANTS INDEX QUARTERLY—DECEMBER 1994 (Ruth Kovacs ed., 1994); THE FOUNDATIONS GRANTS INDEX QUARTERLY—SEPTEMBER 1994 (Ruth Kovacs ed., 1994).

13. Al Kamen and Howard Kurtz, *Theorists on Right Find Fertile Ground; Conservative Legal Activists Exert Influence on Justice Department,* WASH. POST, Aug. 9, 1985, at A1.

14. Mary Hull, *6-Lawyer "Horsefly" Nips Buchmeyer; Vague on Results, D.C. Foundation Seeks the Spotlight,* TEX. LAW., Apr. 29, 1991, at 12.

15. Castagnoli, *What Is the WLF?*

16. Ibid., at 26.

17. Anne Kornhauser, *The Right Versus the Correct; Free-Market Firm Sees Campuses as Fertile Battleground*, LEGAL TIMES, Apr. 29, 1991, at 1.

18. Kornhauser, *The Right Versus the Correct*; Marcia Coyle and Marianne Lavelle, *High Noon for Congressional Habeas Reform*, NAT'L L.J., July 9, 1990, at 5.

19. Ken Myers, *Georgetown Battle Is Concluded*, NAT'L L.J., June 10, 1991, at 4.

20. 861 F. Supp. 551 (1994).

21. *Do Major Corporations Know?* at 29; *Bakke*, 438 U.S. 265 (1978). The Supreme Court struck down a medical school admissions policy that guaranteed a certain number of places for minority applicants as violative of the equal protection clause.

22. *Hopwood: "A Perfect Mess of an Opinion,"* TEX. LAW., Nov. 7, 1994, at 4. Hopwood v. Texas, 78 F. 3d 932 (1996).

23. Joyce Price, *White Painter Sues Set-Asides After Brushoff*, WASH. TIMES, Feb. 27, 1995, at A1.

24. Kornhauser, *The Right Versus the Correct.*

25. THE FOUNDATIONS GRANTS INDEX 1995; THE FOUNDATIONS GRANTS INDEX QUARTERLY—MARCH 1995 (Ben McLaughlin ed., 1995); THE FOUNDATIONS GRANTS INDEX QUARTERLY—DECEMBER 1994.

26. Do Major Corporations Know? at 29; Kornhauser, The Right Versus the Correct; Courtney Leatherman, *A Public Interest Law Firm Aims to Defend the Politically Incorrect*, CHRON. HIGHER ED., Nov. 23, 1994, at A18.

27. Peter Perl, *Coors' Move Spurs Labor Boycott Bid; AFL-CIO Seeks to Blunt Heavy Marketing Effort*, WASH. POST, Oct. 3, 1983, at D1.

28. 476 U.S. 267 (1986).

29. 480 U.S. 616 (1987).

30. 488 U.S. 469 (1989).

31. 497 U.S. 547 (1990); 448 U.S. 448 (1980).

32. THE FOUNDATIONS GRANTS INDEX 1995 and THE FOUNDATIONS GRANTS INDEX QUARTERLY—DECEMBER 1994.

33. Jim Bencivenga, *Young, Brash, and Conservative*, CHRISTIAN SCI. MONITOR, Oct. 5, 1984, at 23; Jeff Nesmith, *Heritage Foundation Stoking the Conservative Fires*, AUSTIN-AMERICAN STATESMAN, Dec. 31, 1994, at A13; Mary Beth Regan and Richard S. Dunham, *A Think Tank with One Idea: The Newt World Order*, BUS. WK. July 3, 1995, at 48.

34: Joanne Omang, *The Heritage Report: Getting the Government Right with Reagan*, WASH. POST, Nov. 16, 1980, at A6; Michael Wines, *Administration Says It Merely Seeks a "Better Way" to Enforce Civil Rights*, NAT'L J. Mar. 27, 1982, at 536.

35: Kathy Sawyer, *Heritage Foundation Gives Reagan Passing Grade*, WASH. POST, Nov. 22, 1981, at A11.

36: *Conservative Think-Tank Sets Proposal for NLRB, Labor and Justice Departments*, BNA DAILY LAB. REP. No. 13, Jan. 19, 1983, at A8.

37. 49 HERITAGE FOUNDATION POLICY REV. 93 (1989); 15 HERITAGE FOUNDATION POLICY REV. 3 (1981); 51 HERITAGE FOUNDATION POLICY REV. 64 (1990); 70 HERITAGE FOUNDATION POLICY REV. 33 (1994); 72 HERITAGE FOUNDATION POLICY REV. 35 (1995).

38. Karl Vick, *Bork, Meese, Chavez Have Their Say on Civil Rights*, ST. PETERSBURG TIMES, Oct. 3, 1989, at 4A.

39. Lars-Eric Nelson, *Dr. King—Hero of the Conservatives?* NEWSDAY, Jan. 16, 1994, at 48.

40. Nesmith, *Heritage Stoking Fires.*

41. Roberts, *Resentment over Preference.*

42. Adam Meyerson, *Hard Times; Losing Ground: American Social Policy, 1950–1980, by Charles Murray*, 31 HERITAGE FOUNDATION POLICY REV. 88 (1985).

43. Gregg Easterbrook, *The Case Against "The Bell Curve"; Book That Links IQ to Race*, 26 WASH. MONTHLY 17 (Dec. 1994).

44. George E. Jones et al., *The Conservative Network; How It Plans to Keep on Winning*, U.S. NEWS & WORLD REP., July 20, 1981, at 46.

45. George Archibald, *Mellowing in the Warmth of Establishment Respect*, WASH. TIMES, Dec. 2, 1991, at A1.

46. David L. Michelmore, *Right Wingers Claim Clinton Lawyer's Death Is a Cover-up*, PITTSBURGH POST-GAZETTE, Apr. 30, 1995, at A1.

47. THE FOUNDATIONS GRANTS INDEX 1995 and THE FOUNDATIONS GRANTS INDEX QUARTERLY—JUNE 1995, MARCH 1995, and DECEMBER 1994.

48. Nesmith, *Heritage Stoking Fires.*

49. Tom Redburn, *Conservative Thinkers Are Insiders; It's Now Their City Hall, and Manhattan Institute Is Uneasy*, N.Y. TIMES, Dec. 31, 1993, at B1; Karen Rothmyer, *Rudy's Raiders: Persistent Critics of Big New York City Government Will Get Their Chance if Guiliani Is the Next Mayor*, Newsday, Oct. 4, 1993, at 29.

50. WASH. POST, June 11, 1995, at C1.

51. June 20, 1995.

52. April 19, 1995.

53. Chuck Lane, *The Manhattan Project; Manhattan Institute*, NEW REPUB., Mar. 25, 1985, at 14.

54. Jason DeParle, *Washington at Work; An Architect of the Reagan Vision Plunges into Inquiry on Race and I.Q.*, N.Y. TIMES, Nov. 30, 1990, at A22.

55. John Leo, *Return to the IQ Wars*, U.S. NEWS & WORLD REP., Oct. 24, 1994, at 24.

56. Rothmyer, *Rudy's Raiders.*

57. Redburn, *Conservative Thinkers.*

58. The Foundations Grants Index 1995 and The Foundations Grants Index Quarterly—March 1995, December 1994, and September 1994.

59. A *Think Tank's Winding Down*, Nat'l J., Dec. 3, 1994; *Linda Chavez Founds Think Tank on Race and Ethnicity*, PR Newswire, Feb. 21, 1995, available in LEXIS, NEXIS Library; Frank Manning, *West Valley Focus: Calabasas; Soka to Offer Talk on Civil Rights "Myths,"* L.A. Times, Apr. 27, 1995, at B3.

60. David Phinney, *Californian Affirmative Action Opponent in Washington*, States News Service, Apr. 5, 1995, available in LEXIS, NEXIS Library.

61. *Affirmative Action: Panelists Debate Merits of Developing Alternative Affirmative Action Policies*, BNA Daily Lab. Rep. No. 69, Apr. 11, 1995, at D12.

62. Tessa Gelbman, *Affirmative Action: Texas-Based Contracting Association Offers Minority Set-Aside Alternative*, BNA Daily Lab. Rep. No. 139, July 20, 1995, at D20.

63. Genaro C. Armas, *Canady Defends Affirmative Action Plan*, States News Service, June 14, 1995, available in LEXIS, NEXIS Library.

64. Federal News Service, Mar. 24, 1995, available in LEXIS, NEXIS Library.

65. Stephen Klaidman, *A Look at Former President Ford's Think Tank Institution*, Wash. Post, Feb. 20, 1977, at F3.

66. Dale Russakoff and Al Kamen, *Bork's Appetite Is Whetted for Place on Supreme Court*, Wash. Post, July 28, 1987, at A1.

67. Federal News Service, Oct. 2, 1989, available in LEXIS, NEXIS Library.

68. DeNeen L. Brown, *Gray in the Debate on Color; Many See Both Sides of Affirmative Action*, Wash. Post, June 5, 1995, at A1.

69. Phaedra Walker, *Roots of Poison in the Ivy*, Wash. Times, Apr. 9, 1991, at G3; Charles J. Sykes, *Illiberal Education: The Politics of Race and Sex on Campus*, Nat'l Rev., Apr. 15, 1991, at 49; Anthony Flint, *A "Likable Guy" Shakes Up Academia with His Politically Incorrect Book*, Chicago Trib., Apr. 19, 1991, at C1.

70. Charles Murray, *Underclass*, Sunday Times, May 3, 1992.

71. For discussion and reviews of The Bell Curve, see Adolph Reed Jr., *Intellectual Brown Shirts: Richard Herrnstein and Charles Murray, Authors of "The Bell Curve,"* The Progressive, Dec. 1994, at 15; Michael Lind, *Brave New Right: Race, IQ, and Genetics in the Charles Murray/Richard Herrnstein Book, "The Bell Curve,"* New Repub., Oct. 31, 1994, at 24; James Powell, *New Ideas About Smarts Stand Logic on Its Head*, Wash. Times, Oct. 31, 1994, at 14; Christopher Caldwell, *The Bell Curve: Intelligence and Class Structure in American Life*, Am. Spectator, Jan. 1995.

72. Rochelle L. Stanfield, *Slogans and Substance*, Nat'l J., Feb. 4, 1984, at 228.

73. *Black Leaders, Public Polled*, Facts on File World News Dig., Oct. 11, 1985, at 760.

74. W. John Moore, *It Pays To Think Right*, NAT'L J., Aug. 15, 1992, at 1923.

75. FEDERAL NEWS SERVICE, *Think Tank.*

76. *They Also Fund PTV Shows; PTV Critic's Funds Are Among "Most Conservative" U.S. Foundations*, COMM. DAILY, Mar. 6, 1992, at 4.

77. THE FOUNDATIONS GRANTS INDEX 1995 AND THE FOUNDATIONS GRANTS INDEX QUARTERLY—JUNE 1995, MARCH 1995, DECEMBER 1994, and SEPTEMBER 1994.

78. Bernard Weinraub, *Hoover Institution Gains Entree to White House*, N.Y. TIMES, Dec. 22, 1980, at D14; Keith Henderson, *A 3,000 Mile Corridor of Power*, CHRISTIAN SCI. MONITOR, Oct. 9, 1984, at 31.

79. Martha H. Peak, *Are We Getting Our Money's Worth From Affirmative Action? Keeping Informed*, 79 Mgmt. Rev. 6 (1990).

80. HERITAGE FOUNDATION POLICY REV. (1982), at 9.

81. *Affirmative Action a Failure, Sowell Tells Heritage Foundation*, BNA DAILY LAB. REP. No. 102, May 25, 1990, at A14.

82. Walter Goodman, *Scholars Debate Affirmative Action*, N.Y. TIMES, May 22, 1984, at B2.

83. Herbert H. Denton, *Economist Sowell Seeks to Organize Conservative Blacks Nationwide*, WASH. POST, Feb. 5, 1981, at A5.

84. *Heavy N.Y. Times Coverage Aids Launch of "Racist" I.Q. Book*, PR SERVICES, Dec. 1994, at 1, available in LEXIS, NEXIS Library.

85. Mark Simon, *Prominent New Fellow at Hoover; Author of Race Critique, Shelby Steele, Signed Up*, S.F. CHRONICLE, May 30, 1995, at A11; Wil Haygood, *Shelby Steele; His Assault on Civil Rights Orthodoxy Has Made Him the New Darling of the Right*, BOSTON GLOBE, June 6, 1991, at 77.

86. Jim Christie, *For Race-Blind Public Policy*, S.F. CHRONICLE, Sept. 2, 1994, at A25; Amy Wallace, *Affirmative Action Battle Builds; Education: "The Mother of All Regents Meetings" Will Be Held in Two Weeks As a Deeply Divided Board Prepares to Consider Changes in UC Admissions and Hiring Policies*, L.A. TIMES, July 6, 1995, at A3.

87. THE FOUNDATIONS GRANTS INDEX 1995 and THE FOUNDATIONS GRANTS INDEX QUARTERLY—MARCH 1995, DECEMBER 1994, and SEPTEMBER 1994.

88. Weinraub, *Hoover Institution Gains Entree.*

89. William H. Peterson, *Worthy Guide to Governance*, WASH. TIMES, Apr. 1, 1995, at C3; Alan McConagha, WASH. TIMES, Feb. 17, 1995, at A9; Gregg Easterbrook, *Ideas Move Nations; How Conservative Think Tanks Have Helped to Transform the Terms of Political Debate*, ATLANTIC, Jan. 1986, at 66.

90. 32 HERITAGE FOUNDATION POLICY REV. 42 (1985).

91. IN ASSESSING THE REAGAN YEARS (David Boaz ed., 1988).

92. 480 U.S. 616 (1987).

93. Terence Moran, *Civil Rights*, RECORDER, Sept. 10, 1991, at 9.

94. 347 U.S. 483 (1954).

95. Ruth Marcus, *Thomas's Conservatism Displayed in Speeches, Writings*, WASH. POST, July 3, 1991, at A15.

96. John Hanchette, *Thomas-Hill Fury Leaves Aftershocks in Capital*, GANNETT NEWS SERVICE, Oct. 29, 1991, available in LEXIS, NEXIS Library.

97. Carl Horowitz, *The Numbers Game at the EEOC*, INVESTOR'S BUS. DAILY, July 7, 1994, at 1.

98. COM. APPEAL, Mar. 26, 1995, at 6B.

99. Steven Pearlstein, *Cato Institute's Unregulated Bash; The Think Tank Celebrates the Opening of Its New Headquarters*, WASH. POST, May 7, 1993, at B1. Mary Beth Regan and Richard S. Dunham, *A Think Tank with One Idea: The Newt World Order*, BUS. WK., July 3, 1995, at 48.

100. Easterbrook, *Ideas Move Nations*.

101. THE FOUNDATIONS GRANTS INDEX 1995 and THE FOUNDATIONS GRANTS INDEX QUARTERLY—JUNE 1995 and MARCH 1995.

102. Warren Brown, *Study Finds Blacks, Whites Begin to Get Similar Pay*, WASH. POST, May 8, 1978, at A10; *Black-White Wage Gap Narrowed*, FACTS ON FILE WORLD NEWS DIGEST, Oct. 27, 1978, at F2.

103. Catherine Gewertz, *Think Tank Reports Gender Gap Narrowing*, UNITED PRESS INT'L, Oct. 30, 1984, available in LEXIS, NEXIS Library.

104. *Education, Not Affirmative Action, Brought Major Wage Gains to Black Men, Rand Study Says*, BNA DAILY LAB. REP. No. 40, Feb. 28, 1986, at A2; Lena Williams, *Data Shows Blacks Slicing Income Gap*, N.Y. TIMES, Feb. 25, 1986, at A21.

105. *Education, Not Affirmative Action.*

106. *Affirmative Action Cuts Not Primary Cause of Poor Wage Gains Among Blacks*, BNA DAILY LAB. REP. No. 86, May 6, 1993, at D13.

107. THE FOUNDATIONS GRANTS INDEX 1995 and THE FOUNDATIONS GRANTS INDEX QUARTERLY—MARCH 1995 and DECEMBER 1994.

108. Jeff Nesmith, *Heritage Stoking Fires.*

109. Torri Minton, *Learning to Value Difference*, S.F. CHRONICLE, Oct. 22, 1992, at D3.

110. Frederick R. Lynch, *Workforce Diversity: PC's Final Frontier?* NAT'L REV., Feb. 21, 1994, at 32.

111. *Labor Study Profiles Company Strategies to Respond to Needs of Changing Workplace*, BNA DAILY LAB. REP. No. 190, Sept. 30, 1988, at A6.

112. Clarence Page, *Base Affirmative Action on Need*, CHICAGO TRIB., Feb. 19, 1995, at 3C.

113. James Bornemeier, *Kemp, Bennett Warn of GOP Rift on Prop. 187*, L.A. TIMES, Nov. 22, 1994, at A1.

114. Gayle Hanson, *Color-Blind Initiative Makes Foes See Red*, WASH. TIMES, Feb. 20, 1995, at 6.

115. FEDERAL NEWS SERVICE, MAR. 7, 1995, available in LEXIS, NEXIS Library.

116. Moore, *It Pays to Think Right*.

117. THE FOUNDATIONS GRANTS INDEX 1995 and THE FOUNDATIONS GRANTS INDEX QUARTERLY—JUNE 1995, MARCH 1995, DECEMBER 1994, and SEPTEMBER 1994.

118. Gail Perry-Daniels, *Welfare Reform Debate Zeros In on Finding Jobs*, CAPITAL TIMES, July 13, 1995, at 6A.

119. *Set-Aside Programs Fail Minorities, Women and Taxpayers, Study Says*, PR NEWSWIRE, June 26, 1989, available in LEXIS, NEXIS Library.

120. *Civil Rights Leaders Urged to Move "Beyond Affirmative Action,"* PR NEWSWIRE, Sept. 3, 1991, available in LEXIS, NEXIS Library.

121. *New Book Charts Decline and Effectiveness of Affirmative Action in America Today*, PR NEWSWIRE, Dec. 16, 1994, available in LEXIS, NEXIS Library.

122. CRAIN'S CHICAGO BUS., July 31, 1995, at 11.

123. CRAIN'S CHICAGO BUS., Apr. 17, 1995, at 13.

124. THE FOUNDATIONS GRANTS INDEX 1995 and THE FOUNDATIONS GRANTS INDEX QUARTERLY—SEPTEMBER 1994 and DECEMBER 1994.

125. Julia Malone, *Black Conservatives Like "Jay" Parker Step into Reagan Limelight*, CHRISTIAN SCI. MONITOR, Feb. 11, 1981, at 4; Mark Muro, *Reading into Thomas' Review Ties*, BOSTON GLOBE, July 19, 1991, at 23.

126. Muro, *Reading into Thomas'*.

127. Louis Jacobson, *Tanks on the Roll*, NAT'L J., July 8, 1995, at 1767.

128. Ronald A. Taylor, *Panel Cites Need-Based Diversity*, WASH. TIMES, Dec. 11, 1991, at A4.

129. Nancy E. Roman, *House to Look at Affirmative Action, Quotas*, WASH. TIMES, Jan. 20, 1995, at A1.

130. Ann Mariano, *Fair Housing Laws under Siege on Hill; GOP Lawmakers Seek Color-Blind Society*, WASH. POST, Feb. 11, 1995, at E1.

131. Catherine Yang et al., *A "Race-Neutral" Helping Hand?*, BUS. WK., Feb. 27, 1995, at 120; Marla Dickerson, *Affirmative Action Opponents: Class-Based Help Would Do More*, GANNETT NEWS SERVICE, Apr. 1, 1995, available in LEXIS, NEXIS Library.

132. Donna St. George, *Preference Question Sizzling Affirmative Action Fans, Foes Seek Middle Ground*, TIMES-PICAYUNE, Apr. 16, 1995, at A1.

133. THE FOUNDATIONS GRANTS INDEX 1995 and THE FOUNDATIONS GRANTS INDEX QUARTERLY—JUNE 1995, MARCH 1995, SEPTEMBER 1994, and DECEMBER 1994.

134. DENVER POST, Jan. 16, 1994, at F5.

135. Romel Hernandez, *Study: Illegals Cost State $70 Million a Year*, ROCKY MTN. NEWS, Apr. 1, 1995, at 5A.

136. Alan Katz, *Provoking Thought; Independence Institute's Role Grows*, Denver Post, Feb. 5, 1995, at C1.

137. The Foundations Grants Index 1995.

138. Melville Ulmer, *Risks in the War on Bias*, Wash. Times, Oct. 18, 1990, at G4.

139. Susan Ferriss, *Report Charges Med School Use of Race Quotas*, S.F. Examiner, June 28, 1995, at A11; K. L. Billingsley, *Medical Schools at UC Hit for Bias*, Wash. Times, June 8, 1995, at A6.

140. The Foundations Grants Index 1995 and The Foundations Grants Index Quarterly — March 1995.

141. Adolph Reed Jr., *The New Victorians*, The Progressive, Feb., 1994, at 22.

Chapter 5

1. Lawrence M. Mead, Beyond Entitlement: The Social Obligations of Citizenship (New York: Free Press, 1986), at 57–60, 94.

2. Note, *Dethroning the Welfare Queen*, 107 Harv. L. Rev. 2013, 2030n. 4 (1994); Joel Handler and Yeheskel Hasenfeld, The Moral Construction of Poverty: Welfare Reform in America (Newbury Park, N.J.: Sage Publications, 1991), at 146–47, 160–61.

3. Ibid.

4. Mead, Entitlement, at 95.

5. *Dethroning*; David Stoesz, *Poor Policy: The Legacy of the Kerner Commission for Social Welfare*, 71 N.C.L. Rev. 1675–80 (1993)

6. Charles Murray, Losing Ground: American Social Policy, 1950–1980 (New York: Basic Books, 1984), at 7.

7. David Trigueiro, *Today's Debt, Tomorrow's Assets*, Calgary-Herald, July 13, 1995, at A4.

8. Murray, Losing Ground, at 24–25.

9. Ibid., at 154–66.

10. Joyce Price, *Families "Not Being Families,"* Wash. Times, Mar. 3, 1994, at A9.

11. Nina J. Easton, *Merchants of Virtue*, L.A. Times, Aug. 21, 1994, at 16.

12. Gertrude Himmelfarb, *Beyond Social Policy, Re-Moralizing America*, Wall St. J., Asia, Feb. 13, 1995, at 6; Dave Lesher, *Huffington on Defensive in Key Goal of Ending Welfare Politics*, L.A. Times, Aug. 19, 1994, at 1.

13. Easton, *Merchants of Virtue*.

14. Ralph Z. Hallow, *An Index of a Culture in Decline*, Wash. Times, Mar. 16, 1993, at A1.

15. Mead, Beyond Entitlement, at 17.

16. *Paternalism as Welfare Reform*, Milwaukee J., Feb. 3, 1995, at 10A.

17. Murray, Losing Ground, at 232.

18. *Dethroning*; Kevin P. Phillips, The Politics Of Rich And Poor: Wealth And The American Electorate In The Reagan Aftermath (New York: Random House, 1990), at 13, 74–75, 87.

19. Donna Cassata, *Republicans Bask in Success of Rousing Performance*, Cong. Q. Wkly Rep., Apr. 8, 1995, Vol. 53, No. 14, at 986.

20. *Kemp Addresses LAMA Convention*, Small Business Press Set-Aside Alert, available in LEXIS, NEXIS Library.

21. Easton, *Merchants of Virtue*.

22. Ibid.

23. David S. Broder, *Beware the Unattached Male*, Wash. Post, Feb. 16, 1994, at A19.

24. Robert Rector, "America's Failed $5.4 Trillion War on Poverty," Heritage Foundation Rep., July 1, 1995, at 23.

25: 141 Cong. Rec. S10334-02 (July 20, 1995) (statement of Sen. Ashcroft).

26. Jonathan Freedland, *New Right Tackles Social Wrongs Under Guise of Cultural Warriors*, Edmonton J., Feb. 5, 1995, at A7; Patrick Goldstein, *Yakity Yak, Please Talk Back*, L.A. Times, July 16, 1995, at 16.

27. Lisa Hoffman, *Boehner: Americans Deserve Meaty Debates*, Cinn. Post, Oct. 22, 1993, at 4A.

28. Edward Walsh, *GOP House "Guerillas" Soften Their Tactics*, Wash. Post, Sept. 30, 1985, at A1; Jeanne Cummings, *Is Go-Getter Gingrich a Prisoner of His Far Flung Political Empire?*, Atlanta J. & Const., Sept. 24, 1994, at A1.

29. Mary Beth Regan and Richard S. Dunham, *A Think Tank with One Idea: The Newt World Order*, Bus. Wk., July 3, 1995, at 48.

30. Christopher Carey, *GOP Tells Firms: Don't Aid Liberals, Donations by May, Anheuser-Busch Catch Eye of Armey's Army*, St. Louis Post-Dispatch, June 25, 1995, at 1A.

31. Peter H. Stone, *Businesses Widen Role in Conservatives' "War of Ideas,"* Wash. Post, May 12, 1985, at F4.

32. Barbara Vobejda, *A Conservative Agenda for the Bush Administration; Heritage Foundation Issues a Bold Blueprint*, Wash. Post, Dec. 9, 1988, at A8.

33. Guy Gugliotta, *A Bold "Budget Plan to Rebuild America," Heritage Foundation Wants to Set GOP's Course*, Wash. Post, Apr. 17, 1995, at A17.

34. Hilary Stout, *Behind the Scenes, GOP's Welfare Stance Owes a Lot to Prodding from Robert Rector*, Wall St. J., Jan. 23, 1995, at A1.

35. Ibid.

36. In Making Government Work: A Conservative Agenda for the States. (San Antonio: Texas Public Policy Foundation, 1992) at 5.

37. HERITAGE FOUNDATION POLICY REV. 58 (1991), at 38.

38. HERITAGE FOUNDATION REP., Backgrounder, No. 967, Dec. 17, 1993.

39. HERITAGE FOUNDATION REP., Backgrounder, No. 875, (Jan. 31, 1992).

40. HERITAGE FOUNDATION REP., Backgrounder, No. 983, Apr. 8, 1994.

41. Heritage Foundation Rep., Issue Bull. No. 200, Aug. 1, 1994.

42. Elisabeth Hickey, *The Defiant Ones: Young Conservatives Steel Themselves Outside the Gates*, WASH. TIMES, Feb. 15, 1993, at E1; Sidney Blumenthal, *Quest for Lasting Power: A New Generation is Being Nurtured to Carry the Banner for the Right*, WASH. POST, Sept. 25, 1995, at A1.

43. Jeff Shear, *GOP Catch Phrase of the 90's: "Defunding the Left,"* BALTIMORE SUN, Apr. 23, 1995, at 1J.

44. *Stop the Subsidies*, INDIANAPOLIS STAR, July 20, 1995, at A8.

45. FEDERAL NEWS SERVICE, Jan. 13, 1995, available in WESTLAW.

46. FEDERAL NEWS SERVICE, Feb. 14, 1995, available in WESTLAW.

47. Anna Kondratas, *Fixing Welfare: Don't Expect Rapid Reform or Quick Results*, SAN DIEGO UNION-TRIBUNE, July 24, 1994, at G1.

48. Regan and Dunham, *One Idea.*

49. Spencer Rich, *Breaking the Cycle of Poverty: Mandate Work Plans, Scholars Suggest*, WASH. POST, Feb. 25, 1987, at A21.

50. Cheryl Wetzstein, *Private Panel Creates Welfare Reform Plan*, WASH. TIMES, May 13, 1994, at A4. The noted analysts are Robert B. Carleson, Charles Murray, Martin Anderson, John Cogan, Linda Chavez, Michael Horowitz, Robert Rector, Peter Ferrara, and John Findley.

51. Charles Krauthammer, *Stopping the Cycle of Babies Having Babies*, CLEVELAND PLAIN DEALER, Nov. 28, 1993, at 2D.

52. FEDERAL NEWS DIGEST, Jan. 26, 1995, available in WESTLAW.

53. Max Boot, *Big GOP Names Aim for the Grass Roots: Empower America Calls for Less Regulation, Less Taxation, Less Government*, CHRIST. SCI. MON., May 6, 1993, at 5.

54. *Empower America Conference to Assess the Clinton Economic Record One Year After the Little Rock Summit*, FEDERAL NEWS SERVICE, Dec. 14, 1993, available in WESTLAW.

55. Kevin Merida, *Balancing the Hill, Hearth, and Home*, WASH. POST, Dec. 11, 1994, at A31; Jill Lawrence, *Republicans Hold Court to Break in Freshman Class*, NEW ORLEANS TIMES-PICAYUNE, Dec. 9, 1994, at A2.

56. FEDERAL NEWS DIGEST, Nov. 11, 1994, available in WESTLAW

57. *Republicans Critical of Clinton's Welfare Reform Plan, Morning Edition*, Nat'l Pub. Radio, June 24, 1994, available in WESTLAW.

58. Michael Rezendes, *The Right Ideas*, BOSTON GLOBE, Feb. 12, 1995, at 67.

59. Cheryl Wetzstein, *Family-Friendly Welfare Bill Ready Christian Groups Back Plan by Gramm*, WASH. TIMES, July 26, 1995, at A8.

60. Freedland, *New Right*.

Chapter 6

1. Laura Duncan, *Painful Decisions: New Business Risks Await Both Plaintiff and Defense Lawyers*, ABA J., Aug. 1995, at 68–69.

2. Michael Steven Smith and Paul F. Oliveri, *About Tort Reform: Injuries to Our Civil Liberties*, NEWSDAY, May 2, 1995, at A26.

3. Martha Middleton, *A Changing Landscape: As Congress Struggles to Rewrite the Nation's Tort Laws, the States Already May Have Done the Job*, ABA J., Aug. 1995, at 57–59.

4. T.R. Goldman, *For Tort Reformers, There's Still the Senate: And They May Face a Tougher Time Than They Did in the House of Representatives*, CONN. L. TRIB., Mar. 20, 1995, at 10.

5. Middleton, *Changing Landscape*, at 59–60.

6. T.R. Goldman, *Prospects Dim for Tort Reform by End of Term: Hindered by Election Politics, Split in Business Community*, RECORDER, Aug. 4, 1995, at 1.

7. Karen Rothmyer, *Rudy's Raiders: Persistent Critics of Big New York City Government Will Get Their Chance If Guiliani Is the Next Mayor*, NEWSDAY, Oct. 4, 1993, at 29.

8. See, e.g., Ron Simon, *Junk Science: Two Sides Square Off*, NAT'L L.J., Apr. 25, 1994, at A17.

9. Smith and Oliveri, *About Tort Reform*.

10. Saundra Torry, *Walter Cronkite Video Helps Stir Up Debate over Tort Reform*, WASH. POST, Sept. 14, 1992, at F5.

11. Stuart Taylor Jr., *A Better Idea for Tort Reform*, CONN. L. TRIB., Feb. 27, 1995, at 17.

12. William G. Castagnoli, *What Is the WLF and Why Is It Challenging the FDA? Washington Legal Foundation*, MED. MARKETING & MEDIA, Apr. 1995, at 26.

13. Ibid.

14. JUSTICE FOR SALE: SHORTCHANGING THE PUBLIC INTEREST FOR PRIVATE GAIN (Washington, D.C.: Alliance for Justice, 1993), at 58.

15. Ibid., at 58–59.

16. Ibid., at 60.

17. *Proponents of Reform*, LEGAL TIMES, Apr. 17, 1995, at S30.

18. T. R. Goldman, *Code Blue for Tort Reform*, CONN. L. TRIB., Aug. 7, 1995, at 6.

19. *Proponents of Reform.*

20. Ibid.

21. Ibid.

22. Mark A. Hofmann, *Big Names Try to Keep Low Profile: Informal Corporate Tort Reform Group Keeps Its Cards Close to Its Vest*, Bus. Ins., April 4, 1994, at 3.

23. *A Lawyer's Pay*, N.J. L.J., May 2, 1994, at 16.

24. *Proponents of Reform.*

25. Encyclopedia of Associations 1996 (Carolyn A. Fischer and Carol A. Schwartz, eds., 1995); *Proponents of Reform.*

26. *Proponents of Reform.*

27. Elizabeth Kolbert, *Special Interests' Special Weapon*, N.Y. Times, March 26, 1995, at Sec. 1, 20.

28. James A. Barnes, *Privatizing Politics*, Nat'l J., June 3, 1995.

29. Saundra Torry, *On the Docket: Trial Lawyers v. Tort Reformers*, Wash. Post, Nov. 21, 1994, at F7.

30. Kolbert, *Special Interests'.*

31. Lee Bowman, *House Passes GOP Measure to Curb Frivolous Lawsuits: Other Bills in Trio of Planned Reforms Limit Damages, Help Fight Product Liability, Securities Fraud Cases*, S.F. Examiner, Mar. 7, 1995, at A11.

32. Mark A. Hofmann, *No Escape from Rhetoric in Tort Reform, Product Liability Debate*, Bus. Ins., Mar. 13, 1995, at 21.

33. Justice for Sale, 47–48 (citing Wall St. J., Apr. 8, 1986, at 9).

34. Nancy E. Roman, *Reformers Protest Huge Jury Awards*, Wash. Times, Feb. 14, 1993, at A1.

35. Ana Puga, *Washington Lobbyists Grind for Battle over Civil Legal System*, Boston Globe, Mar. 5, 1995, at 8.

36. Bowman, *House Passes GOP Measure.*

37. Justice for Sale, at 56–57 (citing Peter A. Bell, *Analyzing Tort Law: The Flawed Promise of Neocontract*, 74 Minn. L. Rev. 1177, 1179n. 7 (1990).

38. Simon, *Junk Science: Two Sides Square Off.*

39. Marc Galanter, *Pick a Number, Any Number*, American Lawyer, Apr. 1992, at 86; *Are There Rough Seas Ahead?*, Ind. Law, Jan. 25, 1995, at 4.

40. Justice for Sale, at 47 (citing *We All Pay the Price*, Insurance Rev., Apr. 1986, at 58).

41. *Rough Seas.*

42. Jack Weinstein, *After Fifty Years of the Federal Rules of Civil Procedure: Are the Barriers to Justice Being Raised?*, 137 U. Pa. L. Rev. 1901, 1909 (1989).

43. Ralph Nader, *Nader's Raid on Corporate Reports: If Tort Liability Is Such a Crippler to American Industry, Why Do Companies Downplay That Effect in Their SEC Reports*, Recorder, May 10, 1995, at 8.

44. Ibid.

45. JUSTICE FOR SALE, at 52.

46. Ibid. at 48 (citing Robert Dee, *Blood Bath*, ENTERPRISE, Mar./Apr. 1986, at 3).

47. *The Quiet Revolution in Products Liability: An Empirical Study of Legal Change*, 37 UCLA L. REV. 479, 481 (1990).

48. JUSTICE FOR SALE, at 50 (citing Michael Rustad and Thomas Koenig, *Punitive Damages in Products Liability*, 3 PROD. LIAB. L. J. 85 (1992).

49. Valerie P. Hans and William S. Lofquist, *Jurors' Judgments of Business Liability in Tort Cases: Implications for the Litigation Explosion*, 26 LAW & SOC'Y REV. 85, 93 (1992).

50. Ibid., at 109.

51. SEAN MOONEY, CRISES AND RECOVERY: A REVIEW OF BUSINESS LIABILITY INSURANCE IN THE 1980s (1992) 17.

52. JUSTICE FOR SALE, at 62 (citing Stephen Labaton, *Product Liability's "Quiet Revolution,"* N.Y. TIMES, Nov. 27, 1989, at D-2.)

Chapter 7

1. Books in this vein include Roger Kimball, TENURED RADICALS: HOW POLITICS HAS CORRUPTED OUR HIGHER EDUCATION (New York: Harper & Row, 1990); Dinesh D'Souza, ILLIBERAL EDUCATION: THE POLITICS OF RACE AND SEX ON CAMPUS (New York: Free Press, 1991); Charles Sykes, THE HOLLOW MEN: POLITICS AND CORRUPTION IN HIGHER EDUCATION (Washington, D.C.: Regnery Gateway, 1991). See also Gertrude Himmelfarb, *What to Do About Education*, COMMENTARY, Oct. 1994, at 21; Dinesh D'Souza, *The Visigoths in Tweed*, FORBES, April 1, 1991, at 81; STUDY WAR NO MORE: UCP'S GUIDE TO UNCOVERING THE RIGHT ON CAMPUS (Cambridge, Mass.: University Conversion Project, 1994)(putting forward the liberal view).

2. Peter H. Stone, *Businesses Widen Role in Conservatives' "War of Ideas,"* WASH. POST, May 12, 1985, at F4. On the movement generally, see Leslie Lenkowsky, *How Philanthropy Can Improve the Quality of Higher Education*, Heritage Foundation Rep. No. 214, July 28, 1989.

3. Karla Vallance, *Campus Confrontation*, CHRISTIAN SCI. MON., Jan. 27, 1983, at B1.

4. Ron Chepesiuk, *Alternative Voices: Liberal and Conservative Newspapers are Emerging Anew on College Campuses*, QUILL, Apr. 1992, at 36.

5. Dudley Clendinen, *Conservative Paper Stirs Dartmouth*, N.Y. TIMES Oct. 13, 1981, at A18. Bob Hohler and Anthony Flint, *Dartmouth Review's Foes; Facing Off-Campus Muscle*, BOSTON GLOBE, Oct. 7, 1990, Metro, at 1.

6. Fox Butterfield, *The Right Breeds a College Press Network*, N.Y. TIMES, Oct. 24, 1990, at A 1.

7. Hohler and Flint, *Foes*.

8. Sidney Blumenthal, *Conservatives Debate Style, Tactics After Dartmouth Incident*, WASH. POST, Feb. 6, 1986, at A3.

9. Marcia Chambers, *Yale Is a Host to Two Meetings About Politics*, N.Y. TIMES, May 2, 1982, at Sec. 1, Pt. 2, at 53.

10. Sidney Blumenthal, *Quest for Lasting Power; a New Generation Is Being Nurtured to Carry the Banner for the Right*, WASH. POST, Sept. 25, 1985, at A1.

11. *Bennett to Help Found Group to Teach Western Classics*, N.Y. TIMES, Sept. 15, 1988, at A22.

12. Carol Innerst, *New Guide Rates G.U., G.W.U. as Free From "P.C.,"* WASH. TIMES, July 15, 1991, at A3.

13. Roger Flaherty, *Campus News Gets Right to the Issues*, CHICAGO SUN-TIMES, Dec. 26, 1993, Sunday News Section, at 10.

14. Butterfield, *Right Breeds*.

15. Chepesiuk, *Alternative Voices*.

16. Ruth Bayard Smith, *The Rise of the Conservative Student Press*, CHANGE, Jan. 1993, at 24.

17. Mary Madison, *Stanford Curriculum Assailed by Conservatives*, S.F. CHRONICLE, Dec. 4, 1993, at A18.

18. The Collegiate Network (program brochure of the MCEA) [1993], at 2–8.

19. Liza Featherstone, *Talkin' 'Bout Their Generation; The Twentysomething Magazine Scene*, COLUM. JOURNALISM REV., July/Aug. 1994, at 40.

20. Ron Chepesiuk, *Conservative Newspaper Beachhead Abroad; Washington-based Madison Center Carries Its Conservative Message to Eastern Europe by Funding Student Newspapers There*, EDITOR & PUBLISHER MAG., July 17, 1993, at 20.

21. THE FOUNDATION GRANTS INDEX 1995 (Ruth Kovacs, ed., 1994).

22. OLIN FOUNDATION, 1993 ANNUAL REPORT at 19.

23. Author's interview of staff member, University Conversion Project, Aug. 1, 1995.

24. Chepesiuk, *Beachhead*.

25. Jerry Walker, *Conservatives Seek Journalism Recruits*, JACK O'DWYER'S NEWSL., Dec. 8, 1993, at Media News, 3.

26. Amy Waldman, *Newt's Minions, Influence of Republican Congressional Staff*, 27 WASH. MONTHLY 20 (MAR. 1995).

27. Thomas Collins, *The Right Is Arming Its Media Guerrillas*, NEWSDAY, Mar. 25, 1990, at 9; LEADERSHIP INSTITUTE, *Train to Win*, 1995 Training Opportunity Catalog.

28. Tony Case, *Promoting Conservative Voices; GOP Booster Morton Blackwell's School for Right-Wing Student Journalists Raised $1.2 Million Last Year to Combat*

the Perceived Liberal Bias of the Press, EDITOR & PUBLISHER MAG., Jan. 8, 1994, at Advertising, 9.

29. Richard Whittle, *GOP Followers Credit Campaign Organizer with Cultivating Political Skills*, DALLAS MORNING NEWS, Apr. 18, 1995, at 1A.

30. Jeffrey Pasley, *Paper Pushers*, NEW REPUB., Dec. 1, 1986, at 24; Charlotte Sutton, *Conservatives Get Ideas Into Print on Campus*, ST. PETERSBURG TIMES, June 24, 1991, at 1A; Larry Gordon, *Papers Proliferate: The Right Presses Case on Campus*, L.A. TIMES, May 1, 1989, at 1.

31. Whittle, *GOP Followers*.

32. THE FOUNDATION GRANTS INDEX 1995.

33. COORS FOUNDATION, 1994 ANNUAL REPORT

34. Mark Johnson, *Compatibility Questionnaire Screens Surge of GOP Job Seekers*, SAN DIEGO UNION-TRIBUNE, Nov. 25, 1994, at A7.

35. EDUCATION AND RESEARCH INSTITUTE, 1993 ANNUAL REPORT.

36. Michael Rust, *Insight*, WASH. TIMES, Jan. 2, 1995, at 24.

37. EDUCATION AND RESEARCH INSTITUTE, 1993 ANNUAL REPORT.

38. THE FOUNDATION GRANTS INDEX 1995.

39. OLIN FOUNDATION, 1993 ANNUAL REPORT.

40. Lyn Nell Hancock and Yahlin Chang, *The Power of the Purse: Wealthy Alums Fight Campus Wars*, NEWSWEEK, May 15, 1995, at 58.

41. Join the Battle of Ideas [program brochure], Intercollegiate Studies Institute [1994].

42. Hancock and Chang, *Wealthy Alums*.

43. THE FOUNDATION GRANTS INDEX 1995; OLIN FOUNDATION, 1993 ANNUAL REPORT.

44. Devin Leonard, *A as in Average: What's Happened to Grading Standards in U.S. Schools*, RECORD, Aug. 9, 1994, at B1, Doug Bandow, *The Bad News: It's Not Just Colleges that Are Politically Correct Today*, WASH. TIMES, Sept. 5, 1994, at A19.

45. David Karp, *A Whiter Shade of Yale?* WASH. POST, June 4, 1995, at F1.

46. Dexter Waugh, *Stanford's Curriculum Feud Raging; Black Students, Impatient with Pace of Campus Reviews, Form Institute, Call for Overhaul*, S.F. EXAMINER, Feb. 21, 1994, at A2; Jane Meredith Adams, *Angry Alums; Conservatives Protesting Stanford Multiculturalism*, DALLAS MORNING NEWS, Dec. 2, 1993, at 12A; Bill Workman, *Conservatives Study Curriculum, Stanford Group Plans Its Own Review of Undergraduate Education*, S.F. CHRONICLE, Feb. 4, 1994, at A21; Mary Madison, *Stanford Curriculum Assailed by Conservatives*.

47. Hancock and Chang, *Wealthy Alums*; Karp, *Whiter Shade*.

48. M. Stanton Evans, *The Bass Dispute at Yale*, WASH. POST, June 24, 1995, at A18.

49. Young America's Foundation, *25th Anniversary Report, 1969–94*, at 8.

50. Ibid., at 12–14.

51. Ibid., at 15–17.

52. Ibid.; Richard Lovegrove, *Weekend Rallies Dot Virginia*, UPI, Feb. 10, 1991, Sunday, BC cycle, available in LEXIS, NEXIS Library.

53. Carol Innerst, *"Ideological Diversity" Blossoms at Liberal College*, WASH. TIMES, Mar. 21, 1994, at A1.

54. Ibid.

55. Young America's Foundation, *25th Anniversary Report*, 1969–94, at 20.

56. Ibid.

57. THE FOUNDATION GRANTS INDEX 1995.

58. WASH. TIMES, Nov. 10, 1995, at A2.

59. Ron Robinson, *America's Campuses: Crisis and Opportunity*, Heritage Foundation Rep., No. 367, Sept. 25, 1991.

60. Keith B. Richburg, *Professors to Be Monitored for Leftism, Conservative Group Fears 10,000 Marxists are Teaching at Universities*, WASH. POST, Aug. 4, 1985, at A7; Alison Muscatine, *Group Monitoring Academia Stirs Support, Concern on Campus*, WASH. POST, Nov. 3, 1985, at D1.

61. ACCURACY IN ACADEMIA, *Fighting for Academic Freedom on America's College Campuses; Why Do College Students Need Accuracy in Academia? How Indoctrination Works* [Information Brochures, 1995].

62. Richburg, *Monitored for Leftism*; Muscatine, *Group Monitoring Academia*; *Student Politics*, THE ECONOMIST, Dec. 7, 1985, at 26.

63. James Ledbetter, *Campus Double Agent: I Was a Spy for Accuracy in Academia*, NEW REPUB., Dec. 30, 1985, at 14.

64. Saul Landau, *Dress Rehearsal for a Red Scare; Students for a Better America*, THE NATION, Apr. 5, 1986, at 482.

65. *Who Is Calling the Shots Now? A Survey of Key Figures and Departments in the Area*, LATIN AMERICA WEEKLY REPORT, Feb. 7, 1986, at 4; Christopher Hitchins, *Minority Report; Reagan on Nicaragua*, THE NATION, Apr. 19, 1986, at 542. See also Leonard Zeskind, *Armed and Dangerous: The NRA, Militias, and White Supremacists Are Fostering a Network of Right Wing Warriors*, ROLLING STONE, Nov. 2, 1995, at 86.

66. Landau, *Dress Rehearsal*.

67. *Les Csorba III*, [interview] HERITAGE FOUNDATION EDUCATION UPDATE, summer 1987, at 4.

68. Ledbetter, *Double Agent*; Landau, *Dress Rehearsal*.

69. *Les Csorba III*.

70. Linda Stewart, *UT Makes Conservative 12-Worst List*, DALLAS MORNING NEWS, June 28, 1994, at 19A.

71. Daniel J. Flynn, *College Instructors Discuss "Queering" of English Classes*, CAMPUS REP., May 1995, at 1.

72. THE FOUNDATION GRANTS INDEX 1995.

73. Kenneth R. Clark, *Power for Sale: From Greenpeace to the Rev. Sun Myung Moon, How PAC's and Lobbies Influence America*, CHICAGO TRIB., Apr. 27, 1986, at 26C; Joanne Omang, *Moon's "Cause" Takes Aim at Communism in Americas*, WASH. POST, Aug. 28, 1983, at A1.

74. John Elson, *Academics in Opposition*, Time, Apr. 1, 1991, at 68; *Death Elsewhere*, DAYTON DAILY NEWS, July 21, 1995, at 6B.

75. National Association of Scholars, Information Pamphlet (1995).

76. Jon Wiener, *A Tale of Two Conclaves: Campus Voices Right and Left*, THE NATION, Dec. 12, 1988, at 644.

77. Letter from Steve Balch, president, National Association of Scholars June 20, 1995 (on file with authors.)

78. NAS Affiliates, *NAS Update*(National Association of Scholars, Princeton, N.J.), spring 1995, at 6.

79. Wiener, *Two Conclaves*.

80. Carol Innerst, *Alexander Takes Aim at Diversity Standards*, WASH. TIMES, Apr. 15, 1992, at A1; Letter from Steve Balch.

81. Valerie Richardson, *Academics Share Blame, Not Solutions, at Convention*, WASH. TIMES, Apr. 17, 1993, at A4.

82. Cathy Young, *He Wants to Teach Integrity in School* [interview with Barry Gross] NEWSDAY, Feb. 25, 1991 at 69; Jacquelin Shaheen, *New Jersey Q & A: Dr. Glenn M. Ricketts; A Voice Against Trendy College Studies*, N.Y. TIMES, Oct. 9, 1994, at 13NJ3.

83. THE FOUNDATION GRANTS INDEX 1995.

84. OLIN FOUNDATION, 1993 ANNUAL REPORT.

85. National Alumni Forum Launched, NAS Update (National Association of Scholars, Princeton, N.J.), spring 1995, at 1–2.

86. National Alumni Forum, *Alumni Organize to Preserve Free Speech and Free Thought at Colleges and Universities; Questions and Answers; About the National Alumni Forum* [1995] (on file with authors). See also James B. Taylor, *Alumni Should Pay Heed Before They Write the Big Checks*, COMMENTARY, May 3, 1995, at A17.

87. National Alumni Forum [list of Council and Committee Members, 1995] (on file with authors).

88. *Conservatives to Fight Campus "Political Correctness,"* ROCKY MTN. NEWS, Mar. 18, 1995, at 42A.

89. Alice Dembner, *Alumni Bring View from Right to Campus*, BOSTON GLOBE, June 24, 1995, at 1.

90. David Greenberg, *The Alumni Are Coming!* LINGUA FRANCA, Jan./Feb. 1996, at 56.

91. Anne Kornhauser, *The Right Versus the Correct; Free-Market Firm Sees Campuses as Fertile Battleground*, LEGAL TIMES, Apr. 29, 1991, at 1.

92. Courtney Leatherman, *A Public-Interest Law Firm Aims to Defend the Politically Incorrect*, CHRON. HIGHER ED., Nov. 23, 1994, at A18.

93. Kornhauser, *Right Versus the Correct*.

94. Ibid.

95. Rosenberger v. Rector and Visitors of the University of Virginia, 115 S. Ct. 2510 (1995).

96. Leatherman, *Public-Interest*.

97. Michael P. McDonald, *Defending Academic Freedom*, Heritage Foundation Rep, No. 371, Nov. 12, 1991.

98. CENTER FOR INDIVIDUAL RIGHTS, 1994–95 ANNUAL REPORT.

99. Kornhauser, *Right Versus the Correct*.

100. Curtis Eichelberger, *A Lesson in Modern-Day Witch Hunts*, ROCKY MTN. NEWS, Dec. 13, 1994, at 4D.

101. *Free Speech Wins One*, WASH. TIMES, Dec. 6, 1994, at A20.

102. *John Elvin*, WASH. TIMES, Oct. 31, 1991, at A6.

103. THE FOUNDATION GRANTS INDEX 1995.

104. Leatherman, *Public Interest*.

105. OLIN FOUNDATION, 1993 ANNUAL REPORT, at 9.

106. Leatherman, *Public Interest*, CENTER FOR INDIVIDUAL RIGHTS, ANNUAL REPORT.

107. McDonald, *Defending Academic*.

108. Leatherman, *Public Interest*; CENTER FOR INDIVIDUAL RIGHTS, ANNUAL REPORT.

109. Bob Sipchen, *Leftists Who Turned Right; Once the Dukes of Radical Chic, Peter Collier and David Horowitz Have Seen the Conservative Light*, L.A. TIMES, June 2, 1992, at E1.

110. Peter Collier and David Horowitz, *Lefties for Reagan; We Have Seen the Enemy and He Is Not Us*, WASH. POST, March 17, 1995, at 8.

111. Sidney Blumenthal, *Thunder on the New Right: A Conference Where the Converted Don't Quite Reach Their Goal*, WASH. POST, Oct. 19, 1987, at B1.

112. Center for the Study of Popular Culture, *Information Brochure* (1995) (on file with authors); *They Also Fund PTV Shows; PTV Critic's Funds Are Among the "Most Conservative" U.S. Foundations*, COMMUNICATIONS DAILY, Mar. 6, 1992, at 4; Alice Kahn, *"Heterodoxy" Has Faithful Readers As Well As Enemies*, STAR-TRIBUNE, June 25, 1993, at 10E.

113. Alice Kahn, *"Heterodoxy."*

114. Sipchen, *Leftists Who Turned Right*.

115. Individual Rights Foundation (Statement of Principles and Short History of the Organization, 1995) (on file with authors).

116. Joyce Price, *Penn's Leniency Said to Abet Censorship*, WASH. TIMES, Sept. 16, 1993, at A4.

117. Dave Gentry, *Full Circle for the Berkeley Free Speech Movement*, WASH. TIMES, Dec. 2, 1994, at A23.

118. Carol Innerst, *Students Try to Weed PC out of Ivy League Schools*, WASH. TIMES, Dec. 3, 1993, at A1; Don Horine, *UF Student: It's Incorrect to be "Politically Correct" on Campus*, PALM BEACH POST, Jan. 24, 1994, at A1; Gentry, *Full Circle;* Horine, *UF Student.*

119. Carol Innerst, *Anti-PC College Students Form an SDS of the Right*, WASH. TIMES, Apr. 5, 1994, at A1; Carl Horowitz, INVESTOR'S BUS. DAILY, May 16, 1994, at National Issue, at 1.

120. Christopher B. Daly, *Group Fights "Political Correctness"; Critics Denounce Campus Crusade as a Front for Conservatives*, WASH. POST, Apr. 23, 1994 at A8.

121. Carol Innerst, *"Free Speech Is a Bad Thing" for Students at Penn Campus; After 106 Years, Magazine Loses Funding for Offending*, WASH. TIMES, Mar. 23, 1995, at A2.

122 Carol Innerst, *Campus Stifling of Free Speech Has Stirred Backlash; Protest Eyes Congressional Action*, WASH. TIMES, Nov. 2, 1994, at A2.

How It Happened and What to Do About It

1. See, e.g., *Gingrich Pushes Agenda—And Pulls Party Along*, BOULDER DAILY CAMERA, Oct. 28, 1995, at A12 (Knight Ridder); James Ridgeway, *Whiplash: Newt Gingrich and His Plans for a New Day in America*, VILLAGE VOICE, Sept. 20, 1994, at 17.

2. See Chapter 1.

3. See Chapter 2.

4. See Chapters 4 & 7.

5. See Chapter 7.

6. See Chapter 4.

7. Larry D. Hatfield and Dexter Waugh, *Liberals Left Behind in Big Battle of the Think Tanks*, S.F. EXAMINER, June 28, 1992, at B7; David Callahan, *Liberal Policy's Weak Foundations*, THE NATION, Nov. 13, 1995, at 568; James W. Singer, *Liberal Public Interest Law Firms Face Budgetary Ideological Challenges*, NAT'L J. Dec. 8, 1979, at 2052.

8. Compare Chapters 6 (tort reform) and 1 & 2 (English-only, immigration). See also Robert Wright, *The Foundation Game: A How-to Guide on Getting a Grant*, NEW REPUB., Nov. 5, 1990, at 21.

9. See Chapter 3.

10. See Joyce Mercer, *A Fascination with Genetics*, CHRON. HIGHER ED., Dec. 17, 1994, at A28.

11. Ibid.

12. Douglas Burton, *To Win the Battle of Ideas, Send in the Think Tanks*, WASH. TIMES, Mar. 6, 1995, at 15. See also Brent Bozell III, *Why Conservatives Should be Optimistic About the Media*, Heritage Foundation Rep., No. 380, Jan. 21, 1992. See *Special Edition, The Right-Wing Media Machine*, EXTRA!, Mar./Apr. 1995 (on conservative funding of right-wing newspapers, talk shows, computer networks, PBS, and books).

13. See Chapter 2.

14. See Chapters 3 & 7; Liz McMullen, *Olin Foundation Gives Millions to Conservative Activities in Higher Education*, CHRON. HIGHER ED., Jan. 22, 1992, at A31; Chuck Lane, *The Manhattan Project; Manhattan Institute*, NEW REPUB., March 25, 1985, at 14.

15. See Ellen Messer-Davidow, *Manufacturing the Attack on Liberalized Higher Learning*, 36 SOC. TEXT 40, 53 (1994); James Atlas, *The New "Opinion Elite,"* Sacramento Bee, Mar. 5, 1995, at F1.

16. Bozell, *Optimistic*.

17. Frank Greve, *Polling Ploy Clouds "Contract" Support*, DENVER POST, Dec. 3, 1995, at 29A.; *Mr. Gingrich, Master of the House*, CHICAGO TRIBUNE, Dec. 21, 1995, at 30.

18. Ibid. See also Burton, *To Win*.

19. Serge Kovaleski, *Gingrich's Guru: Corporate Philanthropist Enlisted to Shape Message*, WASH. POST, Dec. 8, 1994, at A1.

20. See, e.g., Chapter 3, detailing the lavish support the Pioneer Fund provides for IQ research.

21. See Chapter 7 (leadership training, editor training, internships, job placement assistance).

22. See, e.g., James Allen Smith, THE IDEA BROKERS: THINK TANKS AND THE RISE OF THE NEW POLICY ELITE (New York: Free Press, 1991) on the rise of these streamlined, highly effective university wannabes; Easterbrook and Gregg, *Ideas Move Nations: How Conservative Think Tanks Have Helped to Transform the Terms of Political Debate*, ATLANTIC MONTHLY, Jan., 1986, at 66.

23. Charles Trueheart, *Big Man off Campus, Author D'Souza, Leading the Politically Incorrect Crusade*, WASH. POST., Apr. 16, 1991, at B1; Richard L. Berke, *Assistant an Asset in Capital for Rush*, DENVER POST, March 12, 1995.

24. Kovaleski, *Gingrich's Guru*.

25. See Richard Delgado, THE RODRIGO CHRONICLES, (New York: New York University Press, 1995), ch. 3 (on interplay between compassion and competition in American life).

26. See Chapter 2.

27. See Chapters 2 & 7, for example (on media phrases used in the war on immigrants and campus diversity).

28. See Chapter 4, for a description of how conservatives exploit these and other fears.

29. See Tim Wheeler, *Reforming the Academy*, NAT'L REV., July 9, 1990, at 22; Ira Glasser, *The ACLU Finds the 50s Immoral*, DENVER POST, Aug. 6, 1995, at D6 (both on the new nostalgia for earlier times and historical periods).

30. 347 U.S. 483 (1954).

31. Richard Brookhiser, THE WAY OF THE WASP: HOW IT MADE AMERICA, AND HOW IT CAN SAVE IT, SO TO SPEAK (New York: Free Press 1991).

32. 347 U.S. 483 (1954).

33. See generally, Richard Delgado and Jean Stefancic, *The Social Construction of Brown v. Board of Education*, 36 Wm. & Mary L. Rev. 547 (1995).

34. Ibid.

35. Ibid.

36. William Simon, A TIME FOR TRUTH, 206–7, 228 (New York: Reader's Digest Press, 1978).

Bibliography

Aaron, Henry J., Thomas E. Mann, and Timothy Taylor, eds. *Values and Public Policy*. Washington, D.C.: Brookings Institution, 1994.

Aho, James Alfred. *The Politics of Righteousness: Idaho Christian Patriotism*. Seattle: University of Washington Press, 1990.

Alliance for Justice. *Justice for Sale: Shortchanging the Public Interest for Private Gain*. Washington, D.C.: Alliance for Justice, 1993.

Andrews, James. "Conservative Law Groups Adopt Liberals' Model." *Christian Science Monitor*, October 3, 1994, p. 13.

Atwood, Thomas C., ed. *Guide to Public Policy Experts: 1993–1994*. Washington, D.C.: Heritage Foundation, 1993.

Auster, Lawrence. *The Path to National Suicide: An Essay on Immigration and Multiculturalism*. Monterey, Va.: American Immigration Control Foundation, 1990.

Barkun, Michael. *Religion and the Racist Right: The Origins of the Christian Identity Movement*. Chapel Hill, N.C.: University of North Carolina Press, 1994.

Bell, Daniel, ed. *The Radical Right: The New American Right*. Rev. and updated ed. Garden City, N.Y.: Anchor Books, 1964.

Bell, Derrick. *The Age of Segregation: Race Relations in the South, 1890–1945: Essays*. Jackson: University Press of Mississippi, 1978.

————. *And We Are Not Saved: The Elusive Quest for Racial Justice*. New York: Basic Books, 1987.

————. *Confronting Authority: Reflections of an Ardent Protester*. Boston: Beacon Press, 1994.

————. *Faces at the Bottom of the Well: The Permanence of Racism*. New York: Basic Books, 1992.

————. *Race, Racism, and American Law*. 3d ed. Boston: Little, Brown, 1992.

————, ed. *Shades of Brown: New Perspectives on School Desegregation*. New York: Teachers College Press, 1980.

Bellant, Russ. *The Coors Connection: How Coors Family Philanthropy Undermines Democratic Pluralism*. Boston: South End Press, 1991.

————. *Old Nazis, the New Right, and the Republican Party*. Boston: South End Press, 1991.

Bennett, David H. *The Party of Fear: From Nativist Movements to the Militia Movement in American History*. New York: Random House, 1995.

Bennett, William John. *The Book of Virtues: A Treasury of Great Moral Stories*. New York: Simon and Schuster, 1993.

————. *The Devaluing of America: The Fight for Our Culture and Our Children*. New York: Simon and Schuster, 1992.

————. *Index of Leading Cultural Indicators: Facts and Figures on the State of American Society*. New York: Simon and Schuster, 1994.

Berman, Paul, ed. *Debating PC: The Controversy over Political Correctness on College Campuses*. New York: Laurel, 1992.

Bernstein, Richard. "Judge Reinstates Jeffries as Head of Black Studies for City College." *New York Times*, August 5, 1993, p. A1.

Berry, Jason. "Bridging Chasms of Race and Hate." *St. Petersburg Times*, August 22, 1993, p. 6D.

Bloom, Allan. *The Closing of the American Mind: How Higher Education Has Failed Democracy and Impoverished the Souls of Today's Students*. New York: Simon and Schuster, 1987.

Blumrosen, Alfred. *Black Employment and the Law*. New Brunswick, N.J.: Rutgers University Press, 1971.

Boaz, David, ed. *Assessing the Reagan Years*. Washington, D.C.: Cato Institute, 1988.

Bolick, Clint. *Changing Course: Civil Rights at the Crossroads*. New Brunswick, N.J.: Transaction Books, 1988.

————. *Unfinished Business: A Civil Rights Strategy for America's Third Century*. San Francisco: Pacific Research Institute for Public Policy, 1990.

Bonafede, Dom. "Issue-Oriented Heritage Foundation Hitches Its Wagon to Reagan's Star." *National Journal*, March 20, 1982, p. 502.

Bork, Robert. *Political Activities of Colleges and Universities: Some Policy and Legal Implications.* Washington, D.C.: American Enterprise Institute for Public Policy Research, 1970.

—————. *The Tempting of America: The Political Seduction of the Law.* New York: Free Press, 1990.

Bovard, James. *Lost Rights: The Destruction of American Liberty.* New York: St. Martin's Press, 1994.

Bremner, Robert H. *American Philanthropy.* 2d ed. Chicago: University of Chicago Press, 1988.

Brigham, Carl Campbell. *A Study of American Intelligence.* Princeton: Princeton University Press, 1923.

Brimelow, Peter. *Alien Nation: Common Sense About America's Immigration Disaster.* New York: Random House, 1995.

—————. "For Whom the Bell Tolls." *Forbes,* October 24, 1994, p. 153.

Brock, David. "The Big Chill: A Report Card on Campus Censorship." *Heritage Foundation Policy Review,* no. 32 (spring 1985): 36.

Brookhiser, Richard. *The Way of the WASP: How It Made America, and How It Can Save It, So to Speak.* New York: Free Press, 1991.

Buchanan, Ruth, and Louise G. Trubek. "Resistances and Possibilities: A Critical and Practical Look at Public Interest Lawyering." 19 *New York U. Law Review of Law and Social Change* 687 (1992).

Buckley, William F., Jr. *God and Man at Yale.* Chicago: Henry Regnery, 1951.

Burt, Cyril. *The Distribution and Relations of Educational Abilities.* London: London County Council, 1919.

Butler, R. E. *On Creating a Hispanic America: A Nation Within a Nation?* Washington, D.C.: Council for Inter-American Security, 1985.

Cable News Network, Inc. "Both Sides with Jesse Jackson." *CNN,* 9:00 P.M. ET, October 22, 1994. Transcript 147.

Caldwell, Christopher. Review of *The Bell Curve: Intelligence and Class Structure in American Life. American Spectator,* January 1995.

Califa, Antonio J. "Declaring English the Official Language: Prejudice Spoken Here." 24 *Harvard Civil Rights-Civil Liberties Law Review* 293 (1989).

Callahan, David. "Liberal Policy's Weak Foundations." *The Nation,* November 13, 1995, p. 568.

Cantor, David. *The Religious Right: The Assault on Tolerance and Pluralism in America.* New York: Anti-Defamation League, 1994.

The Capital Source. *National Journal* (Washington, D.C.), fall 1995.

The Cato Handbook for Congress: 104th Congress. Washington, D.C.: Cato Institute, 1995.

Cattell, Raymond B. *Abilities: Their Structure, Growth, and Action*. Boston: Houghton Mifflin, 1971.

———. *Intelligence: Its Structure, Growth, and Action*. New York: Elsevier Science Publishing Co., 1987.

Cattell, Raymond B., and H. J. Butcher. *The Prediction of Achievement and Creativity*. Indianapolis: Bobbs-Merrill, 1968.

Chavez, Linda. *Out of the Barrio: Toward a New Politics of Hispanic Assimilation*. New York: Basic Books, 1991.

Cheney, Lynne V. *Telling the Truth: Why Our Culture and Our Country Have Stopped Making Sense; and What We Can Do About It*. New York: Simon and Schuster, 1995.

Cloward, Richard, and Frances Fox Piven. *Regulating the Poor*. New York: Pantheon Books, 1971.

Collier, Peter, and David Horowitz, eds. *Surviving the PC University*. Studio City, Calif.: Second Thoughts Books and the Center for the Study of Popular Culture, 1993.

Common Sense Guide to American Colleges, 1993–1994. Lanham, Md.: Madison Books, 1994.

Compassion or Compulsion: The Immigration Debate and Proposition 187. Golden, Colo.: Independence Institute, 1995.

Conniff, Ruth. "The War on Aliens: The Right Calls the Shots." *The Progressive* 57 (October 1993): 22.

Cooper, Marc. "The War Against Illegal Immigrants Heats Up." *Village Voice*, October 4, 1994, p. 28.

Crane, Edward H., and David Boaz, eds. *Market Liberalism: A Paradigm for the Twenty-First Century*. Washington, D.C.: Cato Institute, 1993.

Crawford James. *Bilingual Education: History, Politics, Theory, and Practice*. 2d ed. Los Angeles: Bilingual Educational Services, 1991.

———. *Hold Your Tongue*. Reading, Mass.: Addison-Wesley, 1992.

Dahlem Workshop (Berlin, Germany, 1992). *Twins as a Tool of Behavioral Genetics*. New York: J. Wiley, 1993.

Daniels, Jessie. *White Lies: Race, Class, Gender, and Sexuality in White Supremacist Discourse*. New York: Routledge, 1996.

Dees, Morris. *Hate on Trial*. New York: Villard Books, 1993.

Delgado, Richard. *The Rodrigo Chronicles: Conversations About America and Race*. New York: New York University Press, 1995.

Delgado, Richard, and Jean Stefancic. "Critical Race Theory: An Annotated Bibliography." 79 *Virginia Law Review* 461 (1993).

———. *Failed Revolutions: Social Reform and the Limits of Legal Imagination*. Boulder, Colo.: Westview Press, 1994.

DeParle, Jason. "Daring Research or 'Social Science Pornography'?" *New York Times Magazine*, October 9, 1994, p. 48.

Deutsch, Martin. *Social Class, Race, and Psychological Development*. New York: Holt, Rinehart, and Winston, 1968.

Diamond, Sara. *Roads to Dominion: Right-Wing Movements and Political Power in the United States*. New York: Guilford, 1995.

——. *Spiritual Warfare: The Politics of the Christian Right*. Boston: South End Press, 1989.

Domhoff, G. William. *The Power Elite and the State: How Policy Is Made in America*. New York: Aldine De Gruyter, 1990.

——, ed. *Power Structure Research*. Beverly Hills: Sage Publications, 1980.

Domhoff, G. William, and Thomas R. Dye, eds. *Power Elites and Organizations*. Beverly Hills: Sage Publications, 1987.

D'Souza, Dinesh. *The End of Racism: Principles for a Multiracial Society*. New York: Free Press, 1995.

——. *Illiberal Education: The Politics of Race and Sex on Campus*. New York: Free Press, 1991.

Dye, Thomas R. *Who's Running America? The Conservative Years*. Englewood Cliffs, N.J.: Prentice-Hall, 1986.

Easterbrook, Gregg. "The Case Against *The Bell Curve*: Books That Link IQ to Race." *Washington Monthly* 26 (December 1994): 17.

——. "Ideas Move Nations: How Conservative Think Tanks Have Helped to Transform the Terms of Political Debate." *The Atlantic*, January 1986, p. 66.

Ellis, John M. "The Origins of PC." *Chronicle of Higher Education*, January 15, 1992.

English First. "Members' Report," vol. 10, no. 2 (spring 1995).

Evans, M. Stanton. *The Liberal Establishment*. New York: Devin-Adair, 1965.

——. *The Theme Is Freedom: Religion, Politics, and the American Tradition*. Washington, D.C.: Regnery, 1994.

Fairchild, Henry Pratt. *Immigration: A World Movement and Its American Significance*. New York: Macmillan, 1919.

Federation for American Immigration Reform. "Are You Concerned About Immigration?" Washington, D.C., 1995.

——. "For Your Information." Washington, D.C., April 1995.

Feldman, Paul. "Figures Behind Prop. 187 Look at Its Creation." *Los Angeles Times*, December 14, 1994, p. 3.

Felten, Eric. *The Ruling Class: Inside the Imperial Congress*. Washington, D.C.: Regnery Gateway, 1993.

Ferguson, Thomas, and Joel Rogers. *Right Turn: The Decline of the Democrats and the Future of American Politics*. New York: Hill and Wang, 1986.

Finn, Chester. *Scholars, Dollars, and Bureaucrats.* Washington, D.C.: Brookings Institution, 1978.

————. *We Must Take Charge: Our Schools and Our Future.* New York: Free Press, 1991.

Fish, Stanley. *There's No Such Thing As Free Speech and It's a Good Thing, Too.* New York: Oxford University Press, 1994.

Foundation Grants Index. New York: Foundation Center, Columbia University Press, 1995.

Fraser, Steve, ed. *The Bell Curve Wars: Race, Intelligence, and the Future of America.* New York: Basic Books, 1995.

Galanter, Marc. "Pick A Number, Any Number." *American Lawyer,* April 1992, p. 86.

Galton, Francis. *Hereditary Genius: An Inquiry into Its Laws and Consequences.* New York: Macmillan, 1882.

Garelik, Glenn. "Born Bad? New Research Points to a Biological Role in Criminality." *American Health* 12 (November 1993): 66.

Gilder, George. *Wealth and Poverty.* New York: Basic Books, 1981.

Gingrich, Newt. *Contract with America.* New York: Times Books, 1994.

Gitlin, Todd. *The Twilight of Common Dreams: Why America Is Wracked by Culture Wars.* New York: Metropolitan Books, 1995.

Goldwater, Barry M. *The Conscience of a Conservative.* New York: Macfadden Books, 1960.

Gottfredson, Linda S. "Egalitarian Fiction and Collective Fraud." *Society* 31 (March 1994): 53.

Grant, Madison. *The Passing of the Great Race; or, The Racial Basis of European History.* New York: Charles Scribner's Sons, 1916.

Green, Mark J., and Ralph Nader. *The Other Government: The Unseen Power of Washington Lawyers.* Rev. ed. New York: Norton, 1978.

Hacker, Andrew. *Two Nations: Black and White, Separate, Hostile, Unequal.* New York: Scribner's, 1992.

Handler, Joel, and Yeheskel Hasenfeld. *The Moral Construction of Poverty: Welfare Reform in America.* Newberry Park, N.J.: Sage Publications, 1991.

Hardin, Garrett James. *Living Within Limits: Ecology, Economics, and Population Taboos.* New York: Oxford University Press, 1993.

Heckman, James J., et al. "IQ, Race, and Heredity: Reactions to Charles Murray's *The Bell Curve* and Its Critics." *Commentary* 100 (August 1995): 15.

Henson, Scott, and Tom Philpott. "The Right Declares a Culture War." *The Humanist,* March/April 1992.

Heritage Foundation. *Mandate for Leadership: Policy Management in a Conservative Administration.* Washington, D.C., 1981.

Heritage Lectures. "Shaping America's Values Debate." *Heritage Foundation Reports*, no. 428 (September 15, 1992).

Herrnstein, Richard J. *I.Q. in the Meritocracy.* Boston: Little, Brown, 1973.

Herrnstein, Richard J., and Charles Murray. *The Bell Curve: Intelligence and Class Structure in American Life.* New York: Free Press, 1994.

Herrnstein, Richard J., and James Q. Wilson. *Crime and Human Nature.* New York: Simon and Schuster, 1985.

Himmelfarb, Gertrude. *On Looking into the Abyss: Untimely Thoughts on Culture and Society.* New York: Knopf, 1994.

———. "What to Do About Education 1: The Universities." *Commentary* 98 (October 1994): 21.

Himmelstein, Jerome L. *To the Right: The Transformation of American Conservatism.* Berkeley: University of California Press, 1990.

Horowitz, Irving Louis. "The Rushton File: Racial Comparisons and Media Passions." *Society* 32 (January 1995): 7.

Huber, Peter. *Galileo's Revenge: Junk Science in the Courtroom.* New York: Basic Books, 1991.

———. *Liability: The Legal Revolution and Its Consequences.* New York: Basic Books, 1988.

Hudson Institute. *Civil Service 2000.* Prepared by William B. Johnston. Indianapolis, 1988.

———. *Opportunity 2000: Creative Affirmative Action Strategies for a Changing Workforce.* Prepared by Clint Bolick. Washington, D.C.: The Administration, 1988.

———. *Workforce 2000.* Prepared by William B. Johnston. Indianapolis, 1987.

Hunter, James Davison. *Culture Wars: The Struggle to Define America.* New York: Basic Books, 1991.

Itzkoff, Seymour. *The Decline of Intelligence: A Strategy for National Renewal.* Westport, Conn.: Greenwood, 1994.

Jacobson, Louis. "Tanks on the Roll." *National Journal,* July 8, 1995, p. 1767.

Jacoby, Russell, and Naomi Glauberman, eds. *The Bell Curve Debate: History, Documents, Opinions.* New York: Times Book, 1995.

Jarrett, Vernon. "Beyondism Has Roots in Racism." *Chicago Sun-Times,* December 21, 1993, p. 25.

Jensen, Arthur Robert. *Educability and Group Differences.* London: Methuen, 1973.

———. *Genetics and Education.* New York: Harper & Row, 1972.

Johnson, George. *Architects of Fear: Conspiracy Theories and Paranoia in American Politics.* Boston: Houghton Mifflin, 1983.

Johnson, Kevin R. "An Essay on Immigration Politics, Popular Democracy, and

California's Proposition 187: The Political Relevance and Legal Irrelevance of Race." 70 *Washington Law Review* 629 (1995).

Katz, Alan. "Provoking Thought: Independence Institute's Role Grows." *Denver Post*, February 5, 1995, p. 1C.

Kaus, Mickey. *The End of Equality.* New York: Basic Books, 1992.

Kazin, Michael. *The Populist Persuasion: An American History.* New York: Basic Books, 1995.

Kemp, Jack. *An American Renaissance: A Strategy for the 1980s.* Falls Church, Va.: Conservative Press, 1979.

Kemper, Vicki, ed. "Do As We Say. . . ." *Common Cause*, April 1995.

Kevles, Daniel J. *In the Name of Eugenics: Genetics and the Uses of Human Heredity.* New York: Knopf, 1985.

Kimball, Roger. *Tenured Radicals: How Politics Has Corrupted Our Higher Education.* New York: Harper & Row, 1990.

Kirk, Russell. *The Roots of American Order.* LaSalle, Ill.: Open Court, 1974.

Kondratos, Anna, and Stuart M. Butler. *Out of the Poverty Trap: A Conservative Strategy for Welfare Reform.* New York: Free Press, 1987.

Kotkin, Joel. *Tribes: How Race, Religion, and Identity Determine Success in the New Global Economy.* New York: Random House, 1993.

Kovaleski, Serge F. "Gingrich's Guru: Corporate Psychotherapist Enlisted to Shape Message." *Washington Post*, December 8, 1994, p. A1.

Kozol, Jonathan. *Savage Inequalities: Children in American Schools.* New York: Crown, 1991.

Kristol, Irving. *Neoconservatism: The Autobiography of an Idea.* New York: Free Press, 1995.

————. *Reflections of a Neoconservative: Looking Back, Looking Ahead.* New York: Basic Books, 1983.

Kristol, William, and Christopher DeMuth, eds. *The Neoconservative Imagination: Essays in Honor of Irving Kristol.* Washington, D.C.: AEI Press, 1995.

Kuhl, Stefan. *The Nazi Connection.* New York: Oxford University Press, 1994.

Lane, Charles. "The Tainted Sources of *The Bell Curve.*" *New York Review of Books*, December 1, 1994, p. 14.

Laughlin, Harry H. *Eugenical Sterilization in the United States.* Chicago: Psychopathic Laboratory of the Municipal Court of Chicago, 1922.

Lenkowsky, Leslie. "How Philanthropy Can Improve the Quality of Higher Education." *Heritage Foundation Reports*, no. 214 (July 28, 1989).

Levin, Michael D., ed. *Ethnicity and Aboriginality: Case Studies in Ethnonationalism.* Toronto: University of Toronto Press, 1993.

Lichter, S. Robert, Linda Lichter, and Stanley Rothman. *The Media Elite: America's New Powerbrokers.* Bethesda, Md.: Adler and Adler, 1986.

Limbaugh, Rush H. *See, I Told You So*. New York: Pocket Books, 1993.

———. *The Way Things Ought To Be*. New York: Pocket Books, 1992.

Lind, Michael. "Brave New Right: Race, IQ, and Genetics in the Charles Murray/ Richard J. Herrnstein Book, *The Bell Curve*." *The New Republic*, October 31, 1994, p. 24.

———. "Calling All Crackpots: A New Conservative Credo." *Washington Post*, October 16, 1994, p. C1.

Lind, William S., and William H. Marshner, eds. *Cultural Conservatism: Theory and Practice*. Washington, D.C.: Free Congress Foundation, 1991.

Litan, Robert, and Peter Huber, eds. *The Liability Maze: The Impact of Liability Law on Safety and Innovation*. Washington, D.C.: Brookings Institution, 1991.

Litan, Robert, and Clifford Winston, eds. *Liability: Perspectives and Policy*. Washington, D.C.: Brookings Institution, 1988.

Locy, Toni. "Not a Penny for Tribute." *Houston Chronicle*, September 11, 1994, p. 12.

Lopez, Gerald P. *Rebellious Lawyering: One Chicano's Vision of Progressive Law Practice*. Boulder, Colo.: Westview Press, 1992.

Loury, Glenn C. *One by One from the Inside Out: Essays and Reviews on Race and Responsibility in America*. New York: Free Press, 1995.

Lutton, Wayne, and John Tanton. *The Immigration Invasion*. Monterey, Va.: American Immigration Control Foundation, 1994.

Lynch, Frederick. *Invisible Victims: White Males and the Crisis of Affirmative Action*. New York: Greenwood Press, 1989.

Martinez, Gebe, and Doreen Carvajal. "Prop. 187 Creators Come Under Close Scrutiny." *Los Angeles Times*, September 4, 1994, p. A1.

Massey, Douglas, and Nancy Denton. *American Apartheid: Segregation and the Making of the Underclass*. Cambridge, Mass.: Harvard University Press, 1993.

Matsuda, Mari, Charles Lawrence, Richard Delgado, and Kimberle Crenshaw. *Words That Wound: Critical Race Theory, Assaultive Speech, and the First Amendment*. Boulder, Colo.: Westview Press, 1993.

McDonnell, Patrick J., and Paul Jacobs. "FAIR at Forefront of Push to Reduce Immigration." *Los Angeles Times*, November 24, 1993, p. A1.

Mead, Lawrence M. *Beyond Entitlement: The Social Obligations of Citizenship*. New York: Free Press, 1986.

———. *The New Politics of Poverty: The Nonworking Poor in America*. New York: Basic Books, 1992.

Mehler, Barry. "African American Racism in the Academic Community." *Review of Education*, vol. 15, no. 314 (1993): 341.

———. "A History of the American Eugenics Society, 1921–1940." Ph.D. thesis. University of Illinois at Urbana-Champaign, 1988.

Messer-Davidow, Ellen. "Manufacturing the Attack on Liberalized Higher Learning." 36 *Soc. Text* 40 (1993).

Miller, Abraham H. "Radicalism in Power: The Kafkaesque World of American Higher Education." *Heritage Foundation Reports*, no. 273 (June 13, 1990).

Miller, Adam. "Professors of Hate." *Rolling Stone*, October 20, 1994, p. 106.

Moore, W. John. "It Pays to Think Right." *National Journal*, August 15, 1992, p. 1923.

————. "Wichita Pipeline." *National Journal*, May 16, 1992, p. 1168.

Murray, Charles. *Losing Ground: American Social Policy, 1950–1980*. New York: Basic Books, 1984.

Nader, Ralph, and William Taylor. *The Big Boys: Power and Position in American Business*. New York: Pantheon Books, 1986.

National Council for Research on Women. *To Reclaim a Legacy of Diversity: Analyzing the "Political Correctness" Debates in Higher Education*. New York: National Council for Research on Women, 1993.

National Press Club. Press conference with Linda Chavez, Jack Kemp, and William Bennett. Washington, D.C., November 21, 1994.

Novak, Michael. *Choosing Presidents: Symbols of Political Leadership*. 2d ed. New Brunswick, N.J.: Transaction, 1992.

Odendahl, Teresa. *Charity Begins at Home: Generosity and Self-Interest Among the Philanthropic Elite*. New York: Basic Books, 1990.

Olson, Walter K. *The Litigation Explosion: What Happened When America Unleashed the Lawsuit*. New York: Truman Talley Books-Dutton, 1991.

Orfield, Gary. *The Closing Door: Conservative Policy and Black Opportunity*. Chicago: University of Chicago Press, 1991.

Osborne, R. Travis, and Frank C. J. McGurk, eds. *The Testing of Negro Intelligence*. Vol. 2. Athens, Ga.: Foundation for Human Understanding, 1982.

Page, Shelley. "Nurture or Nature, Science or Racism: Pursuit of 'Truth' Led to Threats, Personal Losses for Rushton." *Calgary Herald*, January 14, 1995, p. B4.

————. "Philippe Rushton: A Study in Controversy." *Ottawa Citizen*, January 8, 1995, p. B1.

Parks, Ward. "Political Correctness and the Assault on Individuality." *Heritage Foundation Reports*, no. 444 (January 29, 1993).

Perea, Juan. "Demography and Distrust." 77 *Minnesota Law Review* 269 (1992).

Peschek, Joseph G. *Policy-Planning Organizations: Elite Agendas and America's Rightward Turn*. Philadelphia: Temple University Press, 1987.

Peterson, Paul, and Christopher Jencks, eds. *The Urban Underclass*. 1991.

Pfeil, Fred. *White Guys: Studies in Postmodern Domination and Differences*. New York: Verso, 1995.

Phillips, Kevin. *Arrogant Capital: Washington, Wall Street, and the Frustration of American Politics*. Boston: Little, Brown, 1994.

———. *The Politics of Rich and Poor: Wealth and the American Electorate in the Reagan Aftermath*. New York: Random House, 1990.

"Politically Correct." *Wall Street Journal*, November 26, 1990, p. A10.

Political Research Associates. "Covering the Culture War." *Columbia Journalism Review*, vol. 32 (July 1993).

Porter, Rosalie Pedalino. *Forked Tongue: The Politics of Bilingual Education*. New York: Basic Books, 1990.

Pratkanis, Anthony R., and Elliott Aronson. *Age of Propaganda: The Everyday Use and Abuse of Persuasion*. New York: W. H. Freeman, 1992.

Pratt, Larry. *Armed People Victorious*. Springfield, Va.: Gun Owners Foundation, 1990.

Pulliam, Mark S. "Judicial Activists Subvert Will of Majority on Proposition 187." *Washington Legal Foundation. Legal Opinion Letter*, vol. 5, no. 10 (April 28, 1995).

Pye, Michael. "Charles Murray Does Love to Make Trouble." *The Scotsman*, October 17, 1994.

Raspail, Jean. *The Camp of the Saints*. New York: Scribner's, 1975.

Rector, Robert, ed. *Steering the Elephant: How Washington Works*. New York: Universe Books, 1987.

Reed, Adolph, Jr. "Intellectual Brown Shirts: Richard Herrnstein and Charles Murray, Authors of *The Bell Curve*." *The Progressive* 58 (December 1994): 15.

———. Review of *The Bell Curve: Intelligence and Class Structure in American Life. The Nation*, November 28, 1994, p. 654.

———. "The New Victorians." *The Progressive* 5 (February 1994): 20.

Ricci, David M. *The Transformation of American Politics: The New Washington and the Rise of Think Tanks*. New Haven: Yale University Press, 1993.

"The Right Wing Media Machine: A Special Issue of EXTRA!" *The Magazine of Fair*, March/April 1995.

Robinson, Ron. "America's Campuses: Crisis and Opportunity." *Heritage Foundation Reports*, no. 367 (September 25, 1991).

Rose, Douglas D., ed. *The Emergence of David Duke and the Politics of Race*. Chapel Hill: University of North Carolina Press, 1992.

Ross, Irwin. "Bill Simon's Out of the Limelight and In the Money." *Fortune*, May 3, 1982, p. 122.

Rushton, J. Philippe. "Race and Crime: An International Dilemma." *Society* 32 (January 1995): 37.

———. *Race, Evolution, and Behavior*. New Brunswick, N.J.: Transaction, 1995.

Ryan, Alan. "Apocalypse Now?" *New York Review of Books*, November 17, 1994, p. 7.

Schlesinger, Arthur, Jr. *The Disuniting of America: Reflections on a Multicultural Society*. New York: Norton, 1992.

Sedgwick, John. "The Mentality Bunker." *GQ*, November 1994, p. 228.

Sege, Irene. "The Bell Curve: The Other Author: Harvard's Richard J. Herrnstein Didn't Live to Face His Final Controversy." *Boston Globe*, November 10, 1994, p. 91.

"Shedding Light on Liberty Lobby." *News and Record*, June 4, 1995, p. F1.

Shockley, William. *Shockley on Eugenics and Race: The Application of Science to the Solution of Human Problems*. Washington, D.C.: Scott-Townsend, 1992.

Shuey, Audrey. *The Testing of Negro Intelligence*. Vol. 1. Lynchburg, Va.: J. P. Bell Co., 1958.

Siano, Brian. "The Skeptical Eye: Dancing with the Fuhrer—Neo-Nazis Who Deny the Holocaust." *The Humanist* 53 (September 1993): 42.

Simon, William E. *A Time for Truth*. New York: Reader's Digest Press, 1978.

Singer, James W. "Liberal Public Interest Law Firms Face Budgetary, Ideological Challenges." *National Journal*, December 8, 1979, p. 2052.

Smith, James Allen. *The Idea Brokers: Think Tanks and the Rise of the New Policy Elite*. New York: Free Press, 1991.

Smith, James P., and Finis R. Welch. *Closing the Gap: Forty Years of Economic Progress for Blacks*. Santa Monica, Calif.: Rand, 1986.

———. *Race Differences in Earnings: A Survey and New Evidence*. Santa Monica, Calif.: Rand, 1978.

Smith, James P., and Michael Ward. *Women's Wages and Work in the Twentieth Century*. Santa Monica, Calif.: Rand, 1984.

Solé, Andre. "Official English: A Socratic Dialogue/Law and Economics Analysis." 45 *Florida Law Review* 803 (1993).

Soley, Lawrence C. *Leasing the Ivory Tower: The Corporate Takeover of Academia*. Boston: South End Press, 1995.

Sommers, Christina Hoff. *Who Stole Feminism? How Women Have Betrayed Women*. New York: Simon and Schuster, 1994.

Sowell, Thomas. *Civil Rights: Rhetoric or Reality?* New York: W. Morrow, 1984.

———. *Ethnic America: A History*. New York: Basic Books, 1981.

———. *Markets and Minorities*. Oxford, Basil Blackwell, 1981.

———. *Preferential Policies: An International Perspective*. New York: W. Morrow, 1990.

———. *Race and Culture: A World View*. New York: Basic Books, 1994.

———. *The Vision of the Anointed: Self-Congratulation as a Basis for Social Policy*. New York: Basic Books, 1995.

Special Report, Tort Reform Interests and Agendas. "Proponents of Reform." *Legal Times*, April 17, 1995, p. S30.

Steele, Shelby. *The Content of Our Character: A New Vision of Race in America.* New York: St. Martin's Press, 1990.

Stoddard, Theodore Lothrop. *The Rising Tide of Color Against White World Supremacy.* New York: Charles Scribner's Sons, 1920.

Strangers at Our Gate: Immigration in the 1990s. Washington, D.C.: Center for the New American Community, 1994.

Strong, Josiah. *Our Country: Its Possible Future and Its Present Crisis.* Rev. ed. New York: Baker & Taylor, 1891.

Sykes, Charles. *The Hollow Men: Politics and Corruption in Higher Education.* Washington, D.C.: Regnery Gateway, 1991.

Tanton, John. *Rethinking Immigration Policy.* Washington, D.C.: Federation for American Immigration Reform, 1979.

———. Witan IV Memorandum, 1986. Available from People for the American Way, Washington, D.C.

Thernstrom, Abigail. *Whose Votes Count? Affirmative Action and Minority Voting Rights.* Cambridge, Mass.: Harvard University Press, 1987.

"Think Tank with Ben Wattenberg, Guest: Charles Murray." *Federal News Service,* October 14, 1994.

Thomas, R. Roosevelt, Jr. *Beyond Race and Gender: Unleashing the Power of Your Total Workforce by Managing Diversity.* New York: AMACOM, 1991.

Toffler, Alvin. *Powershift: Knowledge, Wealth, and Violence at the Edge of the Twenty-First Century.* New York: Bantam Books, 1990.

Trescott, Jacqueline, and Eve Ferguson. "Chairman Clarence Pendleton, Jr.: The 'Wild Card' of the Civil Rights Commission." *Washington Post,* November 14, 1982, p. H1.

U.C.P's Guide to Uncovering the Right on Campus. Cambridge, Mass.: University Conversion Project, 1994.

Viguerie, Richard. *The Establishment vs. the People: Is a New Populist Revolt on the Way?* Chicago: Regnery Gateway, 1983.

———. *The New Right: We're Ready to Lead.* Falls Church, Va.: Viguerie Co., 1981.

Walls, David. *The Activists Handbook: The Concerned Citizen's Guide to the Leading Advocacy Organizations in America.* New York: Fireside, 1993.

Wattenberg, Ben J. *The Birth Dearth.* New York: Pharos Books, 1987.

Weinstein, James, and David W. Eakins, eds. *For a New America: Essays in History and Politics, from Studies on the Left, 1959–1967.* New York: Random House, 1970.

Wheeler, David L. "The Biology of Crime: Protesters Disrupt Meeting on Possible Genetic Basis of Criminal Behavior." *The Chronicle of Higher Education,* October 6, 1995, p. A10.

Wiener, Jon. *Professors, Politics, and Pop.* New York: Verso, 1991.

Wilson, John K. *The Myth of Political Correctness: The Conservative Attack on Higher Education.* Durham, N.C.: Duke University Press, 1995.

Wooldridge, Adrian. "Bell Curve Liberals: How the Left Betrayed I.Q." *The New Republic,* February 27, 1995, p. 22.

Wright, Robert. "The Foundation Game: A How-To Guide on Getting A Grant." *The New Republic,* November 5, 1990, p. 21.

Yates, Steven. *Civil Wrongs: What Went Wrong with Affirmative Action.* San Francisco: Institute for Contemporary Studies, 1994.

Zeskind, Leonard. "Armed and Dangerous: The NRA, Militias, and White Supremacists Are Fostering a Network of Right Wing Warriors." *Rolling Stone,* November 2, 1995, p. 55.

Index

Cooper Industries, Inc., 99

Coors, Holly, 18, 114

Coors, Jeff, 80

Coors, Joseph, 18, 49, 51, 53, 55, 77

Coors, W. Grover, 55

Coors Foundation, 17, 51, 52, 67, 80, 90, 114, 115, 130, 132

Cornell University, 124

Council for Inter-American Security (CIAS), 17, 122–23, 124

Council for Inter-American Security Committee of Santa Fe, 123

Council for National Policy (CNP), 17, 114

Council on Foreign Relations, 17

Covington & Burling, 49

Cowan, Rich, 134

Cowell Foundation, S. H., 25

cranial size, 41

Crawford, James, 13

Cribb, T. Kenneth, Jr., 121

Crime and Human Nature (Richard Herrnstein and James Q. Wilson), 44

Critical Review, 70

Cronkite, Walter, 12, 99

Crossfire, 87

Csorba, Laszlo "Les," III, 122–23

Cunningham, Bill, 88

Custred, Glynn, 47, 60

Dartmouth Review, 91, 110, 114

Dartmouth University, 124

Darwin, Charles, 34

date rape, 132

D'Aubuisson, Roberto, 123

Davis, T. Cullen, 17

Davis Foundation, Shelby Cullom, 56

de Borchgrave, Arnaud, 18

de la Garza, Anita Cloutier, 14

de Tocqueville Institution, Alexis, 22, 51, 130

Dee, Robert, 107

de-fund the left movement, 89–90

Defender, The, 133

Delattre, Edwin J., 128

Democratic Party, 89

DeVos, Richard, 18

DeVos Foundation, 115, 117

dialogue, refusal of. *See* dogmatism

direct mail appeals, 18–19, 24, 114, 115

diversity, 110, 118, 124

Diversity and Division, 112

diversity training, 73, 132, 134

Divided Mother, The, 59

dogmatism, 153–54

Dole, Robert, 46, 60, 78, 120

Donner Foundation, William H., 59, 63, 67, 128

Dornan, Robert, 120

Douglass, Frederick, 77

Dow Chemical Company, 101, 107

Draper, Mark, 124

Draper, Wickliffe, 24, 37

drive-by shooting, 131

D'Souza, Dinesh, 61, 63, 110, 117, 119, 120

Duke Power, 49

Duke University, 110, 118

DuPont, 102, 103

DuPont, Pete, 89

EEOC. *See* Equal Employment Opportunity Commission

ELA. *See* English Language Advocates

Earhart Foundation, 75, 81, 110, 117, 128

Ebeling, Richard, 119

Education and Research Institute (ERI), 116

Educational Testing Service, 35

Eisenach, Jeffrey, 89

Eisenberg, Theodore, 107–8

El Pomar Foundation, 80

El Salvador. *See* Latin America

Elder, Larry, 88

Eli Lilly, 89

Ellis, Thomas, 38

Emerson, Bill, 10

Emerson Electric, 49

employment discrimination. *See* Civil Rights Act of 1964: Title VII

Empower America, 22, 30, 54, 85, 94–95
End of Equality, The (Mickey Kaus), 93
End of Oppression, The (Shelby Steele), 66
End of Racism, The (Dinesh D'Souza), 62
Engalitcheff Award, 121
English as a Second Language (ESL), 14
English First, 14, 15–16, 123
English First Foundation, 15
English First Political Victory Fund, 15
English Language Advocates, 14, 16
Equal Employment Opportunity Commission (EEOC), 68, 69, 71, 78
Equal Opportunity Act of 1995, 78
Erbkrank (Hereditary Defective), 37
Estrada, Richard, 14
Ethnic America (Thomas Sowell), 65
eugenics, 34–44; evolutionary strategy, 41; Nazi, 24; supergeneration, 42; use of, 42
Eugenics Record Office, 36
Eugenics Research Association, 36
European Journalism Network, 112
European Journalism Program, 112–13
Evans, M. Stanton, 118
Executive Order 10925, 76
Executive Order 11246, 48, 54, 68
expertise, 144–47
Exxon, 49, 102, 103
Eysenck, Hans, 43
Ezell, Harold, 20

Face the Nation, 87
faculty, monitoring of, 121–24
FAIR. *See* Federation for American Immigration Reform
Fairness in Media (FIM), 38
Falwell, Jerry, 18
Family Assistance Plan (FAP), 83
Family Foundation, 17
Family Support Act of 1988, 86
Farrish Fund, William Stamps, 56
Federal Communication Commission (FCC): broadcast licenses, 48; minority tax certificate program, 74

Federal Express, 69
Federal Glass Ceiling Commission, 69
Federalist Society, 110–11, 131
Federation for American Immigration Reform (FAIR), 10, 13, 14, 21, 24–26, 27, 28–29, 30, 31–32
feedback loops, 143
Fein, Bruce E., 61
Feinstein, Dianne, 22
Ferrara, Peter, 116
Feulner, Ed, 18, 94
Fikes Foundation, Leland, 25
Finn, Chester, Jr., 127, 128
First Amendment, 116, 130, 133, 134
First Amendment Coalition (FAC), 134–35
First Year, The, 53
Fish, Stanley, 35
FLA-187, 28
Floridians for Immigration Control, 27, 28
Flowers, William Howard, Jr., 119
FMC Foundation, 56, 64, 67
Forbes, Steve, 94
Ford, Gerald, 61
Ford Foundation, 72
Ford Motor Company, 49, 101, 102, 103
Forked Tongue: The Politics of Bilingual Education (Rosalie Porter), 14
Forrest Gump, 88
Forum for University Stewardship, 117–18, 128
Foster, Ezola, 47
Foundation for the National Capital Region, 64
Fox-Genovese, Elizabeth, 128
Frazza, George S., 103
Free Congress Foundation, 53
Freedom of Information Act, 123
Friedman, Milton, 22, 61, 119
Fullilove v. Klutznick, 52
funding: for anti-affirmative action campaign, 48–49, 51, 52, 55–57, 58–59, 60, 63–65, 67, 69–70, 72–73, 74–75, 77, 79, 80, 81 (*see also* Table 2); for campus re-

Hoover, Herbert, 65
Hoover Institution, 65–67, 112, 118, 127
Hopwood v. Texas, 50
Horowitz, David, 40, 119, 120, 131–35
Horowitz, Michael, 74, 92, 99, 103
Howard, John W., 124, 133
Howard Jarvis Taxpayers Association, 21
Huber, Peter, 96, 99, 106
Huddle, Donald, 26
Hudson Institute, 54, 73–75, 92–93, 99, 111, 127; Commission on Social Justice, 74
Human Genome Project, 39
Hume Foundation, Jaquelin, 56, 67, 70, 79, 81
Hunt, Nelson Bunker, 17
Hyde, Henry J., 78, 135

illegitimacy, 84–85, 93, 94
Illiberal Education: The Politics of Race and Sex on Campus (Dinesh D'Souza), 61, 63
Illinois Citizens for Immigration Reform, 27
immigrants, illegal. *See* Proposition 187
immigrants, legal. *See* Proposition 187
Immigration and Naturalization Service (INS), 20, 21
Immigration Invasion, The (Wayne Lutton and John Tanton), 25
Immigration Moratorium Act, 31
immigration reform, 21, 24, 26–28, 31–32, 35, 60
immigration statistics, 25–26, 27, 28, 29, 30
Independence Institute, 29–30, 79–80
Index of Leading Cultural Indicators (William Bennett), 85–86, 87, 91
Indiana University, 134
Indianapolis News, 116
Individual Rights Foundation (IRF), 133, 134–35
Inside Politics, 87
Institute for Educational Affairs (IEA), 90, 109–11, 127
Institute for Justice, 46, 60, 78–79

Institute for Research in English Acquisition and Development (READ), 14
Institute for the Study of Man, 42, 43
Insurance Information Institute, 106–7, 108
Intellectual Ammunition, 77
intelligence: Anglo Saxon, 43; and personality, 39; tests, 35–36, 39
Intercollegiate Review, 117
Intercollegiate Studies Institute, 116–19, 121, 128
Internal Revenue Service: 501(c)(3) status, 15; investigation of U.S. English, 12
Internet, 112
Invisible Victims: White Males and the Crisis of Affirmative Action (Frederick R. Lynch), 47
Iowa Advisory Commission on Civil Rights, 43
IQ. *See* intelligence
I.Q. in the Meritocracy (Richard Herrnstein), 44
Irvine, Reed, 121, 123, 124
issues: focus on, 140; and media, 142–44; and money, 142; selection of, 141; shuttling of key players between, 145–46

Jackson, Jesse, 63
Jacobowitz, Eden, 121, 125
Jeffries, Leonard, 40
Jencks, Christopher, 93
Jenkins, Woody, 17
Jensen, Arthur, 38
Jewish Community Foundation, 128
JM Foundation, 49, 51, 59, 63, 67, 75, 77, 79, 80, 90, 110, 113, 130, 132
Job Opportunities and Basic Skills Programs, 86
job security, cradle-to-grave, 146–47
John Birch Society, 17
Johnson, Lyndon B., 46, 82
Johnson & Johnson, 103
Johnson Foundation, Robert Wood, 72
Johnson v. Transportation Agency Santa Clara County, 52, 68

militia movement, 17
Model Eugenical Sterilization Law, 35
Modern Age, 117
MOME. *See* Mothers of Multicultural English
Monell Foundation, Ambrose, 64, 67
money. *See* funding
Monsanto, 102, 107
Montgomery Street Foundation, 56, 67, 70, 117
Moon, Sun Myung, 77, 123, 124
Moore, Steve, 22, 31
Moral Majority, 17
Morgan Charitable Trust, J. P., 64, 67
Mothers of Multicultural English (MOME), 13–14
Mott Foundation, Charles Stewart, 75
Mountain States Legal Foundation (MSLF), 48, 51–52
Mountjoy, Richard L., 20, 23
Moynihan, Daniel P., 46
multiculturalism, 13, 29, 60, 109, 110, 114, 116, 117, 118, 123, 124, 126, 132, 134
Murdock Charitable Trust, M. J., 49, 57, 115, 132
Murray, Charles, 33, 43, 44, 55, 57, 58, 61, 62, 80, 84–85, 93
Muskie, Edmund, 115
Mussolini, 42, 43
Myrdal, Gunnar, 71

NAACP Legal Defense Fund, 145, 151
Nader, Ralph, 101, 107, 115
narrative: free market tradition, 148; manliness, 148–49; outrageous event, 149; threat, 149
NAS. *See* National Association of Scholars
National Academy of Sciences, 39
National Alliance, 40–41
National Alumni Forum (NAF), 89, 127–28
National Association for the Advancement of Colored People (NAACP), 66
National Association of Scholars (NAS), 40, 111, 124–27, 128, 129, 134

National Association of Wholesaler-Distributors, 102
National Center for Neighborhood Enterprise, 54
National Conservative Leadership Conference, 119
National Council of Contractors Association, 60
National Empowerment Television, 89
National Endowment for the Arts, 133
National Endowment for the Humanities, 127, 133
National Forum Foundation, 132
National Free Speech Bill, 135
National Immigration Forum, 28
National Journalism Center (NJC), 116, 118
National Origins Quota Act, 35, 38
National Press Foundation, 60
National Public Radio, 58, 94
National Review, 112
nativism, 18–19, 32
nature-nurture debate, 36, 39
Nazi eugenics: texts, 24; leaders, 36; propaganda, 37; revisionism, 43
Nazism, 36, 43
NBC News, 112
Negative Population Growth, 25
negligence, 96
Nelson, Alan, 20, 24
Nelson, John, 47
New Coalition for Economic and Social Change, 76
New Politics of Poverty, The (Lawrence Mead), 86
New Protectionism, The, 59
New Republic, The, 112, 128
news conferences, 34
Newslink, 112
newspapers, conservative, 111–13, 114, 118; liberal, 113, 114–15
Nicaragua. *See* Latin America
Nixon, Richard, 83

Stop the Out-of-Control Problems of Immigration Today (S.T.O.P.-I.T.), 21

Stranahan Foundation, 51, 57, 117, 121, 124

Strangers at Our Gate: Immigration in the 1990s, 30

Students for a Better America, 122, 123

Students for a Democratic Society (SDS), 134

Study of American Intelligence, A (Carl Campbell Brigham), 35

Sumner, Gordon, 18

supply-side economics, 83

Swan, Donald, 42–43

Swarthmore College, 120, 134

Swarthmore Conservative Union, 120

Symms, Steven, 10, 16

Talent, Jim, 85

talk show(s), 23, 39, 85, 88, 106, 131

Tancredo, Tom, 29–30, 79–80

Tanton, John, 10–12, 13, 14, 16, 23, 24, 25

target list, 123

Taxpayers Against 187, 21

Taylor, James B., 120, 121

Taylor Foundation, Ruth and Vernon, 52, 57

Terry, Randall, 17

Texaco, 49

Theme Is Freedom, The: Politics and the American Tradition (M. Stanton Evans), 116

Thernstrom, Abigail, 14, 58

think tanks, 145, 157. *See also various names of think tanks*

Think Tank with Ben Wattenberg, 61, 63

Third Generation, 91

Thomas, Clarence, 48, 54, 68, 77–78

Thomas, R. Roosevelt, Jr., 73

$300 billion tort tax, 96, 106

Time for Truth, A (William Simon), 3, 90

Title VII of the Civil Rights Act of 1964. *See* Civil Rights Act of 1964

tort reform, 96–108; funding, 49, 102–4; legislation, 98, 100, 102, 103, 108; proponents, 96–97

tort tax. *See* $300 billion tort tax

Tower of Babel, 16

training young conservatives, 114–15, 117, 119–20

Trent, Darrell M., 65

Trevor, John B., Jr., 38

Trevor, John B., Sr., 38

TRW, 102

twins study, 39

Unfinished Business: A Civil Rights Strategy for America's Third Century (Clint Bolick), 80

Unification Church, 77, 124

Union of Concerned Scientists, 115

United Organizations of Taxpayers, Inc., 21

United States, future of, 154–57

United We Stand America, 21, 47

University Conversion Project, 134–35

University Information Service (UIS), 119

University of California, 110; at Berkeley Law School, 50; Board of Regents, admissions and hiring policies, 66–67; at Davis, 122–23; at Irvine, 124; at Los Angeles, 124; medical schools, 80

University of Delaware, 40

University of Florida, 134

University of Glasgow, 37

University of Heidelberg, 36

University of London, 41

University of Michigan, 124

University of Minnesota Center for Twin and Adoption Research, 37

University of New Hampshire, 130

University of Northern Iowa, 43

University of Pennsylvania, 121, 124, 134

University of Texas, 124, 134; School of Law, 50

University of Ulster, 42

University of Western Ontario, 41

University of Wisconsin, 124

University Professors for Academic Order, 15, 43, 123